Ius Gentium: Comparative Perspectives on Law and Justice

Volume 63

More information about this series at http://www.springer.com/series/7888

Attila Menyhárd · Emőd Veress
Editors

New Civil Codes in Hungary and Romania

Springer

Editors
Attila Menyhárd
Department of Civil Law, Faculty of Law
Eötvös Loránd University
Budapest
Hungary

Emőd Veress
Department of Law
Sapientia Hungarian University of Transylvania
Cluj-Napoca
Romania

ISSN 1534-6781 ISSN 2214-9902 (electronic)
Ius Gentium: Comparative Perspectives on Law and Justice
ISBN 978-3-319-63326-8 ISBN 978-3-319-63327-5 (eBook)
DOI 10.1007/978-3-319-63327-5

Library of Congress Control Number: 2017946045

Printed on acid-free paper

This Springer imprint is published by Springer Nature
The registered company is Springer International Publishing AG
The registered company address is: Gewerbestrasse 11, 6330 Cham, Switzerland

Preface

Eötvös Loránd University (ELTE) in Budapest is known as Hungary's oldest, largest and most prestigious university. Tuition at ELTE's Faculty of Law began 350 years ago, in 1667, which also means no other Hungarian Faculty of Law has a longer uninterrupted record. Sapientia – the Hungarian University of Transylvania, established in 2001 as a private higher education institution in the multicultural region of Transylvania, Romania, is considered a successor to the great legal academy of Cluj-Napoca, the roots of which go back to 1774 and have emerged as an important centre of legal research. The strong professional connection between the two universities is manifested unambiguously through the fact that numerous lecturers are members of both ELTE and Sapientia, which generates a great opportunity to share legal research experience between the two institutes.

The papers published here are the results of two conferences held on 24 May 2013 and on 20 September 2013 in Cluj-Napoca and in Budapest, thanks to the active cooperation between ELTE and Sapientia. The conferences were dedicated to the new Romanian and Hungarian Civil Codes, as the Romanian "Codul civil" (Act. No. 287/2009) had recently entered into force on 1 October 2011, while the Hungarian "Polgári Törvénykönyv" (Act No. V/2013) has been applicable since 15 March 2014. Additionally, the two countries are connected to each other by their special historical and cultural background, which serves as a solid basis for great cooperation, resulting in the two conferences and the present proceedings from them.

The main purpose of the above-mentioned conferences was to present and discuss the regulation and the fundamental changes related to the new Civil Codes in each study, as well as to highlight the new features and some of the issues of great debate in the new regulations. The concept was that the lectures were organized basically in pairs, and therefore similar topics were presented by lecturers from ELTE and Sapientia, mostly one by one. These topics have reviewed numerous different parts of the civil law. Emőd Veress and Zsolt Fegyveresi provided introspection on the transition towards a monist private law and the persistence of some characteristics of commercial law in connection with the new Romanian Civil Code, while other performers focused on more specific parts of the two Civil Codes, such as the default rules of legal persons and companies in the new Civil Code of Hungary, presented by Zoltán Csehi and András Kisfaludi, key issues in the new regulations on property law, presented by Attila Menyhárd and Szilárd Sztranyiczki, while the topic of intellectual property, presented by Gábor Faludi and Ligia Cătuna also constituted a significant element of the conferences. The law of obligation was a highlighted area of the conferences, and Ádám Fuglinszky discussed some of the structural questions of contractual and extracontractual liability. Meanwhile, Balázs Tőkey provided insight into the new particular agreements in the new Hungarian Civil Code. Then, Johanna Szekrényes discussed unforeseeable changes in circumstances in contracts in the new Romanian Civil Code, and finally Krisztina Constantinescu dealt with both the Hungarian and the Romanian legal systems through the perceptions of simulated contracts. Other specific parts of the conferences were family law and the law of succession, as Orsolya Szeibert delivered a lecture about marriage and cohabitation in the new Hungarian Civil Code, focused on the upcoming challenges of the topic, while the last pieces of the conferences were the two lectures on the law of succession in the new Hungarian and Romanian Civil Code, presented by Hella Molnár and János Székely.

The presentations held at the two conferences provided a great opportunity to present a wide selection of the key regulatory issues of the new Hungarian and Romanian Civil Codes as well as to point out some of the upcoming challenges of the issues discussed. As a verdict on the conferences, it seems fair to declare that the cooperation between ELTE and Sapientia, which has already begun over the past few years, has a bright future and a fruitful continuity lies ahead. Let us share the very first evidence of this highly promising intellectual route through the papers of these conferences with our distinguished readers.

Budapest, Hungary
Cluj-Napoca, Romania
February 2017

Attila Menyhárd
Emőd Veress

Contents

About the Editors

Attila Menyhárd is Full Professor of Private Law, Head of Department and Ddean of Eötvös Loránd University Law School in Budapest, Hungary. He is President of the Advisory Board to the Curia (e.g. highest court in Hungary), Member of the Operative Committee for Recodification of the Hungarian Civil Code and Fellow of the European Centre for Tort and Insurance Law (ECTIL). His research interests cover among other things tort law, contract law, property law, company law, trusts, law and economics, human rights in private law, the relations and borderlines of private and public law and the private law aspects of European law.

Emőd Veress is Full Professor of Private Law and Head of Department at the Sapientia Hungarian University of Transylvania in Cluj-Napoca, Romania, arbitrator and attorney. He is Secretary General of the "Societas – Central and Eastern European Company Law Research Network", Member of the "European Society of Comparative Legal History" and author of a very successful Romanian study book on the general part of the law of obligations and of a monograph on suretyship contracts. His research interests cover among other things law of obligations, creditor protection in company law and insolvency law, comparative private law.

Chapter 1
Legal Persons in the New Civil Code of Hungary

Zoltán Csehi

Abstract Legal persons are the most ancient legal institutions, rooted in Roman law, providing enhanced security as they protect the owner of the asset against the business risk of the legal person's activity. The Hungarian legal system, even in the era of socialist law, also regulated several forms of legal persons as full profit and non-profit organisations. Despite the uninterrupted presence of legal persons, it was only in the 90s that business organisations and also the non-profit organisations became widespread due to the modernisation of the Companies Act on and the revival of civil society. The present study commences by introducing the general structure of the Hungarian Civil Code of 1959 and continues with an analysis of the preliminary issues of the codification of the new Civil Code of 2013. Following that, the author provides a detailed presentation of the general rules on legal persons in the new Civil Code, highlighting the new elements in it (i.e. more freedom and the new default rules regime). In this context, the rules on associations, on foundations are analysed in depth.

1.1 Introduction

Legal persons are creations of the human mind. A legal person is a fiction of the juristic mind that makes sophisticated asset management achievable.[1] This asset management provides security for the original owner of the asset against high business risk and against extraordinary losses. The risk of the activity of the legal person is limited to the assets of that person. The limitation of the risk of asset management provides both full profit and non-profit organisations a special benefit

[1]Overview of the different concepts on legal person: Wieacker, Franz: Zur Theorie der Juristischen Person des Privatrechts, in: Festschrift für Ernst Rudolf Huber zum 70. Geburtstag. (Hrsg.) Forsthoff, E./Weber, W./Wieacker, F. Verlag Otto Schwartz & Co, Göttingen 1973. 339–383.

Z. Csehi (✉)
Faculty of Law, Pázmány Péter Catholic University, Budapest, Hungary
e-mail: csehi.zoltan@nt.hu

A. Menyhárd and E. Veress (eds.), *New Civil Codes in Hungary and Romania*,
Ius Gentium: Comparative Perspectives on Law and Justice 63,
DOI 10.1007/978-3-319-63327-5_1

to keep the personal property of the founder or member of the legal person away from the risk of the activity of the legal person.

The benefits of legal persons were recognised even under socialist laws. State-owned enterprises and other entities showed that this creation of private law is suitable for asset management of any kind. The general rules and the theoretical ones of legal persons were discussed in the socialist legal regime as well, and those theoretical approaches survived in the socialist legal regime.

The socialist state-owned companies had progressively lost their importance in the 1990s; these legal entities should have transformed into classical business organisations, either to public limited companies or to limited liability companies. In 1988,[2] the Companies Act on Companies was passed; based on this legislation, private persons and others could establish commercial companies and conduct business freely. Within 5–7 years, the general business form became the business organisations rather than the previous socialist legal enterprises. Consequently commercial companies, sole entrepreneurs in business and in the economy, cooperatives, and small partnerships, as well as farmers in agriculture, became the dominant business forms in the Hungarian legal culture at the end of the 1990s.[3]

In the socialist area there was neither charitable nor non-profit activities; civil society did not work. From the beginning of the 1990s, new forms of legal persons appeared (primarily in the non-profit sphere) and the number of non-profit organisations grew. The number of foundations grew over relatively few years to over 10,000[4] while their current number is around 20,000.[5] The number of associations has also grown significantly,[6] in 2010 there were 31,321[7] in 2015 34,484.[8] The Act no. II of 1989 on Associations gave widespread freedom for their regulation for both political and non-profit purposes, and the law was reformed in 2011.[9]

A new legal form of charitable organisation was created first, then a special limited liability company was implemented as a new legal form, which is allowed

[2]Act no. VI. of 1988 on Companies.

[3]Sárközy, Tamás: A jog szerepének átalakulása a gazdaságban. A magyar gazdasági jog fejlődése 1988–2005 között [The change of the role of the rules in the economy. The development of business law 1988–2005], in Jakab András – Takács Péter (ed.): A magyar jogrendszer átalakulása 1985/1990–2005. [The transformation of the Hungarian legal system] I–II. kötet, Budapest, Gondolat 2007, 591–606.

[4]Between 1990 and 1995 19,585 – Nonprofit szervezetek Magyarországon, KSH 2005 [Nonprofit organisations in Hungary, Central Statistical Office 2005] 33.

[5]In 2015 19,917 based on the Central Statistical Office, https://www.ksh.hu/docs/hun/xstadat/xstadat_eves/i_qpg005a.html.

[6]Csehi, Zoltán: A civil társadalom szervezeteinek joga Magyarországon [Nonprofit law in Hungary]. Budapest 2007.

[7]Central Statistics Office 2011, STADAT data – http://poratl.ksh.hu/pls/ksh/docs/hun/xstadat/xsatad_eves/i_qpg005ahtml.

[8]See note 5.

[9]Act no. II of 1989 on Freedom of Association.

only to pursue public interest and the generated profit cannot be allocated to the members.[10]

The cooperative was a special legal form in the socialist area and farmers were forced to create cooperatives and provide their personal property and agricultural land to those legal persons.

The regulation of cooperatives has changed several times from the beginning of the 1990s; the legal form itself is now applied to approximately 3,000–4,000 cooperatives[11]; many socialist-era cooperatives have been transformed into business organisations and some of them have closed down or went bankrupt.

Among legal persons, even the legal regulation of established churches has to be mentioned. They were regulated by the Act no IV of 1990[12] and in the Constitution, which means that the Hungarian Parliament approved the laws and church organisations could be recognised as legal persons. This act was replaced by a new act in 2012.[13]

Beyond the various legal persons regulated in the Civil Code, since 1990 several legal persons were created by single acts or as part of other acts. Schools, universities, local governments, forest management, water-supply organisations and mutual insurance associations[14] became legal persons and even about 30 different names and forms of legal persons could be listed. The question of public law entities in private law was especially problematic in practice. For example, when an entity (e.g. a parliamentary faction, as distinct from the political party at large) is recognised by public law, it is a problematic question whether or not private law recognizes that as a legal person. Another related problem was the management of state property—how should the state manage its property, directly or through special state-legal entities? The non-profit law has several different rules in Hungary.[15]

In 1998, the preparatory work on a new Civil Code was launched[16]; it was completed in 2012 and Hungary received a new Civil Code in 2013.[17]

The continuous reform of the legislation related to legal persons preceded the change of the political and social regime in Hungary. First and foremost, the Civil

[10]Act no. XCII of 1993 modified Sections 57–60 of the Civil Code; the rules on charitable limited companies were in force from January 1 1994 until July 1 2009. The new rules are to be found in Act no. IV of 2006 on business companies. All business companies can be non-profit company also; only Section 4 of the Companies Act must be complied with.

[11]Recently Act no. X of 2006 on Cooperatives; however, the New Civil Code provides a new regime for cooperatives in the third book.

[12]Act no. IV of 1990 on Freedom of Conscience and Religion, and on Churches.

[13]Act no. CCVI of 2011 on Freedom of Conscience and Religion, and on the status of Churches, Religious Bodies and Religious Communities.

[14]Act. no. XCVI of 1993 on Free Mutual Insurance Associations.

[15]Csehi, Zoltán: Nonprofit Organisations in Hungary, in Hopt—von Hippel (ed.): Comparative Corporate Governance of Non-Profit Organizations, Cambridge 2010, 325–378.

[16]Decision of the Governement no. 1050/1998 (IV.24.).

[17]On the history of the codification process, see Csehi, zoltán: Überblick über das neue ungarische BGB von 2009, 51 Jahrbuch für Ostrecht 2010, 255–287.

Code regulated foundations (as legal persons) only in 1987, because the Code created in 1959,[18] under a more doctrinaire socialist regime, could not embrace this legal entity for ideological reasons.[19] According to the provisions in 1987,[20] foundations could only be established for public purposes and to serve the public interest, and in this way it constituted the legal basis of charity and endowment in the private sphere.

1.2 Civil Code of Hungary of 1959

In the history of Hungarian private law, the Civil Code was created at the end of the 1950s, more precisely in 1959, during the most difficult years of communism, and it was in force until recently. The Code can be characterised as a short and concise regulation of the basic rules of private law. The Code consisted of less than 700 sections and it is divided into six parts: the first seven sections comprise the first part of the Code, containing introductory rules; the second part consists of Sections 8–87 on Persons (it encompasses Sections 8–25 on natural persons and Sections 27–87 on legal persons); the third part can be found under the title of Ownership (Sections 94–197); then the fourth part contains the Law of Contract (Sections 198–596 on general provisions, compensation, torts, unjust enrichment, rules of certain specific types of contracts); the fifth part contains the rules of Succession (Sections 598–684); and the sixth part consists of Closing Provisions.

The Civil Code of 1959 provides rules on legal persons but these regulations had been effectively emptied of substance after 50 years. There were essentially three sections that set out the general provisions for legal persons, followed by parts which no longer applied (e.g. the rules of state-controlled companies). From this part, there are only six sections applicable to foundations and four sections related to associations.

1.3 Preliminary Issues of Codification

One of the first questions at the beginning of codification was whether to create the Civil Code in an organic, monist form or divided into private law and commercial law. In connection with the concept of the new Civil Code, several discussions were made on the regulation of business organisations and whether commercial contracts

[18]Act no. IV of 1959—Civil Code, as amended many times from 1960. Stefan Szászy: Das neue Zivilgesetzbuch der Ungarischen Volksrepublik, Rabels 26 (1961), 553–573.

[19]Kecskés László: Az alapítványi jog fejlődéséről [The development of the law of foundations] 35 Magyar jog (1988), 104–116; Csehi Zoltán: A magánjogi alapítvány [The private law foundation], Budapest 2006, Hungarian development, 64 et seq.

[20]Law-decree no. 11 of 1987.

should be regulated in a separate commercial act or in a commercial code, or if all these should be put in one general private law code.[21] After a theoretical debate on the monist or double concept of the codification of private law, the monist concept was accepted by the codification committee. Both business organisations and commercial contracts are regulated in a common Civil Code. Another specialty of the new Civil Code is that the new Civil Code contains the rules of family law, which had been regulated in separate code since 1952.[22]

From 1988, Hungarian company law was codified in a separate act and the company-related rules of the European Communities and the European Union were transformed into company law, partly in the Capital Market Act, and partly in other legislation. The legal forms of the European companies law were also introduced.[23]

1.4 Act No. V of 2013: The New Civil Code of Hungary

1.4.1 General Overview

The new Civil Code of 2013 does not contain any general part, does not expand on precepts for legal transactions and does not acknowledge such a general concept of 'contract' as the German BGB (Sections 104 BGB). Some of the abstract legal terms, such as legal act, contract and representation, are still (partly fragmentarily) regulated in the general part of the law of obligation in the New Civil Code.

The new Civil Code consists of eight books and 1,596 sections. The books are the following: book I: Introductory provisions; Book II: Human beings; Book III: Legal persons; Book IV: Family law; Book V: Rights in rem—Property Law; Book VI: Law of Obligations; Book VII: Law of Inheritance; and Book VIII: Closing Provisions.

Next, we will outline the structure of the part about legal persons and summarize the rules on associations and foundations. This is in the third Book of the new Civil Code, consisting of 406 sections and having a huge scope. The structure is the following:

Part I—general provisions of legal person—Sections 1–48, includes rules on groups of companies (Sections 49–62)
Part II—Association—Sections 63–87
Part III—Business organisations—Sections 88–324

[21] Vékás Lajos: Szükség van-e kereskedelmi magánjogra? [Is a commercial private law needed?]45 Magyar Jog 1998/12. sz., 705–714.

[22] Act. no. IV of 1952 on Marriage, Family and Guardianship.

[23] Karel Van Hulle/Harald Gesell (eds.), European Corporate Law, Baden-Baden 2006; Dornseifer (Hg.), Corporate Business Forms in Europe, München 2005; Act no. XLIX of 2003 European Economic Interest Grouping; Act no. XLV of 2004 Societas Europea; Act no. LXIX of 2006 on SCE.

Part IV—Cooperatives—Sections 325–367
Part V—Grouping — Sections 368–377
Part VI—Foundation—Sections 378–404
Part VII—The State—Sections 405–406

From the third book, the general rules, the rules of associations and foundations will briefly be presented here.

1.4.2 Rules on Legal Persons—General Rules[24]

The new element in the new Civil Code is the large scope of general provisions related to all legal persons, including legal persons regulated outside the Civil Code.[25] In the 2008 draft, this part consisted of even more than 100 sections,[26] which long debates and editing reduced to only 48 sections, and at the last moment 14 sections on groups of companies was relocated from the end of this book to Part I.

The rules of the Civil Code establish the new basis and a central concept of legal person, by which a new era is rising in the history of Hungarian civil law. 406 sections of the third book of the Code contain the provisions on the legal persons, divided into the aforementioned seven parts. The different types of legal persons are regulated in separate legal provisions and certain institutions and organisations are declared legal person. These regulations have a mixed result, because there are so many types of legal entities and so many regulations. In the various regulations related to legal persons, the new Civil Code shows a new path and gives new solutions, systematic principles and unified directions by establishing the general rules concerning the legal entities. The new regulations provide more freedom to the parties to their deed of association with a new default rules regime.[27]

---

[24]Csehi Zoltán: A jogi személy a Polgári Törvénykönyvben, [The Legal Person in the Civil Code], in Csehi Z. — Navratyil Z.: A személyek joga a 2013. évi V. törvény alapján. [The Law of Persons under Act no. V of 2013]. Budapest 2013, 55–213.; Csehi Zoltán: A jogi személyek szabályozása az új magyar Polgári Törvénykönyvben és annak tervezeteiben, [Rules on Legal Persons in the New Civil Code of Hungary and its Drafts], in Gondosné dr. Pusztahelyi Réka (ed.): A jogi személyek az új Polgári Törvénykönyvben. Miskolc 2013, 45–86. old.; Sárközy Tamás: Szervezetek státusjoga az új Ptk.-ban [The Rules of Organisations in the New Civil Code]. Budapest 2013; Török Gábor: A gazdasági társaságok közös szabályai, [The Common Rules of Business Associations], Gazdaság és jog, 2013/7–8, 3–9. old.

[25]Kisfaludi András: A jogi személyek szabályozása az Új Polgári Törvénykönyvben, [The rules on legal persons in the new Civil Code] Jogtudományi Közlöny 2014, (július-augusztus), 333–342.

[26]Vékás: Über die Expertenvorlage eines neuen Zivilgesetzbuches für Ungarn, ZEuP 2009, 536 et seq.

[27]See the paper of Prof. Kisfaludi in this volume.

These provisions regulate the legal capacity of the legal person in general, the liability of the legal person, the freedom of establishment, the minimum requirements of the deed of foundation, the name, the registered address, the activity and the assets of legal persons and also the freedom to determine the content of the deed of foundation.

The general provisions related to legal persons set out in the Code (Section 3:1–48) –in order to develop a unified concept of legal person—are universal, which means that they may go beyond the types of legal persons regulated in the Code. The general provisions are applicable not only for the types determined in the Code, but also for other legal persons named and regulated by law in a complementary fashion. This is particularly important with regard to legal persons whose operation and organisation are regulated by law at a relatively superficial level and where legal regulation is lacking.

The provisions of legal persons are extended by the Code, furthermore, to all organisations which are entities without legal personality but are qualified as legal entities by the legislation or by the court in a particular case.

The following are the themes of the regulation of the Code:

1. General rules — the Code regulates here the legal capacity of a legal person and its separate assets;
2. Normative determination of legal personality—the organisation of the legal person
3. The common rules of establishment, general rules of establishment by transaction; the legal determination of the normative system; the legal person is constituted by court registration;
4. The formulation of the principles of the register and its authenticity by legislative provisions;
5. Rules concerning the organisation of the legal person: (i) the competence and operation of its decision-making body; (ii) the management and its power; (iii) the bodies of supervision;
6. Rules of representation
7. The provisions ensuring the lawful operation of the legal person: (i) contesting the resolution of legal person; (ii) the auditor;
8. The common rules of termination of legal persons: (i) termination with succession, (ii) termination without succession; and last
9. The legal capacity of other entities without legal personality.

When the founder or member or shareholder of the legal person is obliged to make a financial contribution, the new Code provides an advantageous legal status that the legal person bears the liability for its debts and obligations and not its founder or shareholder. To lay down the conclusion above, Section 3:2 of the Code needs to be construed and applied together with Section 3:9, particularly with the rule contained in para 2. This is also a new rule, according to which the Code, declares the piercing of corporate veil for all legal persons, including companies, foundations and associations. The assets of the legal person and their management and use are related to the separate liability of the legal person, as declared by the Code in para 1 of Section 3:2. According to the condition of the liability set forth by the norm; this limitation of liability may be applied only where the shareholder or founder respects this legal separation and single life of the legal person, including the separation of its assets, and respects the fact that the asset relates to the activity of the legal person and may not be used for private interests. The shareholder or founder who abuses its limited liability — thus the possibility of limiting the legal person's debts to the assets of the legal person — loses this immunity and shall be responsible for the unsatisfied claims of the terminated legal persons's creditors [para 2 of Section 2 of the Code]. The scope of liability is not determined by the Code; therefore (also in the event of minor misuse) it will be possible that the shareholder or the founder shall be liable for an obligation of a higher amount than the value of the illegally used asset.

Legal persons are created by a legal act of a human being and with court registration. The origin of the birth of the legal person, is the expressed will of the person, a legal act, it means an act of creation. In special cases only one act is not enough for the creation of a new legal person; more acts are needed to establish an association or a business association. This legal act cannot be annulled after the registration of the new legal person, except under special conditions. The nullity of the deed of foundation is regulated separately.

The general rules of the organisation of the legal person consists of a supreme body, like shareholder's meeting, and the management and, if applicable, a supervisory body. The Code regulates the manner of convening, quorum and decision-making procedure of the supreme body of the legal person. The Code also provides incompatibility rules, the duty of confidentiality, nomination, the right to withdraw and liability of members of the management. In order to ensure the supervision of the management, the shareholders, the quota holders or founder have the right to set up a supervisory board. There are general provisions for the representation of the legal person. A legal person is under state supervision; its legality is supervised by the courts, and a shareholder of the legal person has the right to bring an action against the decisions of the legal person. Every legal person can nominate an external auditor. Legal persons have the option to transform, merge and demerge. This part closes with the provisions related to the winding up or termination of the judicial person. A separate act contains the rules of liquidation and bankruptcy, which are not part of the new Civil Code.

The general provisions of legal persons originate partly from the general part of the former Companies Act[28]; while its other part is determined by case law. It is important to know that these provisions are applicable to every legal person, so if the given legal person is a foundation, the general provisions shall apply in the same way as if it were, say, a limited liability company or a legal person regulated outside the Code in a separate act.

---

[28]Act no. IV of 2006 on Companies.

1.4.3 Rules on Associations

The rules on associations changed in 2011 with the new Non-profit Act of 2011. Due to this change, the rules in the Civil Code of 1959 changed for the short time until the new Civil Code entered into force (March 15 2014). Over those three laws, the law of associations was case law, or basically judge-made law.[29]

The New Civil Code provides 25 sections on associations and the general rules on legal persons are also applicable, all together 73 new sections relate and are applicable to associations.[30] This is an essential extension of the written legal provisions on associations and the scope of their regulation was enlarged. In the structure of the New Code the rules on associations follow the general rules for legal persons, and rules on business companies follow the associations. The reason is that the association is the original form of unifying persons for a common goal while a business company has much more precise goal, namely a profit-making business activity.

The possible goal of an association has not changed; associations can be created for any purpose with two restrictions: the association cannot carry out business as its primary purpose and the goal and activity of the association shall not violate the Constitution. Even religious activity can be pursued in the form of an association, provided that this does not violate the specific act,[31] while associations for political activity are governed by a separate act.[32]

The New Civil Code sets out the status of the members of the associations and their rights and obligations. The right to be a member of the association is not a personal right, meaning that this right can be exercised by proxy. Membership is not transferable; it cannot be inherited and does not constitute any quota in relation to the assets of the association. The member is not a quota-holder of the association; the member has no right to the assets of the association. The New Civil Code does not provide any *in rem* or other rights for the member to the assets of the association.

According to the New Civil Code, membership can be terminated: on the one hand the member can terminate his or her membership at any time; on the other hand, the association can terminate his or her membership only if the member does not comply with the requirements of the deed of association. The member can be

---

[29]Lomnici Zoltán: Az egyesületek. 2. bőv. kiad. [Associations, 2nd. enlarged ed.], Budapest 2006—a collection of case law by topic.; Közigazgatási-Gazdasági Döntvénytár [Cases in Administrative and Business Practice of the Supreme Court], especially issue 8–9 of 1999 on foundations and foundations of public law, and issue 8–9 of 2000 on registered NGOs and civil organisations.

[30]Csehi Zoltán: Az egyesület és az alapítvány az új Polgári Törvénykönyvben, [Association and foundation in the new Civil Code], in Grad-Gyenge Anikó (ed.): Egy új korszak hajnalán. Konferencia-kötet az új Polgári Törvénykönyv tiszteletére. Budapest 2013, 77–95.

[31]Act no. CCVI of 2011 on on Freedom of Conscience and Religion, and on Churches, Religious Bodies and Religious Communities.

[32]Act no. XXXIII of 1989 on Political Parties.

excluded by the association if the member violates the deed or the law and the deed of association provides special rules on the exclusion of a member. The deed of association shall also govern the procedure for the exclusion of a member with a guarantee of due process.

The deed of the association can be freely drafted by the members of the association, including the rules on the general meeting, its competence, the detailed provisions to convene it and place of the general meeting. The quorum, voting and protocol of the general meeting shall be laid down in the deed of association. The general meeting has exclusive competence to modify the deed, to make a decision on winding up, merger and demerger of the association, to accept the annual report and to appoint and remove a member of the board and a member of the supervisory board. The management of the association can be a single manager or a body and the management can be appointed by the members of the association. The deed of association may allow non-member management to be elected; in this case, up to one third of the members of the management board can be elected by non-members. The New Code gives detailed rules on the competence of the management, making it easy for non-lawyers to understand those rules.

A supervisory board is to be elected if the number of the association's members exceeds one hundred, or more than a half of the members are not natural persons (legal persons). Legal disputes between the organs of the associations, or between members and the association can be decided by arbitration.

The remaining assets of the association, after its termination, shall be transferred to a non-profit organisation specified in the deed of association. If the deed of the association does not nominate any person, the court of registration shall make a decision on the remaining assets. If the association ceases to exist without any legal successor, and the association has a claim against its management, for example a claim for damages, the member of the ceased association has a right to bring legal action against the management within one year from the date of the deletion of the association from the court register.

Special rules for sport,[33] assurance[34] and other special activity associations[35] will be amended accordingly.

1.4.4 Rules on Business Entities

Hungarian company law was modernised in 1988, was redrafted in 1997 and then again in 2004. A new age came with the New Civil Code: the substantive rules of company law were integrated into the new Civil Code, in Sections 3:88–3:324. The new regulations relate to the general rules on business companies, general

[33]Act no. I of 2004 on Sport.

[34]Act no. LX of 2003 on Assurance and Assurance Activity.

[35]Act no. XCVI of 1993 on Free Mutual Insurance Associations.

partnership, limited liability partnership, limited liability companies and the rules on corporations. Special rules were made on groups of companies and on cooperatives. The rules on Companies House and the registration of companies and their data are contained in a separate act.[36]

1.4.5 Rules on Foundation

The Civil Code of 1959 did not contain any rule on the foundation as an independent legal person. The foundation was introduced in the old Civil Code only in 1987, with just a few sections. Since then, foundation law had also been case law, made by the courts. This case law developed very unique solutions that needed to be changed and a new regime of the foundation in private law was created in the new Civil Code.[37]

The regulations related to the establishment of a foundation (as a legal person) did not essentially change under the new code; the founder or founders shall draw up and sign a deed of foundation and this deed shall be filed for registration at the state court registry. The foundation in private law became a legal person by the act of state registration (by the decision of the court).

A foundation can be established by deed of foundation, by testament or by contract of succession. In those cases, by testament and by contract for succession, the foundation starts to exist only after the death of its founder. A special form of establishment by testament, a foundation is the establishment by the legacy of the testator, in which case the founder will be the person burdened by the legacy. According to the New Civil Code, this kind of trust can be enforced by the state prosecutor and the establishment of the foundation can be enforced before the court.

As far as the foundation is concerned, the most important innovation of the new Civil Code is that foundation can be established not only to pursue a 'long-term public interest' (Section 74/A (1) of the 'old' Civil Code), but any goal, also for private purposes.[38] The foundation can be established only for the 'long-term', for a continuous attainment; for a single temporary goal, there is the foundation based on a legal act as the right form (which will be presented briefly below). It became possible to establish a so-called 'family foundation' and for economic activity without profit earnings. The foundation's goals cannot aim to infringe the law or be against morality; its primary activity cannot be commercial business activity to earn a profit. However, the New Civil Code does not specify the meaning of 'primary activity'. Except for 'family foundation', the beneficiary of the foundation cannot

[36]Act no. V of 2006 on Companies House and the Registration of companies and Winding-Up proceedings.

[37]Csehi Zoltán: Foundation Law in Hungary, in Chiara Perle (ed.): Developments in Foundation Law in Europe. Springer Dordrecht Heidelberg New York London, 2014, 111–135.

[38]See CSEHI note 30.

be the founder, the joinder, the trustee or the members of its management and their relatives. The code contains explicit rules on the disqualification and incompatibility of beneficiaries, management and founders, co-founders.

The limit for the operation of foundations is the prohibition to establish a foundation. Further limitation of the activity relates to the operation of the foundation, due to which foundations cannot join another foundation. The money or assets shall be spent directly to the beneficiaries; no connecting vehicle can be used. The operation of the foundation has to be direct, the goal of the foundation has to be performed by the foundation itself, e.g. its assets and property have to be used directly for the realisation of the goals fixed in the deed of foundation; in this way its activity becomes more controllable. The assets of the foundation are also secured to some extent by further rules: the foundation cannot be a member of another legal entity with unlimited liability; the foundation can only conduct commercial business activities as a secondary purpose, with the restriction that its output cannot be distributed to the founder, the joinder, the trustee or the members of management.

The New Civil Code introduced several new legal definitions into the law of foundations, such as the definitions of the "joinder", the "beneficiary". The joinder is not a founder because the foundation has already been established; the joinder provides assets or an endowment for a registered foundation in return for the exercise of rights stated in the deed of foundation. These rights, such as the right to information or presence in decision-making procedures, are determined freely by the founder. If the founder so decides, the joinder can receive founder's rights as well. In this case, the code shall state that the joinder can exercise his or her founder's rights collectively with the founder or, if there are several of them, with the founders.

The foundation distributes money or other services to the beneficiaries in order to reach its goals. Concerning the beneficiaries, the New Civil Code rules on the conditions of disqualification and conflict of interest and it defines who cannot be a beneficiary, while it also gives the right to the founder to determine the beneficiaries in the deed of foundation. If the deed of foundation does not contain such a provision, the trustee — or management — decides both on who shall be the beneficiary and the nature of his/her support. In the case of a family foundation, the code states who can be its beneficiary, such as the founder, the joinder and their relatives, if the purpose of the foundation is to support the scientific or artistic work of the founder or the joinder, the management of their work or the financial support of the devoted care, maintenance and health provision of these persons, or the financial support of their studies through scholarship or any other means. The family foundation shall support the scientific and artistic heritage and shall grant a multi-generational framework for family support.

As far as the operation of the foundation is regarded, the new regulation changes the hostile nature of the Hungarian case law towards their founder; if there are several founders, it does not always demand the unanimous decision of the persons involved; the new Code makes it possible for the founders to introduce a majority decision-making procedure. The founder's rights will be transferable but not heritable. The founder can authorise the management body to exercise certain founder's rights, while another person can also be appointed for the exercise of founder's rights as a whole.

Regarding the organisation of the foundation, the code regulates the management body and it determines that as the executive and representative body of the foundation. The members of the management body can be appointed by the founder but other solutions for the appointment and withdrawal of the management can also be specified in the deed of foundation. The removal of members of the management body is only possible if the management endangers the aims of the foundation. A supervisory committee can be set up by the founder in order to control the management. There is another change in the provisions compared to the former case law, since the new regulations outline that further executive, consulting and supervisory bodies can be created through the deed of foundation. The New Civil Code contains more rules concerning the property and the assets of the foundation compared to the former regulation: the founder must provide the assets for the foundation within a year from its registration, and the management body is entitled to demand these assets from the founder on behalf of the foundation. If the founder does not fulfil this obligation, his/her founder's rights could be suspended by the supervisory court. In the event of the cessation of the foundation, the persons indicated in the deed of foundation are entitled to receive the remaining assets after the satisfaction of the foundation's creditors, with the special limitation that the assets that could be provided to the founder, the joinder or the granter or their relatives cannot exceed the value of the assets which were provided by these persons.

Concerning the rules of cessation of foundations, the provision could be emphasized, which is contained by Part I the general provisions of legal person of the 3rd Book of the Code and which enable the transformation of the foundation. The possibility of the merger or demerger of foundations could also be enumerated here.

The legal supervision of the operation of the foundation will be provided by the public prosecutor.

Similar to the old Civil Code, the New Civil Code recognizes the form of the so-called foundation based on a simple legal act; however, this foundation can only be established for public purposes. The historical roots of this regulation go back to the 1959 Civil Code, since the 1959 Civil Code did provide for the establishment of foundations for to ideological reasons, instead it regulated the undertaking of a public obligation as a special obligation which is the same as the foundation grounded by legal act. The New Civil Code also contains, in four sections, the legal act for undertaking a public obligation. Any person could undertake an obligation to provide free financial assets for a specific public interest. These assets shall be delivered by the grantor for asset management, who does so to realise the special public interest. If the grantor does not appoint a person for asset management, the court shall appoints this person based on the action of the state prosecutor. The Code regulates the withdrawal of such a trust and also the cessation of the undertaking of obligation.

1.5 Non-Profit Companies

From 1993 the charitable limited liability company was the charity form of business companies. Charitable limited liability companies could be established only for public benefit purposes and the non-distribution constraint was applicable. Act no. IV of 2006 introduced the so called non-profit company to the Hungarian legal system. Since 2006, non-profit companies can be established in different legal forms, such as a limited liability company, partnership, limited liability partnership, or limited liability company by share, but the "public purpose" requirement was eliminated. A non-profit company cannot do business for profit sharing but the "charity" purpose is not required in order to set up a non-profit company and no other restriction is given except the non-distribution constraint. The new Civil Code does not provide any rule on non-profit companies, this issue is a part of the private autonomy. The act on Companies House provides special rules on non-profit companies.[39]

The new charity law[40] was enacted in 2011; the new act is still in force.[41] This act completes the rules on foundations and associations.

1.6 Conclusion

The new Civil Code of Hungary of 2013 shows a new way of regulation of legal persons in private law. This regulation differs from the solution of the Romanian Civil Code of 2011 and also from the new Czech Civil Code of 2012.[42] Business forms and non-profit legal persons are regulated within the same code and the Code provides 48 general rules for all legal persons in private law, all those that are regulated within the Code and also for those that are out of the scope of the Code.

---

[39] § 9/F of Act no. V of 2006 on Companies House (see note 36).

[40] [Charity and donation law in Hungary], Gemeinnützigkeits- und Spendenrecht in Ungarn, in R. Walz—L. von Auer—Th. von Hippen (Hrsg.): Spenden- und Gemeinnützigkeitsrecht in Europa, Tübingen 2007, 511–570.

[41] Act no. CLxxVI of 2011 on freedom of association, charity status, and operation and support of civil organizations.

[42] Lubos Tichy—Rita Sik-Simon: A Cseh Köztársaság új Polgári Törvénykönyve [The new Civil Code of the Czech Republic], Magyar Jog 2013, 748–753.

Chapter 2
Default Rules on Companies in the New Hungarian Civil Code

András Kisfaludi

Abstract The starting point of the present study is that company law has been incorporated into the new Hungarian Civil Code. Company law had been regulated separately over the centuries and under different social structures, but this scheme was overwritten by the new Hungarian Civil Code, despite it being not only tradition but also considerable counter-arguments that were against this incorporation. The most significant impact of the placement of company law into the Hungarian Civil Code arises from how it is regulated. Upon examination of the pros and cons of mandatory and default rules, and taking the internal and external characteristics of the relationships regulated by company law into consideration, the Hungarian legislator voted for a blended solution: default rules shall primarily be applied except for when the protection of a third party's interest justifies the mandatory rules. Chapter by chapter, this study unfolds the debate on the proper place for the regulation of companies (by separate law or in the Civil Code), then analyses the regulatory methods and finally presents the actual regulation regime of the new Hungarian Civil Code and reveals some of its consequences.

2.1 Introduction

The title of this study contains two implied statements that are worth closer examination for understanding the driving force behind the choice of regulatory method in the new Hungarian Civil Code with regard to companies. The first statement is that the Civil Code, which came into force on 15 March 2014, includes among many subjects other than the regulation of companies. This basically changed the previous situation when company law was regulated in separate law and, being so, it was a certain distance away from the core of the civil law, although it was acknowledged that it belongs to the domain of the civil law.

A. Kisfaludi (✉)
Civil Law Department, ELTE Eötvös Loránd University, Budapest, Hungary
e-mail: kisfaludi@ajk.elte.hu

A. Menyhárd and E. Veress (eds.), *New Civil Codes in Hungary and Romania*, Ius Gentium: Comparative Perspectives on Law and Justice 63,
DOI 10.1007/978-3-319-63327-5_2

The second relevant statement included into the title is that the Civil Code regulates companies by default rules, i.e. by rules from which company members may deviate if they want to. It is also a new element in the regulation of company law that will have a more serious impact than the placement of the regulations in the Civil Code. The two abovementioned statements are interrelated. Whether companies can be regulated in the Civil Code is dependent on how we perceive these institutions. If we treat them as private institutions, they can be the subject matter of private law regulation, and legal regulations having a private law nature allow it to be questioned whether their regulation should be mandatory or not.

The aim of this study is to examine what reasons led the legislator to regulation by default rules, how this regulation works, who and what kind of advantages may be gained from such a regulation, and what kind of problems in application can be anticipated.

In Sect. 2.2 I will address the arguments that were raised in the discussion about the proper place of regulation of companies, and try to explain why it was a defensible and progressive solution to insert the body of company law legislation into the Civil Code. Section 2.3 will describe the possible regulatory methods that could have been applied in the regulation of company law in the Civil Code and summarise the advantages and disadvantages of different solutions. In the next section (Sect. 2.4), I will present the actual regulations that were enacted in the new Civil Code in this respect and in the Conclusion (Sect. 2.5) I will deal with some possible consequences and problems of the relevant rules.

2.2 In or Out of the Civil Code?

It is one of the basic characteristics of a code that it aims to regulate its subject matter as a whole; it tries to cover a certain field of law in its entirety. The new Civil Code had the same principle from the very beginning of its preparation. The Concept of the Code was drawn up by the Codification Committee and confirmed by a governmental decree in 2003.[1] These Principles laid down the general requirement that the Code should regulate the legal relationships belonging to the domain of civil law as broadly as possible.[2] However, this expectation could not mean that the Code covers all the relevant relationships without exception.

[1]It was ordered that the Draft of the Concept of the new Hungarian Civil Code should be published and discussed by the Government Decision No. 1009/2002. (I. 31.) Korm. After expert discussions, the Concept was modified by the Codification Committee and the final version was confirmed by Government Decision No. 1003/2003. (I. 25.) Korm. The Concept was published in a special edition of the Official Journal (Magyar Közlöny) in February 2003.

[2]The Principles of the New Civil Code was approved by Government Decision No. 1003/2003. (I. 25.) Korm. and published in the (Magyar Közlöny 2003/8.) as an attachment of the same decree.

On the one hand, taking the constitutional rules on the hierarchy of the sources of law, the legislator cannot forbid regulating the same subject matter in another piece of legislation on the same level of the hierarchy. The new Civil Code is an ordinary act of Parliament, and because such an act has no special status, one of the subject matters of the Civil Code can therefore be a subject matter of any other piece of legislation given by the Parliament. These special laws may modify the Civil Code, provide additional regulation or even contradict the code.

On the other hand, the concept of an omnipotent code has some substantive limits as well. Regulating legal relationships of a similar character is not a value in itself. The main advantage of such a piece of legislation is that the rules included in a code are governed by the same regulatory concept and principles, and they constitute a coherent and interrelated system, in which the parts of the system can co-operate with each other smoothly, because the notions within the system have the same meaning and the possible contradictions show themselves more obviously than in if they are regulated in different laws and, therefore, such contradictions can be avoided more easily. However, these advantages are not limitless. A code should keep the same level of abstraction, more or less. Rules having some technical character should not be included into the code even if their subject matter belongs to civil law regulation. The legislator had to find a balance in deciding how far the scope of the code should be extended. Where the advantages of coherent and systematic regulation overwhelm the disadvantages of very detailed, particular and technical rules, regulation in the Code can be justified.[3]

With the abovementioned regulatory principles of the Code, it was obvious that a general Civil Code had to determine what kind of persons could become participants in a civil law relationship, otherwise the regulation would have been incomplete. A coherent and overall regulation inevitably needs to regulate the question of who can hold rights and obligations in civil law relationships.

It was out of question that, beside natural persons, legal persons can also be subjects to such relationships. What kind of legal persons can be the subject of civil law regulation and to what extent these legal persons should be regulated within the Civil Code was, however, disputed. The main problem was organisations that do not have their roots in private autonomy but in public functions can also appear in civil law relationships. Such organisations are generally regulated in public law, where the approach to the regulatory subject matter and, consequently, the method of regulation is quite different from that of private law. These public organisations normally fit into a hierarchical system in which the participants are not equal; some of them are superior to others. Private law is not an appropriate tool for regulating such relationships. It can handle relationships between parties having equal rights and having the freedom to enter into legal relationships at their own risk. Consequently, the new Hungarian Civil Code only includes the specific regulation of those legal persons with internal and external relationships of a private character.

[3]Vékás, Lajos: Preliminary Theoretical Questions of the New Civil Code (Az új Polgári Törvénykönyv elméleti előkérdései); HVG-Orac Budapest, 2001, Chapter 1.

As for the companies[4] it is well known that historically they were strongly connected with the state; they were founded by an act of the state, and their function was not only to organise economic resources of their investors for a common economic goal, but primarily to provide a state concession for certain economic activities that were not allowed for those who were not parties to the company. It is obvious that such types of companies cannot be typical private law institutions, because they do not fit into the concept of private law regulation.

However, the situation has changed dramatically in this respect. As a result of gradual development companies have been freed from direct state intervention. The role of the state has been limited to normative legal regulation and registration. Within the framework of legal regulation it is in the competence of private actors to decide to form of a company and to determine the rules of the operation of the company. Furthermore, if the conditions of the formation of a company laid down in general laws are observed by the founders, the state cannot refuse its registration; consequently, the state has no right to decide in an individual case whether it is possible to form a company or not.[5]

In such circumstances, companies became private institutions that could become subject to regulation under private law. Being so, company law legislation could be a natural part of the new Civil Code.

Inevitably, there were some counter-arguments against including company law legislation in the Civil Code. These arguments went in different directions and included:

(i) Hungarian legal traditions justified separate company law legislation;
(ii) Company law is a mixed body of law, not only containing substantive private law rules but also public law and procedural rules;
(iii) Company law is a rapidly changing field of law, and regular modification would jeopardise the stability of the Code;
(iv) Company law legislation necessarily contains a series of technical rules that do not reach the level of abstraction that is a feature of the whole Civil Code.

It is worth noting that these arguments did not question that company law belongs to the domain of civil law. This approach was expressed in positive law as well. In the former legislation,[6] commercial companies were regulated in a separate

---

[4]Company in Hungarian legal terminology is a general term for organisations formed by the will of the members, who pursue economic or business activity through this organisation whose property is provided originally by the members and where the profit of the economic activity can be divided among the members. This general term embraces not only those organisations which are qualified as companies or corporations in common law systems but also business partnerships and limited partnerships. However, for the purpose of this paper I use the term of company for the business associations.

[5]These principles are expressly laid down in the new Hungarian Civil Code in Section 3:4(1) and (4).

[6]Speaking about old legislation I mean the laws prior to the new Civil Code. The new Civil Code is Act No. V of 2013 which came into force on 15th March 2014.

law[7]; however, there was a rule providing that in those matters where this separate law had no special regulation then the rules of the Civil Code must be applied.[8] In the new situation, when company law legislation is an integral part of the Civil Code, it is more obvious that general civil law rules are applicable to the field of company law.

As to Hungarian legal traditions, it is true that the companies had been regulated in a separate law, not in the general Civil Code. This goes back to the middle of the nineteenth century, when Hungarian company law legislation started and it reached its peak in the Hungarian Commercial Code,[9] which covered the regulation of commercial companies in general. However, one should not overlook the fact that at this time Hungary had no Civil Code at all and so there was no choice as to whether companies were regulated in a Civil Code or a Commercial Code. The regulation of commercial relationships was needed to strengthen the triumph of capitalism over feudalism, and the Commercial Code was a weapon in the battle between these two social systems. A general Civil Code was not absolutely necessary, and Hungary did not have such a code until 1959. At this time, there was a socialist economic and social system which was based on state ownership and the direct state management of the economy. This system did not need, and the more, could not have handled significant privately-owned companies, so it was obvious that the Civil Code did not contain regulations on them. Summarising these facts, we can conclude that when there were private companies there was no Civil Code, and when there was a Civil Code there were no private companies. In current circumstances, where we have both private-sector companies and a new Civil Code, legal tradition cannot be decisive. The current situation is completely different from any former situation, therefore the reference to legal tradition is meaningless.

The statement that the existence and the operation of companies is influenced by different branches of law is true in itself, but it does not follow from this fact that the law shall reflect this complexity with a unified, comprehensive Act. In a legal system where private law and public law legislation is basically separated, such a separation can be maintained in the field of company law as well. The substantive private rules can be regulated by civil law, specifically by the Civil Code, while the connected rules—e.g. the rules on registration of companies, the rules of state supervision over the activity of the companies, the rules on competition matters, the rules on taxation and accounting—can be laid down in separate rules, and it is not necessary to mix the regulation of these matters with private law rules. The new Civil Code follows the principle of leaving procedural and other non-private law matters to separate laws, and tries to keep the Code as pure substantive legislation. The same principle could be followed in the field of company law legislation. Similarly to the former situation, when substantive company law was regulated in

[7]Act No. IV of 2006 (this act was ineffective from the date of coming into force of the new Civil Code, i.e. from 15 March 2014).

[8]Section 9(2) of Act No. IV of 2006.

[9]Act No. XXXVII of 1875.

an independent piece of legislation and the related matters were regulated in separate laws, the rules of the former Companies Act can be taken over by the Civil Code, and the other laws can keep their separate function, and this separation can even be strengthened by the new legislation. The separation of substantive law from related legal matters was not perfect in the former legislation and cannot be perfect in the new Civil Code either. At a certain point, the substantive company law legislation contains, for example, procedural rules that shall be applied in the enforcement of substantive law. The new Civil Code is intent on purifying the regulations of substantive law[10]; however, the result cannot be total separation. There are still some rules of a procedural character, but fewer of them than in the former legislation.

Looking back to the modern history of the Hungarian company law legislation it is true, that the frequency of the change of the law was particularly high. The Companies Act of 1988 (which was the first company law legislation after the Commercial Code of 1875 and the law on limited liability companies in 1930) was replaced by a brand new act in 1997, and then this new one was substituted by a new law in 2006. That Companies Act was in turn repealed by the new Civil Code in 2014. One could have the impression that company law requires completely new overall regulation every nine years, on average. However, a code should not be changed so frequently. A code should reflect stability, and subject matters that are best served by more flexible regulation cannot be the subject matters of legal regulation according to a code. Taking these theoretical requirements as granted, company law can still be a proper subject matter for its regulation in the Civil Code, because frequent changes in the regulatory regime are not a necessity. There have been no such changes in the social and economic system that could necessitate the introduction of a totally new Act on company law. The company law system has not fundamentally changed; the principles of company law have remained unchanged and so any alteration that was necessary in company law could have been realised by simple modification of the existing law.

The other great change that could have had an impact on company law legislation was Hungary's accession to the European Union, but our earlier company law legislation had been already harmonised with the European law so it could not justify a brand new Act on company law either. Complete alignment with European law could have been completed by modifying the existing laws. Furthermore, the changes in European law with regard to companies are not too frequent to preclude the regulation of company law in a Civil Code.

Finally, the opponents of company law regulation within the Civil Code allege that company law is burdened by a lot of technical rules concerning the operations of companies, and such operational rules are below the abstraction standard of the

[10]The regulations on expelling company members can be mentioned as an example. The former legislation not only had rules on the conditions, the substantive basis of expulsion, but gave also special rules of the legal procedure aiming at such expulsion. The new Code left out these procedural rules with the aim of these special terms being regulated by procedural rules, e.g. by a Civil Procedural Code.

Code. In my opinion, substantive company law regulations should always be reflections of conflicts of interests of different groups connected with the company. Sometimes these conflicts are not obvious, and may remain covered by the appearance of technical norms. It is said, for example, that the rules on the competence of different company organs or on the necessary proportion of votes in decision making are mere technicalities, and therefore they do not fit into the Civil Code, which is designed for handling real conflicts. However, after a deeper analysis, one can conclude that the company law rules having a *prima facie* technical character handle genuine conflicts of interest. Competence rules are relevant in the conflict between company shareholders and its management. The voting rules have an impact on the relationship between the majority and minority shareholders. These operational rules are indeed rules handling conflict of interests and doing so they have precisely the same character as any other classical civil law rules; therefore they reach the abstraction level of the Civil Code.

Summarizing the above arguments, I believe that it is an amply justified conclusion that company law matters having a civil law character need to be regulated in the Civil Code and also that such regulation is possible.

2.3 Regulatory Methods in the Civil Code

Civil law regulation can basically follow two different methods. One possibility is to introduce mandatory legal norms that have to be applied unconditionally; consequently, the parties to the legal relationship are not allowed to depart from such regulations according to their will. The second option is to set up default rules from which the interested parties can deviate by their common will.[11] Such rules will be applied only if the parties do not agree otherwise.

The choice of the applicable method is not arbitrary. Rules regulating legal relationships having an absolute structure (i.e. legal relationships where only one party is determined personally and everybody else is obliged to refrain from breaching the rights of the named obligee) cannot be default rules, because it is impossible to reach an agreement among all interested parties, since the obligors are not and cannot be determined individually. Furthermore, deviation from the legal rules cannot be acceptable if the parties' agreement upon such deviation results in external effects. If the rights or obligation of a person who is not a party to the agreement on deviating from the legal rules could be influenced by the agreement, it could transfer costs to a third party, which would be inconsistent with the principle of private autonomy that governs private law in general.

[11]These two methods in their pure version, as they are described here, are the extremes. There are some further possibilities in between. For example the legislator may limit the directions or measures of the deviation from the rules, or may regulate the possible alternative rules as well, letting the parties to choose a readymade alternative provision instead of the general rule.

That is why property law is regulated overwhelmingly by mandatory rules. Since everybody is obliged to observe the rights of the owner, everybody is subject to a certain property law relationship, where only the owner is individualised. However, the owner cannot agree with every other interested person upon the alteration of the rules regulating the property law relationship.

In the field of law of obligations (and especially in contract law), the situation is different. Contracting parties are personally identified, and their contractual agreement has legal effect only on the parties; there are normally no external effects. Contracting parties may negotiate with each other on the rules of their legal relationship without transmitting the impacts of such a negotiation onto unknown third parties. As such, the rules on contract law can generally be default rules, allowing the parties to deviate from them and substitute the law with their own agreement. Introducing regulation by default rules needs an explicit order from the legislator. The legal rules are rules by definition, ultimately applicable and enforceable by the state. If the legislator does not stick to the unconditional application of a legal rule, it has to express this will. In the Civil Code, such regulations can be found in connection with all types of obligations and there is also a special provision on contracts, stating that the parties may deviate from the legal rules.[12] As a matter of course, there are certain cases where the default provisions cannot provide satisfactory regulation, even in contract law. In such exceptional cases the Code forbids deviation by special rules.

The legal relationships regulated by company law are special from this point of view. Their special nature comes from the fact that company law relationships are mixtures: the shareholders of the company are identified, so they can negotiate with each other and can reach an agreement on deviation from the law; however, the aim of their agreement is to form or operate a company which is a legal entity and is distinct from its shareholders. The aim of the existence of a company as a legal person is to facilitate this organisation in entering into legal relationships with third parties under its name, separately from its members. At this point, however, the company law relationships necessarily have an external effect.

Having this mixed nature of company law relationships, the method of legal regulation is not self-evident. There are arguments for and against both methods. In the following chart I summarise the possible advantages and disadvantages of regulating company law by mandatory or default rules.

	Advantages	**Disadvantages**
Mandatory	• Certainty • Lower direct transaction costs	• Unable to follow individual requirements
Default	• Flexibility, • Adjustable to individual requirements, • Lower costs in general	• Regulatory objectives could be missed • More need for judicial interpretation

[12]Sections 6:1(3) and 6:59(2) of the Civil Code.

In my view, costs and flexibility are interconnected. It can be true that mandatory regulation is safer, because the parties do not bear the risk of autonomous regulation, and at the same time cost-effective, because the parties do not spend money on deviating from the regulations (since it is forbidden). However, these advantages are only virtual or much smaller than the advantages of regulation by default rules. The safety created by mandatory rules is much more expensive than default regulation. It may happen that mandatory regulation involves lower actual costs, but society has to pay a very high price for that. The price is a great volume of lost opportunities.

It is unlikely that the legislator could regulate company law relationships in such a diverse and complex way as the parties would ideally like. However, if regulation consists of mandatory rules then the parties have no right to add their own initiatives to this regulatory framework. Instead, they have to accept mandatory regulation or try to circumvent the rules that hinder them from reaching their goals. In the first case, the cost of mandatory regulation is that the rules applicable to the company are not effective; they do not best serve the needs and interests of the parties. The second option has great risks and therefore it also entails costs. The most obvious risk of such an attempt is that the legal system does not allow agreements that are in contradiction with the mandatory rules to be enforced; consequently, the parties may not reach the result they aimed at the time of entering into the contract.

As a matter of course, such costs have to be borne if the reason for regulation is to protect of third parties who are not participating in the contract. However, where the agreement of the parties has no external effect, mandatory rules cannot be justified. In theory, even mandatory rules could provide effective regulation, but in practice, with such a complex and diverse arena as companies, the legislator's attempts to map and regulate all the possible needs and solutions that the parties might have without affecting third parties' interests is impossible. That why arguments that the method of regulation should be chosen on the basis of which version needs more exceptional rules are specious. Even where there are mandatory rules, the number of possible alternative solutions is infinite. If the legislator identifies some of these possible solutions and allows their application by enabling provisions, it does not mean that only these exceptions are necessary and that there is no need for any further alternatives.

Under default rules, it is not the legislator who is expected to conclude what parties might need in all individual cases. The parties themselves will fulfil this task, and they will find the best solution for themselves, without any rule that specifically fits their expectations. Instead, the default rules try to find the most common solutions that match the needs of most interested parties, and being so, that could be applied in the majority of cases. The function of the default rules is to serve as a model. If this model is acceptable to the parties, they are exempted from negotiating over these terms, and in this way they can spare costs and effort.

Obviously there is no guarantee that legal regulation by default rules will meet the requirements better than mandatory regulation. However, in the former case, the mistake of the legislator can be corrected by the parties. Such a correction is not cost-free, but in the long run it can show what would be a more effective legal prescription, and as a consequence it may result in better regulation. Mandatory regulation does not leave room for manoeuvre; the parties have to follow the rule (at least on the surface and, covered by the appearance, they can try to find a better solution at a higher cost), and by doing so it hinders the development of an effective law.

2.4 The Solution of the New Civil Code

Taking all the arguments described in the foregoing chapter into account, the Hungarian legislator decided that the companies will generally be regulated in the new Civil Code by default rules, and mandatory rules will be applied only when the protection of a third party interest makes it necessary.

The relevant section of the Code reads as follows:

"Section 3:4

(1) Legal subjects may freely agree upon the formation of legal persons by a contract or a deed of foundation or articles of association, and may establish the organisation and operational rules of the legal person.
(2) In the course of regulation of the organisation and the operation of the legal person, as well as the members' or founders' relationships towards each other and towards the legal person, the members or founders may deviate in the deed of foundation from the law on legal persons, with the exceptions prescribed in Subsection (3).
(3) The members or founders of the legal person shall not deviate from the law if
    (a) the deviation is forbidden by law;
    (b) the deviation obviously infringes the rights of company creditors, employees and minority members, or hinders the state control of the legality of the company's operation."

In my opinion, this text nicely reflects the dual nature of the company law relationships and tries to separate internal matters, where there is no risk of third party effects, from external connections, where the company members' agreements could have effects on third parties. Subsection (2) contains the basic rule in this respect. This is the enabling rule, allowing the parties to deviate from the law. However, this allowance is not limitless. The deviation from the law is accepted only in internal relationships, i.e. in relationships between the company members or between the company and its members. Furthermore, in the field of company organisation—even if there are not always prima facie interpersonal relationships—deviation is allowed, because the effects of regulation are generally limited to the company.

Although in the field of company relationships described in Subsection (2), the principle is regulation by default rules, one should note that, even in this field, situations may occur where the agreement between the parties has an external effect. The cited provision therefore forbids regulation under certain conditions in order to avoid such unintended cases.

The most obvious situation when the parties are not allowed to deviate from the law is when the wording of the act clearly and individually expresses this prohibition [Section 3:4(3)a]. There are many instances in the Code where the rule itself provides that an agreement different from the legal rule is null and void. The Code itself does not explain the reason for such a prohibition as a matter of course, but—if the legislation is correct—there always must be a good justification for that, and the valid justification could be the protection of the third parties. However, the legislator was not completely sure that all rules from which deviation shall be prohibited can be identified and therefore introduced a general prohibition, in which the relevant third party interests are specified, and any deviation from the law which could harm these interests is prohibited. With this rule the system of prohibition is complete, and covers any situation where deviation is not acceptable, even if the specific prohibition is missing.

2.5 Conclusion

The method of regulation of companies in the new Civil Code was broadly debated in public and in the legal profession. There are fears of ambiguities and uncertainties in interpretation and application of the new law. It is not worth denying that there will be some obscurity and disputes concerning whether the deviation from certain legal rules is acceptable or not. However, I believe this price is not too high for the advantages deriving from this new method of regulation. These advantageous outcomes can be summarised as follows:

1. Company founders will be able to design their company individually, in accordance with their individual circumstances. The internal relations can be adjusted to the needs of the parties, and in this way companies may better serve their members' interests
2. The agreements of the company members will be enforceable, because any agreement deviating from the law will not be illegal.
3. Having the above mentioned advantages, the new regulatory method does not overlook third party interests; the law provides all-inclusive protection to third parties.

Chapter 3
The New Romanian Civil Code—Difficulties in the Transition Towards a Monist Private Law

Emőd Veress

Abstract The new Romanian Civil Code repeals not only the previous Civil Code, but the Romanian Commercial Code as well. Thus the separate regulation of civil and commercial law ceased, and Romania has transitioned to a monist private law. This process, however, cannot be considered unambiguous and free of contradictions. The dualistic character of private law is not related only to the coexistence of distinct civil and commercial codes; the dualistic nature is given by the fact that different rules are applied to the same type of obligations. This is exemplified by the cases when commercial transactions (for example, sales contracts) are determined by at least partly different standards compared to the similar civil law transactions. Ultimately, it is irrelevant whether these specific standards are included in a separate code, the Civil Code or special laws; private law can still be classified as dualistic. In fact if we approach it from this perspective, the Romanian system of private law obligations can be divided into at least three subsystems, civil law, commercial law and consumer law obligations. The present study examines the implications of the entry into force of the new Civil Code and deduces that the majority of the determining factors of former commercial obligations are retained and developed through the introduction of the notion and special regulation of professional contracts.

1. On October 1, 2011 the new Civil Code of Romania (Codul civil), that is Law no 287/2009 (hereinafter abbreviated as C. civ.) entered into force. At first sight it seems that we are witnessing a new wave of civil law codification in Central and Eastern Europe, as new Civil Codes have been adopted not only in Romania, but in Hungary and in the Czech Republic as well. In my opinion it is an exaggeration to talk about a "wave" of codification as the creation of the new Civil Codes can be traced back to very different reasons. It is more of a coincidence that the new Codes were drafted on the historical scale almost simultaneously.

E. Veress (✉)
Sapientia University, Cluj-Napoca (Kolozsvár/Klausenburg), Romania
e-mail: emod.veress@sapientia.ro

A. Menyhárd and E. Veress (eds.), *New Civil Codes in Hungary and Romania*,
Ius Gentium: Comparative Perspectives on Law and Justice 63,
DOI 10.1007/978-3-319-63327-5_3

In Romania the new code is perceived as a great achievement, even though the degree of elaboration of some legal institutions, the accuracy and the level of detail of drafting is not always the same, it is not uniform.

The significance of the new C. civ. is even greater than that of the previous Civil Code, as the new code also replaces and integrates the former Commercial Code, and thus, on October 1, 2011 Romania virtually transitioned from a dualistic system of private law to a monist one, in which one and not two separate codes (the Civil Code and a separate Commercial Code) regulates the fundamental issues of private law. Currently, the new Civil Code includes the fundamental rules on the business law (of obligations) as well.

The "old" Romanian Civil Code was created in 1864. Its basic model was the French, Napoleonic Civil Code established in 1805. In the second half of the 1800s in Romania, an agrarian country underdeveloped from economical point of view compared to Western European realities, the Civil Code represented the asset of accelerated modernisation: it was a "baseless form", lacking real social embeddedness. According to Lucian Boia, a well-known Romanian historian, in the process of modernisation of Romania the greatest problem was the coordination between old socio-cultural habits and imported institutions and rules.[1]

2. The 1864 Civil Code was liberal and capitalist in its character. In the context of Romanian social realities it was alien. In the 1800s, the concepts of freedom, equality and fraternity, the spirit of the French *Code civil* were rather far from the ideologies of the agrarian society basically still classified into boyars and peasants. Nevertheless the Civil Code was proven to be one of the basic tools of compelling and shaping the above mentioned agrarian society into a bourgeois society. The Civil Code gradually formed and re-shaped social relations in a process that was not without contradictions.

The causes of this historical phase shift are evident, as Romania was still the subject of the Ottoman Empire at the time of the adoption of the old Civil Code (although Turkish control had weakened starting with the end of the 1700s). Romania would only gain complete independence from the Ottoman Empire as the consequence of the Russo-Turkish War of 1877–78, that means more than a decade after the adoption of the Civil Code.

The timeless nature of this code, finalized (translated and compiled) in a few weeks, is shown by the fact that it survived through enormous historical turmoils of the 20th century, and until 2011, it served as the overall legal framework of the most important elements of human life.

Replacing it was not a necessity. For example, the French model, though with several amendments, is still in force. Therefore several professional opinions have been formulated against a new Civil Code stating that in order to respect traditions, to preserve continuity and proper legal institutions, a well designed and comprehensive reform of the old 1864 Civil Code would have been sufficient in the name of continuity instead of accepting the new C. civ.

---

[1]Lucian Boia, *De ce este România altfel?* Humanitas, Bucharest. 2012. 38.

Ceasing the application of the old C. civ. is not a fast process. The two, the old and the new Civil Codes may need to be applied in parallel for decades.

If on September 30, 2011 someone signed a 25 year term bank loan agreement and a related real estate mortgage contract, the application, interpretation, effects, termination, the resolving of the related disputes would happen under the previous regulations, those in force at the moment of signing the agreements.

This means that there can be legal disputes in the future in which the regulations of the old Civil Code need to be applied. The amendments of previously signed contracts however will be formulated under the new code. Therefore, with respect to such agreements, it is possible that regarding the original parts of a particular contract the old Code civil needs to be applied, while in the case of the clauses modified after October 1, 2011 the new C. civ.

3. The study of law is impossible without the use of proper historical perspective. Eric Hobsbawm, one of the greatest historians of the 20th century wrote that "*Most young men and women at the century's end grow up in a sort of permanent present lacking any organic relation to the public past of the times they live in.*"[2] It is obvious that this cannot lead to a healthy vision of the world: historical knowledge, more specifically knowledge on the history of law is essential for a benchmark in order to understand and assess the present, to develop a critical approach and the ability to evaluate.

There are generally two types of approaches to the codification of private law.

On the one hand there is the *dualistic understanding of private law.* In this system, private law can be divided into two sub-systems: civil law and commercial law, distinct from the former. That means that trade, more exactly business has a separate private law. The *raison d'être* of the dualist system is supported by the basic argument that business activity needs speed, clarity, maximum predictability, stronger creditor protection, which cannot be guaranteed to the necessary extent by civil law that follows general interests, ensures the balance between creditor rights and debtor protection possibilities. The origin of the dualistic system can be traced back to urban commercial customary systems (*lex mercatoria*) that appeared and existed next to inflexible feudal private law but were separate from it. Historically, two private laws were developed, different from the formal point of view as well: there was a separate road for the formation of civil law, and another one for the development of commercial law (lex mercatoria), which was freer, less affected by social distress and less bound to political transformations. The development of lex mercatoria started as early as the second half of the 11th century, next to a feudal context, in particular in relation with maritime trade. For example, the text of the Tabula Amalfitana containing 66 articles has been preserved (its full title being *Capitula et ordinationes Curiae Maritimae nobilis civitatis Amalphe*), which was drawn up in the era of the first Crusade (1095) in the Republic of Amalfi. The separate development of the lex mercatoria resulted in the large-scale commercial codifications of the 19th century.

[2]E. J. Hobsbawm: *Age of extremes: the short twentieth century, 1914-1991*, London, 1995. 3.

The emergence of the dualistic principle is indicated by the French regulations on land and sea trade (1673, 1681), as well as the French Commercial Code (1807), the Spanish Commercial Code (1829), the common Commercial Code of the German states (1861), the commercial code of the unified German state (1897), the Italian Commercial Codes (1865, 1882). It becomes clear from the examples and the dates that the dualistic concept characterised the great codifications of the 19th century. It is the period of the creation of the Hungarian Commercial Code (Act no. XXXVII. of the year 1875) based on the common Commercial Code of the German states.

The second alternative is the *monist approach to private law*. In this system there is no separate commercial law, civil and business transactions are evaluated under the same regulations.

It was deduced even in the golden age of the dualistic approach, in the 19th century, that the separation of civil and commercial law has external, relative, historical reasons, and that separation would put the unity and security of law at risk.

The most recent codes of civil law clearly aim to assert the monist approach. For example, since 1942, Italy has switched to the monist conception through its then adopted Civil Code (*Codice Civile*). The French, German, Austrian legal systems, however, still maintain the tradition of the dualistic regulation.

The main argument to transition to a monist system is that the once difficult general private law has changed and accelerated to such an extent that it can now ensure the flexibility of trade as well, and there is no need for a separate commercial law. General private law has become very much like old commercial law. In this transformation commercial law had an important role, several achievements of which were taken over by civil law, gradually increasing the flexibility of separate civil law for it to be applicable to commercial relationships as well. "Independent" commercial law has formed civil law (more precisely the law of obligations) to its own image, and as such—in the states which transitioned from the dualistic approach to the monist one—it basically liquidated itself. The new Hungarian Civil Code also codifies several solutions developed in commercial, business environments, as well as commercial judicial practices as general rules.

4. Romanian private law is traditionally built on the dualistic concept. On the one hand Romania adopted the (former) Civil Code (*Codul Civil*) as the overall source of private law. As mentioned previously, the old Romanian Civil Code was drafted in 1864 along the lines of the French Code civil ("Code Napoléon"), over six weeks, based on the draft of the Italian Civil Code, the Belgian Mortgage Law and the previous Romanian regulations. It came into force in 1865. On the other hand, the Commercial Code (*Codul comercial*) that came into force in 1887 also had an important role. Its model was the 1882 Italian Commercial Code (*Codice di Commercio*), but elements of German, Belgian, French origin can also be traced in the text. At the time of its adoption it was extremely modern. It consisted of 971 articles. It is true, however, that it soon became apparent that by itself it could not regulate the whole of commerce, that is why there was need for the gradual adoption of several special commercial laws.

During the soviet type dictatorship, the Commercial Code (C. com.) was never repealed, it was simply not applied: the C. com. became obsolete due to the elimination or at least strong limitation of private ownership, the introduction of planned economy, the nationalization of companies, as well as to the creation of state-owned enterprises, becoming the almost exclusive subjects of economic life and regulated by means of administrative law.

After the regime change (1989) however the Commercial Code was applied again. The fate of the Romanian C. com. is thus very interesting: it outlived its own model (the Italian Commercial Code was repealed during the Second World War, when the original Italian legal system transitioned to monist private law with the 1942 Codice civile), it survived totalitarianism and after 1989 it was resurrected together with capitalism, its natural environment.

But the Commercial Code proved to be less stable over time than the Civil Code, as after the regime change its most important parts, such as company law and insolvency law had to be re-regulated in separate laws as the texts of the C. com were no longer suitable to ensure the necessary framework to rebuild capitalism and to make possible the transition to a market economy after the fall of the totalitarian regime.

5. From October 1, 2011, with the entry into force of Law no. 287/2009, Romania transitioned to a monist system. The new Civil Code repealed not only the previous Civil Code, but the Romanian Commercial Code as well.

Thus Romania is currently one of those states where private law is of a unified (monist) character, meaning that the general rules on business life are also included in the Civil Code.

According to Article 3 of the new Civil Code, *the provisions of this code will be applied to legal relationships between professionalists and between these and any other entities. The professionalists are those who run enterprises.*

The entry into force of the new C. civ. provoked a lively debate regarding the future of commercial law (private law of business), and whether commercial law was going to be eliminated or not. Is the age of commercial law as a specialization in legal practice, as academic discipline, as research field gone by? The answer in my opinion is definitely negative.

6. The unification of private law is essentially a positive phenomenon as it makes issues clearer. The Civil Code includes family law, the general regulation of contracts and several (but obviously not all) special contracts, the general regulations of companies, the separate regulations relating to persons previously originating from the 50s. The categories of separate commercial contract law and commercial acts were eliminated together with the separate legislation of contracts. So what is actually eliminated is separate commercial contract law? There will be no double regulation for example in the case of sales agreements or mandate contracts as before.

Nevertheless, in my opinion commercial law remains a relatively autonomous subdivision of private law.

Professor Stanciu D. Cărpenaru from Bucharest published an 800 page long volume in 2012 entitled *Handbook of Romanian Commercial Law—Based on the new Civil Code* (Tratat de drept comercial român. Conform noului Cod civil), which has a telling title, expressing his standpoint on the matter.[3] The author does not consider commercial law to have been eliminated in spite of the entry into force of the new monist C. civ.

The continuation of commercial law is not this obvious in the opinion of others. For example Law no. 31 of 1990 on trading companies had its title changed at the beginning of 2013 with the deletion of "trading", the present title being Law no. 31 of 1990 on companies (*Legeanr. 31/1990 a societăţilor*). This is misleading because the law does not include the general regulation of companies (which can be found in the Civil Code next to the regulations on simplified companies and companies without legal personality), nor regulations on other types of companies (there are separate laws on co-operative companies as well). Law no. 31 of 1990 only regulates the five types of former "commercial" companies recognized in Romania (general partnership—*societate în nume colectiv*, simple limited partnership—*societate în nume colectiv*, joint stock company—*societate pe acţiuni*, limited joint-stock partnership—*societate în comandită pe acţiuni* and limited liability company—*societate cu răspundere limitată*). There is a debate between the group of lawyers who exaggerate the monist approach and the ones who have a much more moderate attitude.

Anyway, the monist conception introduced by the Civil Code is appropriate.

The unification of private law was an issue even in the golden age of commercial law codification. Let us mention one example: the Italian professor Cesare Vivante (who passed away 70 years ago), one of the most original thinkers and reformers of commercial law, professor of the Bologna, Parma and Rome faculties of law, argued for the unification of private law.

However there is no need to exaggerate the monist approach and to force it in contexts where there is no need for it.

The Civil Code, as it was before, is a "mother right" which does not preclude the existence of special laws in many aspects of economic life. The Civil Code cannot include the whole of company law, the insolvency law or private law regulation of capital market's. As opposed to this, the Hungarian legislator innovatively incorporated company law—specifically the aspect regarding private law—into the Civil Code, like in Italy, although in the case of insolvency law this could have not worked. The pursuit for completeness would disrupt the Civil Code's framework in any state.

The practice of commercial law and its recognition as an academic discipline does not depend on a substantive Commercial Code. The Commercial Code has worked only partly as basic regulation for commercial law, which was rather decisively comprised of special laws.

But most importantly, several peculiarities of commercial law are maintained in the system of the new Civil Code as well. This means that in the respect of contract

[3]Stanciu D. Cărpenaru, *Tratat de drept comercial român. Conform noului cod civil*, Universul Juridic, Bucharest. 2012.

law, within the framework of the new Civil Code there are specific solutions, which are to be applied only in the case of business-related legal relationships. Private law of contracts is now practically tripartite: alongside classical civil contract law, which stands at the base of general contract law, special business (professional) and special consumer contracts are also present whith specific legal norms (and issue of a distinct fourth subdivision, i.e. administrative contracts, can be also raised).

The survival of the Commercial Code's certain peculiarities is worth reviewing in the system of the new Civil Code.

One example is the presumption of joint and several liability in the case of business-related legal relationships (C. civ., Article 1446). Joint and several liability is a tool of creditor protection): the creditor can claim the whole payment from any debtor, and any debtor's lack of enforceable possessions will not be the creditor's risk, but the risk of the co-debtors. The joint and several debtor is bound to fulfil the entire commitment even when the co-debtor does not. The debtor's joint and several liability is an assurance for the creditor, because even if some of the co-debtors are unable to perform, other solvent and fulfilling co-debtors can be forced to execute the whole payment. In the case of debtor's joint and several liability, the creditor does not need to share his or her demands between multiple debtors. In the case of professional legal relationships, if there are multiple debtors, not the divisibility of the claim, but the joint and several liability is the default rule.

The automatic placing in default is a similar business-related legal institution (Civil Code, Article 1523). The expiration of deadline automatically places in default the professional entity, resulting that the creditor will be given the option of unilateral termination of contract. Within a classical private law relationship the expiration of deadline is not sufficient, the obligor must be formally requested (by court bailiff or registered letter) to fulfil, and a compliance date shall be fixed, otherwise unilateral termination of contract is of no effect. The creditor may only choose unilateral termination if the debtor does not meet the deadline given in the notice either. (Submission of legal proceedings also places the debtor in default, but if he performs within reasonable time after the receipt of the notice, the applicant cannot request legal fees.)

Ad probationem, in the case of legal transactions over 250 RON the transaction shall be given the written form of a private document, otherwise, in case of a dispute, the existence and content of the legal transaction cannot be proven in court, for example trough witnesses.

But when it comes to professional contracts, evidence of witness is allowed independent of value range (for details, see Article 309 of Law no. 134 of 2010).

In the case of several types of contracts, different rules are applied regarding business-related legal relationships, the characteristics of limitation rules or regulations of interest are also displayed differently in the case of professional contracts. The detailed overview of these is not my task now.

It should be also noted that important contracts in business life could not be included in the new Civil Code, given that the regulation of all types of contracts on the level of the Civil Code is impossible. For example, leasing will be retained in separate legislation, as well as franchise, and factoring, too (here basically, the legal definition is only one sentence which does not even include all the essential elements of factoring; in Romanian law, factoring is floating between being a nominate or innominate contract, but obviously, it is frequently applied in business).

Nowadays economic life is very difficult to analyse based on isolated aspects of private law. The legal regulation of business is the blend of public and private law. Under these circumstances, unifying the private law regulation of economic life is not something to be feared.

The basic issue is much more important: the new Civil Code has brought such reform in Romanian law, as the adoption of the first democratic Constitution (1991) did (even if it is still contested in some of the legal solutions provided).

As the Commercial Code has not been able to regulate the economy in every detail, the Civil Code cannot do it by itself either. After the regime change, conditions for the modern market economy had to be created by adopting special laws, since the Commercial Code was already outdated in many respects. Alongside the new Civil Code there is also a number of special laws (such as the Law no. 31 of 1990 on companies), and their significance is outstanding in terms of regulating business life.

7. The introduction of a unified private law code in Romania is to be appreciated, but the fact that the monist approach does not prevail and cannot absolutely prevail should be made aware. Commercial law, despite the disagreements, lives on, on the one hand through the Civil Code rules regarding professional legal transactions, on the other hand through special laws. There is also a minority opinion of legal scholars that a new Commercial Code should be drafted and adopted.

8. The adoption of the new Civil Code, even if a more thorough professional preparation and a more prudent implementation would have been desirable, is an important step in the development of Romanian civil law. The new Civil Code is more than a simple translation (which was the case of the former Civil Code). If we wished to evaluate it by summarizing, the new Romanian Civil Code has multiple models; these models are applied properly in the most of the cases, being an outcome of independent intellectual work. Its significance is not reduced by the isolated arguable passages or problems found in its text. Obviously, this Code cannot and should not be considered a flawless creation. Not a single code is a complete literary masterpiece, but an act, which should stand the test of application, and when necessary, deliberate corrections should be carried out on its text.

Chapter 4
The Persistence of Some Characteristics of Commercial Law in the Monist Romanian Civil Law

Zsolt Fegyveresi

Abstract Romania's new Civil Code came into force on October 1, 2011, having been adopted by the Romanian Parliament with Law no. 287 of 2009. The new Civil Code did not only replace the old Civil Code of 1864, but also the Commercial Code of 1887 and the Family Code of 1954. Thus the dualistic or even pluralistic system of private law was replaced by a "monist" law system and the separate regulation of civil and commercial law legal relationships ceased.

4.1 Overview

The new Civil Code does not use the words ***trade or commercial***, instead it talks about legal relationships between ***professionalists***, and ***professional*** legal acts. According to Article 3 of the new Civil Code, *the provisions of this code will be applied in respect to legal relationships between professionalists and the relations between these and any other legal entities. The professionals are those who run companies.*

Of course, the entry into force of the new Civil Code raises the question whether one could speak of independent commercial law or not. Is this made possible by the new Civil Code and the monist legal system of private law? Does commercial law exist at all?

The scholarly literature is of the view that the law of professionalists represents one of the legal areas of civil monist law.[1] According to some, we are witnessing

---

[1]Şerban Beligrădeanu: Consideraţii în legătură cu efectele caracterului „monist" al Codului civil român actual asupra fiinţării, în continuare, a unui „drept comercial" în România. *Dreptul*. 2012/9. p. 24.

Z. Fegyveresi (✉)
Sapientia University, Cluj-Napoca (Kolozsvár/Klausenburg), Romania
e-mail: fegyveresi@veress.ro

A. Menyhárd and E. Veress (eds.), *New Civil Codes in Hungary and Romania*, Ius Gentium: Comparative Perspectives on Law and Justice 63,
DOI 10.1007/978-3-319-63327-5_4

the commercial *legalization* of civil law.[2] Most of specialists are of the opinion that commercial law still exists, its independent existence cannot be doubted.[3]

Therefore we can conclude that the reglementation of civil legal relationship needed to be modernized, taking into consideration that the text of the Civil Code from 1864 has not been changed for nearly a century and a half in extremele important matters. One of the fundamental ideeas of the new Civil Code was the unification of civil and commenrcial law, so the obligations and contracts would be regulated by the same code—including also the commercial ones.[4]

The present article aims to explore the persistence of commercial law in the light of the old and new regulations regarding trading obligations, with a special regard to sales contracts. It is obvious that some features of the Commercial Code continue to be present in the system of the new monist Civil Code; in some cases these features function as general principles in classical private law obligations.

The general provisions regarding commercial transactions were part of the Civil Code of 1864, and civil law was the mother right. The first article of the Commercial Code states that *the law is applied in commerce, and wherever the law does not have provisions, the* Civil Code *is applicable.* However, the Commercial Code had specific provisions regarding commercial transactions as well. Title V of book I of the Code contained the general provisions regarding trading obligations, while title VI regulated commercial sales agreements.

There were different provisions regarding sales agreements, but other professional obligations as well:

- bidding and the acceptance of bidding
- determining contract purchase price and place of performance
- the time and place of the conclusion of the contract
- the responsibility of the seller regarding latent defects
- the regulation of interests
- the joint and several liability of obligants
- the end of the waiting period
- the ban of retract litigious or evidence of witness
- the regulations regarding limitation

[2]Gheorghe Piperea: Profesionistul şi întreprinderea sa. *Curierul judiciar*. 2012/1. p. 19.

[3]Lucian Săuleanu: Specificul obligaţiilor asumate de profesionişti în contextul dispoziţiilor noului Cod civil. *Revista română de jurisprudenţă*. 2012/1. pp. 266-267.

[4]Flavius Baias: *Proiectul Noului Cod civil – un demers necesar*, în „Curierul judiciar“, nr. 3/2009.

4.2 The Purchase Price

The purchase price of sales agreements was regulated by two articles of the 1864 Civil Code, Articles 1303 and 1204. According to these, the purchase price shall be determined by the parties, and it needs to reflect the seriousness of the intentions of the parties. In case, however, the purchase price is not determined by the contracting parties, a third party can be entrusted with determining it.[5]

But what is the fate of the transaction if this third party cannot or will not determine the purchase price of the contract? In the case of civil law transactions the contract does not have any legal effect, although the Civil Code does not contain this *expresis verbis*, the legal literature and case law clearly demonstrates it. Thus the question regarding the legal basis for such case law is valid. The answer can be found in the French Code Civil, Article 1592 stipulating that if the third party named by the parties cannot or will not determine the purchase price, the sales transaction cannot be concluded. This article was probably left out of the Romanian Civil Code of 1864 due to a translation error.

In contrast, the Commercial Code had the following provisions regarding the purchase price: if the person designated by the parties does not determine it, the parties need to name another person, or, if they cannot agree on this person, he/she would be appointed by the court. The judge does not determine the purchase price, but assigns a person who is required to determine it. The Commercial Code also made it possible in the case of commercial transactions, that if the parties do not agree on a specific purchase price, it would be determined later on, in a manner determined in the contract.[6] We can see that the legislature was more lenient regarding commercial transactions, thus emphasizing the importance of commercial obligations.

Regarding the determination of the purchase price, the Civil Code partly takes over the provisions of the Commercial Code. In connection with sales, the Commercial Code allowed the parties to determine a specific purchase price later, in a manner stipulated by the contract. The new Civil Code extends this provision to every sales contract; in fact, in the case of any sales transactions; if the third party designated by the contracting parties does not determine the purchase price, the court shall appoint an expert to determine the purchase price at the request of the interested party.

Article 1233 of the new Civil Code contains a special provision regarding the determination of the purchase price of contracts between professionalists, a provision taken over from the Commercial Code. If the purchase price is not specified in the contract, and the parties do not decide upon the way in which to determine it in the future, the law presumes that the parties took into consideration the purchase prices of services from the same area, functioning based on the same conditions, or

---

[5]Stanciu D. Cărpenaru: *Tratat de drept comercial român*. Bucharest, Universul Juridic, 2012. p. 474.

[6]Lucia Uță: *Contracte civile și comerciale*. Bucharest, Hamangiu, 2011. pp. 34-36.

if this does not exist, a reasonable and fair price. In the case of contracts concluded by professionalists, the law is more flexible and as such it does not assign the determining of a purchase price to the competence of the court, thus allowing for the liberty of the contracting parties.[7]

This rule has several legislative inspirational sources, including Article 55 form the United Nations Convention on Contracts for the International Sale of Goods (CISG), which referring to the payment of the price states that: where a contract has been validly concluded but does not expressly or implicitly fix or make provision for determining the price, the parties are considered, in the absence of any indication to the contrary, to have impliedly made reference to the price generally charged at the time of the conclusion of the contract for such goods sold under comparable circumstances in the trade concerned. Another legislative inspirational source of this text is Article 5.1.7 from the UNIDROIT Principles of International Commercial Contracts (2010), which also is inspired from Article 55 of the CISG. These reglementations have the necessary flexibility to meet the needs of trade.

4.3 The Joint and Several Liability of Obligants

The Civil Code of 1864 discusses joint and several liability from both the points of view of creditors and debtors. In civil law the general rule was the divisibility of obligations, meaning that every creditor could claim from each debtor only the amount owed by that particular debtor, and only that part of the debt that particular debtor owed. In the following I analyse the regulations solely from the obligant's side. Under Article 1041 of the Civil Code of 1864, joint and several liability cannot be assumed, thus in the case of a sales agreements the contracting parties had to formulate express provisions regarding this issue.

Unlike the provisions of the Civil Code, the Commercial Code regulated joint and several liability only for the side of the obligant. If the issue of joint and several liability was raised by the creditor, the provisions of the Civil Code had to be considered. In the case of trading obligations, the obligants were jointly and severally liable to the creditor, if the parties did not stipulate otherwise in the contract. Thus the Civil Code presumed the joint and several liability of the obligants. The regulations regarding trading obligations in fact reversed the provisions of the Civil Code: what was an exception in civil law became a rule in commercial law.

The joint and several liability of the obligants in trading obligations was an effective warrant in cases where the co-obligor was insolvent. The obligants were jointly and severally liable for the whole obligation, while the creditor could claim

---

[7]Antoniu Flavius Baias: *Noul Cod Civil. Comentariu pe articole*. Bucharest, C.H. Beck, 2012. p. 1299.

and force the whole debt out of any of the obligants. The paying obligant then could turn to the other co-obligors and could claim the payment of their part of the debt.[8]

Article 1446 of the new Civil Code took over another special provision from the Commercial Code: the presumption of joint and several liability regarding business or professional legal relationships. Thus, in such legal relationships the main rule is not the divisibility of the claim, but joint and several liability. The Code does not make it possible for the parties to stipulate otherwise regarding liability in the contract. The rebuttable presumption of joint and several liability in the Commercial Code is irrebuttable presumption in the Civil Code.[9] In an other opinion the joint presumption of obligants contracted in the course of business has only a relative character and it can be removed in that case if the creditor accepted the obligation to be divisible.[10]

4.4 The End of the Waiting Period

The Civil Code of 1864 stipulated in relation with synallagmatic contracts, such as sales agreements, that if the obligant does not execute, the creditor could file for forced execution or the termination of the contract, and in both cases could require compensation as well. The termination of the contract could be declared by the court based on the legal action of the concerned party, however, following the examination of the substantial part and circumstances, it could also give the debtor a waiting period to fulfil the obligations. If the debtor did not execute by the end of the waiting period, the court ruled the termination of the contract and obligated the debtor for the payment of compensation. If the parties had included a resolution clause in the contract, the court could only examine whether the conditions for resolution were met and could not give a waiting period. The Code of Civil Procedures also included several provisions prohibiting waiting period, for example if the debtor was subject to bankruptcy or insolvency procedures.

In contrast, the provisions of the Commercial Code prohibited the possibility of allowing for a waiting period in the case of trading obligations. Article 44 of the Commercial Code stipulated that in the case of trading obligations, the judge, in contrast to the provisions of the Civil Code, cannot give the debtor a waiting period, thus ensuring a greater efficiency and a higher level of security to commercial transactions.

In order to apply the prohibition, three conditions needed to be met simultaneously:

---

[8]Stanciu D. Cărpenaru 2012. p. 482.

[9]Lucian Săuleanu: Specificul obligaþiilor asumate de profesionişti în contextul dispoziţiilor noului Cod civil. *Revista română de jurisprudenţă*. 2012/1. p. 268.

[10]Emőd Veress: *Drept civil. Teoria generală a obligaţiilor*. 2nd Edition, Bucharest, C.H. Beck, 2016, p. 230.

- the obligation of the debtor results from a synallagmatic contract;
- the contract should include a deadline determined by the parties; if the contract does not have such a deadline, the court could determine the completion deadline, this however should not be taken for the deadline of the waiting period;
- the obligations of the debtor should be of a commercial nature.

The new Civil Code does not regulate the allowing of a waiting period in the case of trading obligations. In regulating placing in default (Article 1522), the legislator obliges the obligant to notify the debtor in writing or through application to fulfil its obligations. In the notice, the obligant needs to determine a period of completion, and if he/she fails to, the debtor is required to complete the obligations within a reasonable time. If he/she fails to do so, the creditor has the right for the unilateral termination of the contract. The new Civil Code regulates the automatic placing in default as well (Article 1523). The obligant is automatically in default if any of the following conditions is met:

- if the debtor fulfilled effectively his/her contractual obligations only within a certain period of time, but the deadline is not met;
- if the debtor's action made the completion in-kind of the obligation impossible;
- if the debtor breached a *non-facere* obligation;
- if the debtor had clearly indicated his intention not to fulfil his/her obligation to the creditor;
- in case of the repeated refusal or failure to perform a continuous obligation;
- *if the debtor did not perform the payment obligation and this obligation results from the operation of a business (professional legal entity);*
- if the obligation results from a prohibited, non-contractual action.

We can see that the expiration of the term automatically places the professional legal entity in default and the obligant can unilaterally terminate the contract, while in classical private law legal relationship the obligant has to notify the debtor in writing, and can only terminate the contract unilaterally if the debtor does not perform.[11]

4.5 Evidence of Witness

The Civil Code of 1864 contained several procedural law provisions as well, thus, under Article 1191, legal transactions above 250 lei needed to have the form of private document or of authentic instrument so that in case of any disputes, their existence and content could be proven. Thus, evidence of witness was excluded in

[11]Veress Emőd: Új Polgári törvénykönyv Romániában - a monista magánjogra való áttérés nehézségei. *Grosschmid Working Papers*. 2014/3. http://jog.sapientia.ro/data/gbpapers/gb20143.pdf (2016.10.22.).

this case. The last paragraph of the article however made evidence of witness possible in the case of legal transactions above 250 lei, if agreed by the parties.

The Commercial Code stipulated that in the case of trading obligations, evidence of witness is allowed in every case, where the court considers that there is need for it in a certain dispute, regardless of its value. If the Commercial Code required documentary evidence, evidence of witness was possible only when allowed by the Civil Code. Thus, unlike the provisions of civil law, where the judge could not reject evidence of witness in the cases stipulated by the law, in commercial law the judge could ponder this possibility.

The regulation of evidence of witness in the case of legal transactions was transferred to the new Code of Civil Procedure (Article 309 of Law 134 of 2010), which took over the regulations from the two old codes (Civil Code, Commercial Code). Legal transactions above 250 lei need to have the form of private document or of authentic instrument so that in case of any disputes, their existence and content can be proven. In professional legal transactions evidence of witness is permitted regardless of value, if the following conditions meet: by the testimony of witnesses is intended to prove a legal act against a professional, the legal act was closed by a professional during exercise of his business, for the legal act not to be required a written *ad probationem* ammunition by a special law.[12] Therefore we can see that there is a limitation of testimonial ammunition regarding to the legal acts closed by professionals during exercise of their professional activity.

The new Civil Code regulates the possibility of evidence of witness regardless of value: in the case of necessary deposit and accommodation deposit agreements. In both cases evidence of witness is allowed: not just the delivery can be proven by witness but the nature and value of the thing delivered.

4.6 Conclusions

We can notice that the new Civil Code has several specific regulations regarding professional legal relationships, but in parallel with the Code, there are several special regulations regarding business life (Law no. 31 of 1990 on companies, law 85 of 2014 on insolvency prevention and insolvency procedures, etc.). In the different regulations of professional legal transactions and special legal provisions we can recognise the specificities of commercial law.

The "monist" approach does not have an absolute effect in the provisions of the new Civil Code, and it was not the aim of the legislature to have every private legal relationship regulated by one single code. The absolute effect could be realized only if the same rules were applied to identical types of obligations. In this case however there are different rules being applied to identical types of obligations. This is how the dualist characteristic is created and not by the existence or two or more codes.

[12]Gabriel Boroi-Mirela Stancu: *Drept procesual civil*, Bucharest, Hamangiu, 2015, p. 455.

A separate code is not the prerequisite of the existence of commercial law. The text of the new Civil Code is the best evidence for the continuity of commercial law.

Regarding the autonomy of commercial law we must destinguish the difference between legislative and scientific autonomy. Commercial law as a branch of law and as a subject of study has continued to exist also in those countries which adopted the monist system in the reglementation of private law, despite other opinions. After the entrance into force of the Civil Code in 1942 in Italy—which took the place of the old civil and commercial code—the italian jourist, Mario Rotondi considered that commercial law which had just been born in Italy, has already seen its final sunset.[13]

References

Anca Gheorghiu: Comercialitatea în condiţiile Noului Cod civil, *Revista de drept comercial*. 11/2011.

Antoniu Flavius Baias: *Noul Cod Civil. Comentariu pe articole*. Bucharest, C.H. Beck, 2012.

Flavius Baias: Proiectul Noului Cod civil - un demers necesar, *Curierul judiciar*. 3/2009.

Gabriel Boroi-Mirela Stancu: *Drept procesual civil*, Bucharest, Hamangiu, 2015.

Gheorghe Piperea: Profesionistul şi întreprinderea sa. *Curierul judiciar*. 2012/1. p. 19.

Lucia Uţă: *Contracte civile şi comerciale*. Bucharest, Hamangiu, 2011.

Lucian Săuleanu: Specificul obligaţiilor asumate de profesionişti în contextul dispoziţiilor noului Cod civil. *Revista română de jurisprudenţă*. 2012/1. pp. 266–267.

Şerban Beligrădeanu: Consideraţii în legătură cu efectele caracterului „monist" al Codului civil român actual asupra fiinţării, în continuare, a unui „drept comercial" în România. *Dreptul*. 2012/9.

Stanciu D. Cărpenaru: *Tratat de drept comercial român*. Bucharest, Universul Juridic, 2012.

Veress Emőd: Új Polgári törvénykönyv Romániába—a monista magánjogra való áttérés nehézségei. *Grosschmid Working Papers*. 2014/3. http://jog.sapientia.ro/data/gbpapers/gb20143.pdf (2016.10.22.).

Veress Emőd: *Drept civil. Teoria generală a obligaţiilor*. 2nd Edition, Bucharest, C.H. Beck, 2016.

[13]Anca Gheorghiu: Comercialitatea în condiţiile Noului Cod civil, *Revista de drept comercial*. 11/2011. p. 129.

Chapter 5
Property Law in the New Hungarian Civil Code: Key Issues

Attila Menyhárd

Abstract One of the particularities of the regulatory structure of civil law legal relationships is that they are built on relatively few system-forming elements. The identification and contextual recording of these elements necessarily determine the other parts of regulation. Regulation cannot be successful without determining these basic regulatory elements, which underlie the regulation as theoretical principles or are even expressed in a normative manner. These key points in property law are the concept of numerus clausus of property rights, the abstract concept of property, the definition of the scope of the objects of property, the transfer of ownership of movable property, and the prohibition of lex commissoria in the law of liens.

Codification, especially with regard to regulations that already exist and are in force, is a multi-layered and multi-dimensional task. The basic approach followed in the course of revisiting property law for the new Civil Code (2013)[1] was to specify the key points of regulation that necessarily determine certain further elements including the choices between regulatory alternatives which influence other rules, then analysing if alternative solutions provide a better choice than the Civil Code (1959). As such, the basic aim was to provide regulation that meets practical demands as far as possible. The result was that there are no better regulatory alternatives and so the Civil Code (2013) did not introduce dramatic changes in property law.

For this process, it is necessary to identify the legal policy objectives and aspects of codification techniques that will support the decisions made in the course of codification and determine the choices between the alternatives. A particular feature of the law of rights *in rem* is that the decision in the key questions typically means a

[1]Civil Code (2013).

A. Menyhárd (✉)
Civil Law Department, ELTE Eötvös Loránd University, Budapest, Hungary
e-mail: menyhard@ajk.elte.hu

A. Menyhárd and E. Veress (eds.), *New Civil Codes in Hungary and Romania*,
Ius Gentium: Comparative Perspectives on Law and Justice 63,
DOI 10.1007/978-3-319-63327-5_5

choice between two possible models, which can be of equal value, but require different regulations. In the course of the drafting of the new Civil Code, the key issues included the principle of *numerus clausus* of *in rem* rights, the definition of the concept of ownership rights, the objects of ownership, the concept of the thing, the system of transfer of ownership over movable property and the system of collateral property, as well as the legal quality of possession. Certain elements of the regulations necessarily reflect the consequences of the decisions made on these questions.

The rights *in rem* rules of the Civil Code (1959) were built to a significant extent on the drafts of the pre-World War II and achievements of judicial practice. The effective law is the result of the organic development of the efforts to codify Hungarian private law. The property rights rules fit clearly into the process that, starting from the 1900s, has resulted in increasingly polished and practical draft texts, which, relative to the nature of the law of rights *in rem*, were open and flexible. We can regard the effective statute as an enhanced and polished version of the Private Law Bill of 1928. The socialist idea of property arising as the ideological background of the Civil Code (1959) had not affected the fundamental structure of the regulations; it only appeared at the regulatory level in a few provisions. Hence, in the course of revisiting the rules of rights *in rem* in the new Civil Code, there was no need for a comprehensive reform that could affect the foundations and the basic structure of the regulations. The changes to the regulations aimed primarily at better conformity with practical demands.

The central organising principle of the regulation of property law in Hungarian law—similarly to other continental legal systems—is the abstract concept of property. The abstract concept of property appears in the indivisibility of partial interests in property: there is always only one ownership over one thing, and all other rights *in rem* regarding the thing can be only rights *in rem* in another thing. More than one person can have proprietary interests in one thing only in the form of joint ownership. In the case of joint ownership, partial proprietary interests are not divided, but all co-owners are entitled to every one of them in the same manner. The "flexibility" of property is due to this view, which regards others' rights *in rem* in the thing as temporary, with the caveat that although the owner can be limited in all partial interests of ownership that can be named, with the termination of them its ownership regains its original unlimited nature; that is, the essence of ownership is not altered by the limited nature or lack of partial interests. Ownership cannot be merely looked at as the sum of partial interests, even if the partial interests cannot be exhaustively listed, because ownership prevails even in the event of the assignment of the exercise of all partial interests–which, in theory, can probably be regarded as finite: ownership remains unaltered even if the "box" of interests is entirely empty.[2]

[2]Merryman, 927.

5.1 The *Numerus Clausus* Principle

The principle of exclusivity and the substantive limitation of rights *in rem* (the *numerus clausus* of rights *in rem*) is a natural attribute of our present day thinking on property law, which has two conceptual bases. One of the conceptual bases is a feature of historical evolution, which can be traced back to the development of civil ownership. The system of feudal divided property—as the property law reflection of vassal arrangements—meant the long term, conditioned rights of the use and utilisation of land(s), which rendered the property non-negotiable for both the principal owner and the using owner. This divided ownership provided partial interests for utilisation, limiting and thus making the object of ownership non-negotiable. Contemporary property rights could loosen this limited ownership in two ways: they either made the utilisation rights negotiable, or ruled out the possibility of generating long term non-negotiable utilisation rights with respect to land. English law followed the former path, while continental laws chose the latter. The principle of *numerus clausus* means from this historical perspective that the legislature reserves the right to identify the content of property rights and the partial interests of property rights. In this way, parties are prevented from creating long term limited ownership by which they would render assets non-negotiable. The other explanation of the *numerus clausus* principle follows actually from the *in rem* nature of proprietary rights, i.e. that these rights are enforceable against third parties (all other persons). If the parties could freely establish new rights *in rem* or modify the content of them through contract then getting to know the content of rights *in rem* would entail high transaction costs for third persons, but these can be avoided by type constraints and fixed content. Thus, for example, the position of the holder of beneficial ownership and the precise legal standing of the beneficial owner can be identified by third persons without further examination of the origin of the legal relationship. A high level of standardisation of property rights can develop as a result of the principle of the exclusivity of rights *in rem*, and this makes the legal relationships in the law of rights *in rem* transparent and thus decreases transaction costs.[3] There is no need for this in such, relatively structured, legal relationships that establish rights and obligations for only one party in relation to another party.

The principle of *numerus clausus* of property rights implies the exclusive authority and freedom of the legislature to identify the scope and content of the *in rem* rights that can be established. At the same time, however, it is the task of the legislator to provide rights *in rem* that are suitable for satisfying practical demands which places a major onus on the legislature,[4] since the market cannot substitute for this. The new Civil Code does not create new rights *in rem* and does not modify the content and system of establishment of them; however, with the correction of the existing rights, it strives to ensure that the existing "supply" aligns with the demand arising in practice.

---

[3]Hansmann/Kraakman, 39.

[4]Merrill/Smith, 69.

5.2 The Object of Ownership: The Thing

The starting point for reconsidering the concept and objects of ownership was that it is the function of the law covering property in general to provide protection to positions which can be exploited in society and in the economy. This determined the task of the legislator in the course of preparing the property law rules for the Civil Code (2013). Three main tasks were identified. First, the law has to define the protected positions, by establishing the rights belonging to them; second, the regulations have to define what kind of protection should be provided over these positions; and third, the law has to describe how these positions can be transferred and, in general, how the position of the beneficiary of these position, i.e. the position of exercising the rights (and fulfil obligations) and entitlement to protection can be allocated to other persons. There were four categories of positions identified that may be relevant in patrimonial law: things, rights, debts and contractual positions. The Civil Code (1959) defined the object of ownership as things and extended the rules of ownership to certain assets that are not corporeal things (esp. to sources of energy). The Civil Code (1959) did not extend the objects of ownership to rights and debts, primarily on the grounds that they are either rights that are part of property or debts which are covered by the law of obligations. In the course of preparatory work on the Civil Code (1959) the legislators came to the conclusion that rights and debts are not necessarily transferable and their content is so heterogeneous that they cannot be brought under one abstract definition. Under the preparatory work for the Civil Code (2013) there were strong arguments for extending the scope of ownership to transferable rights, debts and contractual positions, including the money held in a bank account. From this also follows that money paid out can be claimed back with a claim for restitution of unjustified enrichment but not with a property claim. One of these arguments was that, in the context of the right to property, the constitutional concept of property covers these assets as well and such an extension could have provided conceptual homogeneity in the law. Another argument was that, as these assets are transferable, they present the most important features of property as well and can also be the objects of in rem rights such as collateral or usufruct. Hence, there seem no grounds for rejecting them as possible objects of ownership. There also are assets that cannot be described either as things or as rights but are deemed objects of property, such as shares in private limited companies. Other assets, such as goodwill, internet domain names, copyrights, patents or trademarks, also have some attributes of ownership, although they also miss some other attributes of ownership.

5.2.1 Objects of Ownership: Tangible Things

The starting point of preparatory work in this aspect was that the legislator has a wide playing field in defining the objects of ownership but, in order to decide if such immaterial assets should be defined as objects of ownership, the purpose of ownership first had to be defined. It has been found that the main goal of ownership is providing protection to the owner in the event of unlawful interference with his or her ownership rights. Protection can be provided by giving the right to the owner to reclaim his/her property back if it was taken (*rei vindicatio*) or to claim its separation from the estate of the possessor in the event of liquidation and have it delivered to its owner. The underlying idea was that, although due to their commercial value and their transferability such assets can be deemed objects of property, their "owner" cannot be deprived of them and the position of having immaterial assets (rights, debts and contractual positions) cannot be interfered with. Thus, defining them as objects of ownership would have no practical value while it would require difficult and specific regulation in the context of possession, joint ownership and rules such as excluding the limitation of proprietary claims. Defining immaterial assets as objects of ownership would be pointless and also unnecessary. If the basic tasks of regulation (defining protected positions and describing changes to these positions) are completed in the Civil Code as whole, there is no need to give the position of ownership to these assets.

The rights of the creditor of debts and the rules of transferability of debts (assignment) are provided in the law of obligations. Debts can be the object of collateral (liens) as well as of usufruct. The creditor cannot be deprived of his or her claim. Defining debts as object of ownership would not add anything, neither in the context of protection nor in the context of transferability and this also holds for contractual positions or transferable rights. Whether rights, debts or contractual positions are transferable can only be assessed according to the legal norm creating and defining them. The Civil Code cannot give a general rule on assessing the transferability of such immaterial goods, as they are as manifold as the legal norms creating them. There is still, however, one further difference between corporeal things and immaterial goods. As immaterial goods cannot be possessed, delivery cannot be required for their transfer. If delivery (*traditio*) is required for transferring ownership or passing of risk in the context of contract law, this cannot be done with such assets. This quality distinguishes immaterial goods and corporeal things at the level of the regulatory structure, provided that delivery is required for transfer of ownership or passing of risk. As a result, the New Hungarian Civil Code provides that things of a tangible nature, being capable of being possessed, are the objects of ownership. The provisions pertaining to things also applies to money and securities, including natural resources that can be utilised as things.[5] Natural resources cannot be defined as things in the traditional sense of the word, as they do not have physical limits, but this extension of the concept of things resulted from court practice and was already accepted in the Civil Code (1959) in order to penalize the illegal use of electricity under the crime of theft. The category of immaterial or incorporeal things does not exist in Hungarian property law.

[5]§ 5:14 Civil Code (2013).

Money held in a bank account is not the object of property but a debt of the bank vis-á-vis the holder of the bank account. The grounds for adopting this solution and strengthening the court practice in this respect was that while money in cash (bank notes and coins) has a physical reality, this does not hold for money in a bank account. Transferring the money to the bank results in the bank acquiring ownership of the banknotes and coins (except specific forms of deposit), and appears as an increase of the balance of the account. Accepting that this increase is an object of ownership too would result in duplicating reality and creating assets without reality behind them. Above the view that law should not provide such multiplication of the real world, it was unforeseen how such assets could behave in the event of liquidation. Due to these considerations, in the system of the Civil Code money is the object of ownership in its physical form but not so for money in a bank account. Banknotes and coins that are no longer used as tools of payment are antiquities and fall under the category of corporeal things and can be owned as such. Specific rules provided for money are not to be applied to them.

Information is not the object of ownership either but is protected as a private secret under the regime of protecting inherent rights of persons and intellectual property law. The significant difference between things and information is that while its owner can be deprived of a thing this is not true for information, which can be passed on but the original holder of it still will own it, even if acquired, used or copied illegally. As such, extending the scope of protection of ownership would only be an empty rule in property law, because protecting its lawful holder cannot be provided with the rules covering ownership. The provisions pertaining to things shall apply to animals in accordance with the statutory provisions to be applied to them according to their nature. This rule expresses a moral value and aims at harmonising private law with criminal law, which penalizes the mistreatment of animals.

5.2.2 Objects of Ownership: Land

The property law of the Civil Code (2013) follows the traditional division of objects of ownership into tangible things and land (immovables). The specific rules for establishing *in rem* rights and the transfer of ownership for land provided by the rules covering the system of land registration make this distinction relevant. The concept of land (immovable) is an abstract one. Land is what is registered as such in the land register. In the Hungarian system of land registration, all land is registered, and so no unregistered land is to be assumed. All other things, which are not registered as land in the land register, are to be seen as tangible things. From this it also follows that differentiation between tangible things and land is not according to the nature of the things; land is an abstract legal concept. Defining land (immovable) as a thing is an abstraction as well. Differences in the regulation of property in tangible things on the one hand and immovables on the other hand are primarily relevant insofar as the consequences of the content of land register for acquiring rights concerning immovables are provided. The most important effect of land register is that *bona fide* buyers who relied on the content of the land register are protected. This protection is provided as a limitation of the claims of the original owner, which is triggered after a certain period of time has elapsed. A person holding some title in material law, or who is expected to obtain some right upon the cancellation of an entry may bring an action for cancellation against a third party who acquired the registered right in good faith for counter-value and with relying on an unlawful entry or an entry that became incorrect subsequently, relying on the completeness and the probity of such entry, within six months from the date of delivery of the resolution on the originally invalid entry in the case of the person holding the title in material law, or, in the case of the person becoming entitled as a result of deletion, within six months from the date of delivery of the resolution on the registration of acquisition made on the basis of an entry that became incorrect subsequently, if the resolution was delivered to him. If delivery of resolution did not take place, the action for cancellation may be brought within a period of three years from the effective date of the entry.[6] Thus, the position of persons acquiring title in reliance upon the content of the register in good faith and for counter-value cannot be challenged after three years. This consequence of protecting reliance brings the legal effects of land registration very close to that of securities (e.g. bills of exchange).

The purpose of ownership is to provide the protection of assets against unlawful interference. Interference with property rights can be assumed only in positions that can be defined (limited) in space. As such, chattels can be the object of ownership by their nature but this does not hold for land. Land is defined by the contents of the land register, with an identification number and which is described on a map belonging to the number. According to the strict interpretation, land is a part of the surface of the Earth circumscribed by the boundaries drawn on the map without assuming three-dimensional extension.[7] It has, however, never been questioned that the privilege and the right to use and utilise the space above and below the surface is allocated to the owner of the land. It is, however, also clear that protection should not exceed the interests of the owner. Legal systems have basically two options for defining ownership of land. They either provide that ownership of land covers the space above and below the surface (up to the sky and down to the middle of the Earth) as well, but the owner does not have the right to prevent interference in the depth or at the height where it cannot serve his or her interests or draw the limits of ownership (or, more correctly, the boundaries of land as a thing) where the prevention of interference cannot serve the interests of the owner. The Hungarian legislator followed the latter option. Land is deemed a thing and as such an object of ownership. The ownership of real estate property covers the airspace above the land and the land mass underneath to the extent of potential use of the property.[8]

[6] 5:187. § Civil Code (2013).

[7] Almási, 86.

[8] 5:17. § (1) Civil Code (2013).

Assessing the extent of potential use requires a comprehensive approach. The natural qualities of the estate, trends in the technical development of exploitation in the foreseeable future and the regulatory framework all are to be taken into account in the course of assessing the potential use of the property.

In the course of the preparatory work, the extension of the scope of rights *in rem* arose in connection with the possible introduction of leasehold as a transferable right, which was also known in pre-World War II Hungarian law, but this idea was finally abandoned.[9] It appeared that the divided ownership rights to the building and to the land properly resolved situations in this respect, so the circle of rights *in rem* has not been expanded with the individual right *in rem* providing a transferable right to build on the plot. In this context, however, the regulations became more flexible with respect to two points, primarily to make it more suitable for the satisfaction of economic demands arising in practice. On the one hand, the Civil Code (2013) does not tie the option of establishing the building and the land on which it stands as separate real estates to the construction of the building, and it also makes it possible for the owner of the real estate to choose to have the land and the building on it entered in the land register as separate properties.[10] If the land and the building standing on it are the property of different owners, they may assign a third party effect to their agreement—if they concluded one—covering specific rights and obligations concerning the rights of the owner of the building to use the land. In order to assign this *in rem* effect to their agreement, the fact thereof has to be entered in the land register. It is justified to extend the binding effect of such an agreement (between the owner of the land and the owner of the building) to third persons acquiring the land or the building, because without this the original interests, allowing separate ownership rights for the owner of the land or the plot protected in the agreement (for example, the extent, the due date, and manner of payment of the user's fee, the extent and limitation of land use and other mutual obligations) could not be enforced if ownership changed. Hence, if the agreement has been registered, a transfer of property cannot result in losing the position of a party acquired by the contract for use of the land. For this, it was necessary to require that this agreement applies to third persons as well,[11] primarily including persons who obtain ownership rights, beneficial ownership rights, or right of use on the plot of land or the building. The extension of the binding effect of the agreement on third persons can be accepted only and to such an extent, when and if the content of this agreement can be made available to the third persons. That is why the new Civil Code requires the obligation of the submission and registration of the agreement in the land register. The failure of submission does not affect the validity of the agreement, but it excludes the enforceability of the agreement vis-á-vis third persons. Naturally, this is applicable to all amendments of the agreement, too.

---

[9] Szőke, 6.

[10] § 5:18 (2) Civil Code (2013).

[11] § 5:19 (1) Civil Code (2013).

5.3 Transfer of Ownership

The question whether delivery is needed for transfer of ownership of chattels or the contract itself may pass ownership is a central issue from the point of view of the structure of the Civil Code. If the contract itself transfers ownership, the division of civil law into property law and the law of obligations can be questioned and its justification may be lost. The Civil Code (2013) maintained the system where delivery is required for transfer of ownership. In this system, the contract creates the title of the transfer and the obligation to deliver the chattel by establishing the right for the transferee to claim delivery from the transferor. Ownership of the chattel is passed upon delivery, which is assumed to be a legal transaction (like a contract) with the legal effect of transferring ownership. Delivery of chattels or registration of a title in land, however, cannot transfer ownership if the contract creating the title was invalid.

Delivery is the transfer of possession. Transfer of possession shall be governed by the provisions on the conclusion and validity of contracts.[12] This rule attempts to express that delivery itself is a legal transaction too, as contracts are, but it does not create obligations (as contracts do) but its legal effect creates *in rem* rights. Thus, if possession was passed on a basis other than acquiring ownership (i.e. as deposit or use), or it was performed by an incapable person or by an unauthorised person then passing possession could not result in acquiring ownership.

Transfer of possession can be performed upon the conveyance of physical control of the thing on the basis of an agreement for that purpose; done by means of an agreement between the possessor and the acquirer of possession if the party acquiring possession already has physical possession of the thing as a secondary possessor (*brevi manu traditio*); if the transferor maintains physical possession of the thing as a secondary possessor (*constitutum possessorium*) according the agreement of the parties; it can be completed upon the possessor relinquishing physical possession of the thing if so agreed by the possessor and the acquirer of possession (*longa manu traditio*); or, if the thing is held by a third party, transfer of possession shall be considered completed upon conveying the claim for the thing to the party acquiring possession, if so agreed by the possessor and the acquirer of possession (*cessio vindicationis*).[13] The main argument for maintaining the system where delivery is needed for transferring ownership was that, in systems where the contract itself is enough to transfer ownership, it is very difficult to manage risks being passed in cases of transferring goods to be produced or obtained by the transferor in the future. It is, however, relatively easy to recognise that the systems where delivery is required and the ones where the mere contract transfers ownership stay very close to each other. In cases of *brevi manu traditio*, *constitutum possessorium*, *longa manu traditio* and *cessio vindicationis,* delivery is performed with the agreement of the parties without any changes in the physical status of the thing.

[12] § 5:3 (1) Civil Code (2013).

[13] § 5:3 Civil Code (2013).

The law requires only that which of the parties possesses the thing and under what title (owner, lessor, borrower etc.) is made clear.

In cases of transferring ownership over land (immovables), delivery is required as a contractual obligation of the transferor. As the legal effect of registration of title in the land register is acquiring ownership, failure to deliver in contracts for transferring land is a breach of contract triggering the consequences of delay in performance in contract law but does not hinder title from passing. If the transferee was the registered owner of the land but delivery was not performed in spite of the contractual obligation of the transferor, the transferee has the choice of evicting the transferor who became an unlawful possessor, claiming it to be done by the transferor as specific performance of his contractual duty, or to terminate the contract and restoring the original state.

5.4 Possession

There is a long history of debates over the legal nature of possession. It was a basic question of rethinking the regulation of the Civil Code if possession is a transferable right or a fact with certain legal consequences. It also had to be considered if intent (*animus*), actual possession (*corpus*) or title (*causa*) were necessary in order to establish possession. The Civil Code (2013) postulates that possession is a right of the possessor and not a mere fact with legal consequences. Thus, possession can be transferred and can be the subject of succession as well. Legal entities can also be possessors and the incapacity of persons does not preclude acquiring possession either. Intent and actual possession shall be relevant in the course of establishing or acquiring possession and losing it and the title is relevant in deciding who shall have the (stronger) right of possession if there are competing claims. Someone who acquired possession shall be a possessor, as long as he or she did not lose it. Losing control over the thing temporarily does not result in losing possession. The possessor is the person in possession of a thing as his own, or who keeps possession of a thing under temporary right. Where there is a person who maintains actual possession of a thing under temporary right (secondary possessor), the person from whom the possession actually originates shall also be considered a possessor (principal possessor). The person from whom a thing is temporarily conveyed without legal basis to the actual control of another person is also deemed a possessor.[14] Possession can be acquired by getting actual control over the thing or by transfer of possession[15] and can be lost by definitively abandoning physical possession of the thing, if possession of the thing is acquired by others[16] or by transferring it. Whether the possessor is a primary (*possessio*) or a secondary

[14] § 5:1 Civil Code (2013).

[15] §§ 5:2 and 5:3 Civil Code (2013).

[16] § 5:4 Civil Code (2013).

(*detentio*) one is relevant only in their relationship but there are no further consequences of that. This distinction was used in order to describe positions (e.g. by transfer of possession) but is relevant only if it has to be decided that one of the parties has the right to possess against the other, which is to be assessed according to the title of possession. Right of possession is allocated to the owner as a general right, being part of ownership rights. Thus, possession over land (immovables) and over tangible things is treated on an equal footing in Hungarian private law.

5.5 Content of Ownership

It is another starting point of Hungarian private law followed in the Civil Code (2013) that ownership as an abstract right consists of the right to possess, use or utilise the thing and the right of disposition (alienation and encumbrance). The owner is entitled to use and enjoy the benefits of a thing, and shall bear the expenses of the thing, as well as the risk of losses if no compensation can be demanded from anyone. The limits of the rights of the owner are described with a general clause, which establishes that when using a thing, the owner shall refrain from engaging in any conduct that would needlessly disturb others, especially his or her neighbours, or that would jeopardize the exercise of their rights.[17] This rule allows courts a wide playing field to decide if the owner shall bear the limitation of his or her property rights in order to protect the interests of others. At the centre of court decisions is the counter-weighing and balancing of the interests of the parties involved. The courts may not only establish if disturbing others is necessary or not in the given case and whether to prohibit actions but they also can specify how the owner is entitled to exercise his or her rights by setting time limits or the mode of use.[18] Courts also can impose specific obligations on the owner in order to prevent the disturbing effects of his or her activity[19] or prohibit the activity and implement preventive measures in order to avoid the risk of causing damage.[20] Disturbing others is understood in a wide sense. Not only emissions (noise, smoke, stink, works etc.)[21] but making video records from the neighbouring land can also be an unlawful act, even the people on it are unrecognisable.[22]

Regulatory or statutory permits to pursue some activity within specified limits do not necessarily make the interference of the rights of others lawful under private law. In Hungarian legal theory, practice and tort law regulations, there seems to be a Chinese wall between the regulation of administrative law and civil law. This wall

[17]§ 5:23 Civil Code (2013).

[18]Supreme Court, Legf. Bír. Pf. IV. 21 023/1984. sz. (BH 1985/344).

[19]Supreme Court P. törv. I. 20 295/1991. sz. (BH 1992/100).

[20]Supreme Court, Legf. Bír. Pfv. III. 22.140/2000. sz. (BH 2003/64).

[21]Supreme Court, Legf. Bír. Pfv. I. 21.139/2001. sz. (BH 2005/50).

[22]Supreme Court, Legf. Bír. Pfv. I/A. 22. 539/1999. sz. (EBH 2001. 519).

is built with the autonomous concepts of unlawfulness and fault in tort law, which are independent from administrative regulation. According to the autonomous concept of unlawfulness, it follows that, even in the absence of the infringement of a statutory provision, unlawfulness of the conduct in private law can be established, even if it was in compliance with a statutory provision or an administrative permit.[23] The Civil Code (2013) did not change this view and leaves the way open to maintain this approach.

The restraint on alienation and encumbrance established by contract still significantly improves the position of creditors, even if it does not affect the obtaining of rights by bona fide third persons obtaining them for consideration. The improvement of the position of creditors with a restraint on alienation and encumbrance, which can be established the most freely, may facilitate access to credit. Based on the enforcement rules, the contractual restraint on alienation and encumbrance does not weaken the position of creditors, and, therefore, the restriction aspects of the restraint on alienation and encumbrance developed in pre-World War II private law are not decisive today. To prevent the debtor from alienating the object of the collateral can be in the creditors' vital interest, because, for example, in the event of selling for an insolvent person, in the course of the enforcement, the creditor may "lose" the right to the securitisation of the thing. Meanwhile, the assumption of the obligation in itself does not make the debtor's situation impossible.

Compared to the Civil Code (1959), the Civil Code (2013) provides for the possibility of the establishment of contractual restraint on alienation in a broader sense, not only in the event of transfer. However, not even the new regulations allow that the restraint on alienation and encumbrance can become an independent security, because it expects that it will continue to serve the provision of specific[24] rights. Related to this is that the restraint on alienation and encumbrance—with regard to real property- can only be registered in the real estate register if there is a primary secured right (mortgage, right to reclaim gift, right to purchase, etc.) also registered. The independence of the restraint on alienation and encumbrance from the secured rights would have limited by much too great an extent—even without protectable interests—the transferability of things and real property ownership, which would have contradicted the abstract concept of property, on which the rights *in rem* rules of the Civil Code (2013) rest. The restraint on alienation and encumbrance is tied to the securitisation of certain rights, by which the right-holder whose rights the restriction protects can always be identified. The restraint on alienation and encumbrance is not a self-serving restriction but a specific right and, because of this, it can be established in order to provide security to the holder of specific rights.

---

[23]Lenkovics, 324.

[24]§ 5:31 Civil Code (2013).

5.6 Adverse Possession

Acquiring ownership via adverse possession became a controversial issue in the context of its relevance concerning the right to property as protected by the European Convention of Human Rights.[25] It may be argued that rules that provide acquiring ownership by law on the grounds of possession without the consent of the owner and without providing compensation to the owner losing his or her property is unfair and unjust. The basic aim of providing the opportunity to acquire ownership is to create incentives for the party possessing a thing as his or her own to invest in land. The Civil Code (2013) basically upheld the system of acquiring ownership via adverse possession. A person who has had uninterrupted possession of a real estate property for fifteen years, or any movable property for ten years as his or her own, shall acquire ownership through adverse possession. Upon the acquisition of ownership of movable property by way of adverse possession, the rights of a third party on the thing shall cease if they had arisen before the adverse user acquired possession, if the required duration of adverse possession has expired concerning them, except where the adverse user did not act in good faith in respect of those rights. Title shall be considered acquired by way of adverse possession after five years if the possessor acquired possession of the real estate property from the owner by means of a written contract, which gives him or her the right to demand registration of his/her title in the real estate register if the contract meets the prescribed formal requirements and if the possessor has paid the amount of consideration.[26]

5.7 System of *in rem* Security Interests

The Civil Code (2013) upholds the system of *in rem* security interests. The law of security was one of the most sensitive issues of codification due to the demands of practicality and the economy. It is true that it is a field of private law where there can be a great gap between the idea of the legislator and reality. There may emerge such forms of security which, in their content, significantly differ from the aims of the legislator but, at a formal level, comply with typical legal institutions.[27] This provokes legislation as well as practice to react and raises the question whether the door should be kept open to practical attempts and, if yes, to what extent and with what tools this should be allowed. The regulation of liens was also one of the most sensitive issues of codification in Hungary. The central issue was whether transfer of ownership, assignment or option for security purposes should be allowed or prohibited. These transactions were often used in practice in order to provide as

[25] *J.A. Pye (Oxford) Ltd* v *The United Kingdom* (ECHR, 30 August 2007, App no. 44302/02).

[26] §§ 5:44 and 45 Civil Code (2013).

[27] Wiegand, 283.

strong as possible a position to the creditor. Although assignment and option for security purposes were basically accepted in Hungarian court practice, the validity of transfer of ownership for security purposes was questioned in court practice, as well as in the literature. The strongest argument against accepting that, instead of establishing liens, the debtor may transfer ownership of the thing provided as security to the creditor and could buy it back by paying the debts was that in this way the parties might circumvent the regime of liens and mortgages, which provides protection to the debtor too. This question was strongly debated over the past decades in Hungary.[28] This discussion made it clear that this issue cannot be solved on the basis of the internal logic of private law but needs to be addressed as a policy issue. Finally, the most decisive argument for prohibiting such transactions was that they undermine the regime of liens and mortgages. The key rule of regulation of liens and mortgages is the prohibition of *lex commissoria*. This rule, providing that any agreement concluded for transferring ownership of the pledged property to the lien holder at the time of opening the right to satisfaction shall be null and void, was maintained in the Civil Code (2013), too.[29] Transfer of ownership for security purposes was found incompatible with this rule, as in such transfers the parties not only agree to the direct acquisition of ownership by the creditor but they perform it too. Such transfers were declared as null and void, but this rule was revisited after the Civil Code came into force. The prohibition has been softened as it applies only to contract where one of the parties is a consumer and it is the consumer who undertook such an obligation.[30]

In the practice of financing on credit, assignment for security purposes was a widely used and accepted form of security. Its logic and structure was similar to that of transferring ownership for security purposes insofar as the debtor assigned its claim against third persons to his or her creditor who, as assignee, acquired the claim (debt) and had the right to collect it if his/her debtor (assignor) failed to pay. Driving it out from the system could have caused practical problems regarding financial transactions but the rules covering pledges on debts (claims) bring the creditor into the same position as the assignee of a security assignment, which presumably will be functionally equivalent to assignment by security and can eliminate the problems that arises from the absence of assignment for security purposes.

The changes in the law of collateral brought a simpler structure to *in rem* security. According to the concept of lien, the holder of it has the right to seek satisfaction prior to other claims against the property pledged as security for his or

[28]Szabó Gábor Zoltán (Gazdaság és Jog 1998/3), 13 and A visszavásárlási joggal kombinált adásvételi szerződésről (Gazdaság és Jog 1998/10) 17, Gárdos István, 18.; Gárdos István/Gárdos Péter (Polgári Jogi Kodifikáció 2004/1–2.) 33.; Gárdos István/Gárdos Péter (Gazdaság és Jog 2005/3. sz. 13–18); Lajer and Leszkoven, 23 ff.

[29]5:136. § Civil Code (2013).

[30]Act no. LXXVII of 2016 on the Amendment of the Civil Code, § 19. The § 6:99 of the Civil Code as amended reads as: "Any clause in which a consumer undertakes the commitment for the transfer of ownership, other right or claim for the purpose of security of a pecuniary claim, or for the right to purchase, shall be null and void."

her claim upon the failure of the obligor of the secured claim. There are two basic forms of lien, depending on whether the creditor acquires possession of the object of the lien or the lien is registered in land register, another register for specific things (esp. vehicles) or to the register of collateral. Due to the flexible regulation, the parties are free to agree upon the secured claims as well as the objects of lien. Lien may be established on one or more existing or future, conditional or unconditional pecuniary claims of a specific amount or the amount of which can be determined. If the lien is not arranged for a pecuniary claim, the lien shall guarantee the claim for damages resulting from the failure to satisfy a claim, or shall guarantee other receivables.[31] The pledged property may be described by type and quantity, or by a detailed description, by which it may be identified. The description may also pertain to certain assets which do not yet exist, or over which the lienor has no right of disposition.[32] Land charges and floating charges are driven out from the system. Land charge, as an abstract right, was used to provide security for re-financed loans and also used in the grey economy to hiding the actual basis of the claim and the legal relationship between the parties behind it. In order to keep the advantages of land charge in providing security for re-financed loans, separated lien was introduced to the system. According to the new law, the holder of the lien shall be allowed to transfer the lien—under contract, to guarantee his or her debt—without having to transfer the secured claim to the holder of his/her debt. Based on the separated lien, the rights of the lien holder shall pass on to the party acquiring the lien. The contract on the transfer of the lien shall specify the claim to which the seceded lien pertains. This contract shall be concluded in writing. The transfer of the lien shall be considered effective in dealings with third parties as of when the separated lien holder is registered in the real estate register, land register or collateral register, or when the third party receives notice on the assignment of the lien in accordance with the provisions on assignment. The holder of the separated lien shall exercise his or her rights stemming from the lien without jeopardising the recovery of the original secured claim. Upon the termination of the claim secured by a separated lien, the separated lien shall revert to the original lien holder. The separated lien holder shall be entitled to reassign the lien to the original lien holder before the termination of the secured claim. The separated lien must be transferred together with the claim secured by the separated lien.[33]

References

Almási Antal, A dologi forgalom. Budapest, 1910.
Gárdos István, A biztosítéki célú tulajdonátruházásról. Gazdaság és Jog, 6/1998. sz. 18–21.

[31] 5:97. § Civil Code (2013).
[32] 5: 89. § (4) Civil Code (2013).
[33] 5: 100. § Civil Code (2013).

Gárdos István/Gárdos Péter: Van-e a fiduciárius biztosítékoknak helyük a magyar jogban? Vitacikk. Polgári Jogi Kodifikáció, 2004/1–2. sz. 33–47.

Gárdos István/Gárdos Péter: Ismét a fiduciárius biztosítékokról. Gazdaság és Jog, 2005/3. sz. 13–18.

Hansmann, Henry/Kraakman, Reinier, Property, Contract, and Verification: the Numerus Clausus Problem and the Divisibility of Rights, The Harvard John M. Olin Discussion Paper Series, 2002, Vol. 10, No. 388, Harvard Law School, John M. Olin Center for Law, Economics and Business.

Lajer Zsolt/Leszkoven László: A bizalmi (fiduciárius) biztosítékokról. Polgári Jogi Kodifikáció, 2004/1–2. sz. 23–33.

Lenkovics Barnabás, A környezetszennyezés polgári jogi szankciói in: L. Asztalos/K. Gönczöl (ed.), Felelősség és szankció a jogban (Liability and sanction in the law) (1980) 317 ff.

Merrill, Thomas W./Smith, Henry E., Optimal Standardization in the Law of Property: The Numerus Clausus Principle, The Yale Law Journal, 2000, Vol. 110, No. 1, 1–70.

Merryman, John Henry, Ownership and Estate (Variations on a Theme by Lawson), Tulane Law Review, 1974, Vol. 48, 916–945.

Szabó Gábor Zoltán, A visszavásárlási joggal kombinált adásvételi szerződésről. Gazdaság és Jog, 1998/3. sz. 13–14.

Szabó Gábor Zoltán, A visszavásárlási joggal kombinált adásvételi szerződésről. Gazdaság és Jog, 1998/10. sz. 14–17.

Szőke Irén, Az elbirtoklás, a használati jogok és a birtokvédelem bírói gyakorlatának elemzése és annak tanulságai, Polgári jogi kodifikáció, 2002/3, 3–18.

Wiegand, Wolfgang, Kreditsicherung und Rechtsdogmatik. In Berner Festgabe zum Schweizerischen Juristentag 1979. Hrsg. von Bucher, Eugen—Scladin, Peter. Bern–Stuttgart, 1979, Verlag Paul Haupt, 238–308.

Chapter 6
Property Law in the New Romanian Civil Code

Szilárd Sztranyiczki

Abstract Taking into account the recent change in Romanian civil legislation, we consider the present scientific material very useful for an overview of this institution under the auspices of the New Civil Code. The national legal provisions set clear, therefore, that the property is divided into two institutions, the public property and the private property. Property classification is very important in this form, for us to understand the legal nature and the applicable regime for each type of property. Moreover, the property right, either private or public, it has an elite regulation in most European laws, but also in universal laws the respect for it and the guarantee of this right can be also found in the fundamental human rights, in the international treaties, and in the constitutions of different nations. We will try, therefore, to offer a brief overview of the new Romanian legislation in the mentioned field, which is already harmonized with European legislation, the result being the New Romanian Civil Code. We believe that the interpretation should be considerably more extensive, but—pragmatically—we will try to capture the main theoretical and practical features, to denote the importance of this institution.

1. The Notion of the Right to Private Property Property right is closely linked to patrimony and in the Romanian doctrine it has been proposed that it is also linked to the owner. The new Civil Code (in the following: NCC)[1] recognizes *the priority of private property in relation to public property*. This is the reason why Article 554, para 2 stipulates that *if the law doesn't state the contrary, the applicable dispositions of private property rights are also applied to public property rights, but only to the degree that these dispositions are compatible with the latter*. In the NCC, private property rights are regulated by Article 555–692, and public property rights by Articles 858–875.

[1]The New Civil Code entered into force on 1 October 2011.

S. Sztranyiczki (✉)
Sapientia University, Cluj-Napoca (Kolozsvár/Klausenburg), Romania
e-mail: sztranyiczkisz@kv.sapientia.ro

A. Menyhárd and E. Veress (eds.), *New Civil Codes in Hungary and Romania*, Ius Gentium: Comparative Perspectives on Law and Justice 63,
DOI 10.1007/978-3-319-63327-5_6

The standard definition of the right to private property is found in the NCC Articles 555, para 1: *private property is the right of the owner to possess, use, and dispose of goods exclusively, absolutely, and perpetually, within the limits defined by the law.*

This definition, in our conception, is far from being complete.[2] This is why in defining property one must start from the legal concept of the right to property, comprised of the prerogatives (attributes) recognized by law, on the one hand; on the other, these prerogatives are exercised without the intervention of other persons who form a general, passive, and undefined subject. In addition, there are many situations in which some of these attributes or all of them are exercised by a person other than the owner on the basis of another real right derived from the right to property. Examples include the usufructuary, to whom the law grants attributes of possession and use of the object of the usufruct, or the superficiary, who can also exercise the attributes of material and legal disposition beyond the attributes of possession and use.

To the question of how an owner differs from other persons entitled to parts of a property, who exercise some of the attributes of the owner, the response is that the owner of the property exercises his/her attributes in *his/her own power and in his/her own interest*. In *his/her own power* means that he/she is not legally subordinated to anybody, except the law, and all the other persons exercising real rights are obliged to be aware of this. In *his/her own interest* means that the exercise of the right to property is done exclusively to satisfy the property owner's own interests, without obligations toward other people.

When we define the right to private property, we focus first and foremost on the general definition of property. The form of private property is stipulated in Article 136.5 of the Constitution, and in Article 552 of the NCC. In the context of putting our civil rights on new foundations with the adoption and implementation of the NCC, private property has become dominant (not only in a theoretical sense), as the goods that make up private property are in a general civil sphere, which makes them overwhelmingly important in ensuring the permanent material needs of the members of society. The dominating force of private property, in contrary to public property, derives from the fact that it is found in commerce, and the healthier and more responsive its sphere is, the greater the development of a competitive economy of society, satisfying general and particular interests. In contrast, public property is outside the civil sphere, and within the system of ***property, private property is the norm, while public property, through its strict system, constitutes an exception***. The constitutional guarantee and protection of private property is also found in Article 44, para 1 of the fundamental law, which stipulates that *the right to private property, as well as debts and claims against the state are guaranteed;* and

[2]There was a similar definition in Article 480 of the old Civil Code, which was criticized by many authors. See C. Stătescu, Bîrsan, C. 1980. *Civil Law. The General Theory of Real Rights.* Bucharest: Editura Universității din București. pp. 31–32.

in Article 44, para 1 of the Constitution, according to which *private property is protected and guaranteed equally by the law, regardless of the titleholder.*

Private property, besides the Constitution and NCC, is also regulated in a series of normative acts, organic and ordinary laws, including Law No. 18/1991 of the Land Registry, Law No. 7/1996 regarding Cadaster and Real Estate Registry, and several others. The most complete regulation of the legal system of the right to private property is in the NCC. Stătescu, Bîrsan

As far as terminology is concerned, from the evolving legislative conceptions and the attributes of property law, the following notions are used: *private property, particular property,* and *the state's or the territorial-administrative units' private domain.*

The given definition leads to the exercise of the three attributes in one's own right and own interest, regardless of whether they are exercised directly, or through persons to whose benefit certain real rights have been granted (usufruct, location, superficies, etc.).[3]

Starting from the legal conception of the right to private property and appreciating the specific position of the owner, one can define the **right to private property** as *a real right that confers upon the title holder the attributes of possession, use and disposition of a good, appropriated in private form; attributes which he/she can exercise in their totality, in his/her own power and own interest, in an exclusive, absolute and perpetual manner, respecting the material and legal limits defined by law.* Exercising private property is realized through the correspondence that must exist between legal capacity and subjective right.

The conclusion drawn from this definition is that it takes into consideration the legal content of the right to property, comprised of the totality of attributes recognized as belonging to the owner.[4]

In the modern age there is a new method of analysis that tends to show that private property is not easily confined to the simple stature of a subjective law; even though this may be complex, it fulfills a real social function. This new dimension justifies the restrictions on the exercise of property right, which today are more and more numerous, emphasizing the tendency that property ceases to be an intangible and absolute subjective right in order to become, along with family, a suple and orderly institution in the service of the community.

At the same time, one notes a concerted universal or regional action of some organizations in order to adopt some norms for the protection of human rights, including the right to property. In addition to the *Universal Declaration of Human Rights* adopted by the UN in 1948, of special importance is the *European Convention of Human Rights and Fundamental Liberties* adopted by the member states of the European Council in 1950, which came into effect in 1950 and in our

[3]Cf. I. Sabău-Pop, *Acquiring the right to property.* Accent Publishing House, Bucharest, 2000, p. 45.

[4]O. Ungureanu, C. Munteanu, *The content and definition of private property rights in the light of new Civil Code,* in Roumanian Journal of Law, nr. 3/2013, pp. 102–109.

country on June 20, 1994. According to the additional Protocol No.1, *any physical or legal entity has the right of having his/her goods protected. Noone can be deprived of one's property unless for the purpose of public utility and according to the conditions stipulated in the law and the general principles of international law.*[5]

On the other hand, returning to the idea of the social function of property, the second paragraph of the same text states that the dispositions are not of a nature to fulfill the rights of sovereign states to adopt laws that they deem necessary to regulate the use of private property goods, according to general interest.

Called upon to consider the applicability of a regulation of the European Council, the Luxembourg Court decided that *fundamental rights, property rights in particular, cannot generate absolute prerogatives, only prerogatives limited by their social functions. Such restrictions respond effectively to the Union's general interests, and so they cannot constitute an exaggerated and intolerable intervention, which could posit the existence of the guaranteed right.*[6]

2. Subjects to the right to private property From the definition, in principle, it follows that the right to private property can belong to any subject of the law: physical entities, legal entities, the state, and territorial-administrative units.[7]

Similarly, according to Article 553, para 4 of the NCC, *goods, objects of private property, regardless of the title holder, are and will stay in the civil sphere even though the law doesn't provide for it. They can be expropriated, be the object of judicial execution and can be acquired in any way stipulated in the law.* Therefore, immovables (land and constructions) in private ownership are in the general civil sphere, so they can be expropriated and acquired in any way regulated by the law (convention or contract, legal and testimentary inheritance, accession, usucaption, and court order). In the case of private property land, since it is part of the civil sphere, the right to property is transmissible in its entirety, or in its dependent parts.

Exceptions to the norm—according to which property rights can be acquired absolutely by physical and legal entities—are those expressly stipulated in the law. There were and there are cases of special incapacities and legal inalienabilities:

(a) *Special incapacities*:

- *foreign citizens, expatriates and legal persons can acquire the right to private ownership of land, in the limited conditions stipulated by Article 44, para 2 of the Constitution and Law No. 312/2005.*

---

[5]*European Convention on Human Rights, as amended by Protocol no. 11.* European Treaty Series, no. 5, Strasbourg, 2001, p. 27.

[6]Court of Justice of the European Community, 1991, Cause Georg Von Deetzen C. Hauptzollampt Oldenburg, C 44/1989, Bulletin CJCE, No. 18-1, p. 2.

[7]Some authors inculde ad hoc collectives in the category of subject private property rights, for details see S. Văcăruş, *Obştile de moşneni, obştile de răzeşi, comunităţile grănicereşti de avere şi composesoratele ca subiecte de drept, în lumina legislaţioei fondului funciar*, in Law, nr. 10/2000, pp. 16–24.

As far as private ownership of land is concerned, Article 44, point 2 of the Constitution recognizes the possibility of acquiring property rights over land by foreign citizens and expatriates, but only under conditions resulting from Romania's joining the EU and other international treaties that Romania is a part of, based on reciprocity, according to the conditions stipulated by organic law. According to this constitutional text, which is repeated by Article 6, para 1 of Law No. 312/2005, in addition to the fulfilment of special conditions, the general condition of reciprocity[8] in such treaties is obligatory. So far, Romania has not signed such an international treaty, which allows certain foreign nationals and expatriates to acquire land in Romania.

Law No. 312/2005 referring to the acquisition of private property right over lands by foreign citizens, expatriates, and other foreign legal entities, grants the possibility of acquisition of property rights over lands to these categories of people, delayed until Romania's joining the European Union (January 1, 2007), and under the conditions of international treaties that Romania is a part of.

According to Article 5, para 1 from Law No. 312/2005, *the citizen of a member state, the expatriate with residency in a member state or in Romania, and the legal entity constituted according to the legislation of a member state can acquire property right over agricultural lands, forests and forest land 7 years after the date of Romania's joining the European Union*. This special limitation will be implemented on January 1, 2014, when the seven-year period stipulated in the legal text above expires. *(This special incapacity was fulfill on the date of 1st January 2014, when the term of 7 years prescribed in the legal text above-mentioned has expired, therefore currently interdict is not applied anymore.)*

Exceptions to this general rule were:

(I) farmers, who carry out independent activities and are either citizens of member states or expatriates with domicile in a member state, who establish their residency in Romania, or expatriates with domicile in Romania. These persons acquire the property right over agricultural lands, forests, and forestlands according to the same conditions applicable to Romanian citizens, from the date of Romania's joining the European Union. The state of being a farmer must be proved with issued documents in each case, either by the suitable authorities of the member state or the state of origin, or by the

[8]The reciprocity condition has many exceptions in international law. As a rule, international treaties have a sinalagmatic character, establishing reciprocal rights and obligations for both parties. However, in the context of the constitutional text, reciprocity becomes obligatory. In international law the reciprocity condition has a second meaning: certain problems can be resolved through agreement of states or on the basis of reciprocity. Namely, reciprocity is a principle of solution, of solving the problems between the states, in the absence of a treaty. Article 6, para 1 of Law No. 312/2005 states the condition of reciprocity: *The foreign citizen, expatriate and legal entity belonging to tertiary states cannot acquire the right to private ownership of land in more favorable conditions than those applicable to a citizen of a member state and to the legal entity constituted according to the legislation of a member state.*

certificate issued by the Romanian Ministry of Agriculture, Forests, and Rural Development. All these persons have the obligation not to change the designation of the agricultural lands, forests, and forestlands before the expiration of the seven-year period, stipulated in Law No. 312/2005, Article 5, para 1;

(II) the citizen of a member state who is not a resident in Romania, the expatriate who is a non-resident in Romania with domicile in a member state, and the legal entity who is a non-resident constituted according to the legislation of a member state, can acquire property right over land for the purpose of secondary residency and secondary headquarters, respectively, 5 years after Romania's joining the European Union (1 January 2012);

- *foreign citizens and expatriates can acquire the right to private ownership of land through legal inheritance, according to the conditions stipulated in Article 44, para 2 of the Constitution.*

Therefore, through legal inheritance foreign citizens can in fact acquire the right to private property. *Per a contrario* such individuals cannot acquire the right to private property in case of testimentary inheritance. Taking into consideration the principles guiding the application of civil law in time, foreign citizens and expatriates can acquire the right to private ownership of lands in Romania from the effective date of the Revision Law of the Romanian Constitution No. 429/2003, but only if the succession case in reference to which the legal inheritance is exercised was opened after this date.

(b) *Cases of legal inalienability*:

- *requirement of the authentic form of legal acts disposing of immovable goods (lands and constructions)*;
- *land acquired according to the criteria in Article 19, para 1, Articles 21 and 43 of Law No. 18/1991 of the Land Registry, cannot be expropriated through agreements inter vivos for a period of ten years from the beginning of the year following the one in which the property was registered, under the sanction of absolute voidness of the expropriation act, and the acquired apartments by tenants or title holders of apartment contracts (apartments which are not restituted in nature to the former owners or their heirs) cannot be expropriated for a period of ten years from the date of purchase, according to Article 9, last paragraph of Law No. 112/1995*;
- *exercise of the right to preemption*[9] *in selling movables and immovables*. The right to preemption was defined in the scholarly literature as *the subjective civil right recognized by law to certain titleholders, which gives priority to such individuals to purchase unincorporated agricultural areas, seriatim, and under*

---

[9]Cf. Fr. Deak, *The right to preemption*, in Law No. 7/1992, pp. 34–43; Gh. Beleiu, *The Right to Preemption Regulated by Law No. 18/1991 of the Land Registry*, in Law No. 12/1992, pp. 3–15; E. Chelaru, *The Right to Preemption Regulated by Law No. 54/1998*, in Law No. 8/1998, pp. 19–25.

other conditions prescribed by law.[10] Evidently, the cited author only consulted the provisions of Law No. 18/1991 of the Land Registry valid at that time. Article 1730, para 1 of the NCC defines the right to preemption as follows: *according to the conditions established by the law or contract, the title holder of the right to preemption, called preemptor, can purchase a good with priority.*

Therefore, the right to preemption is a priority right to purchase a good, according to the conditions established by the law, or through convention. At the same time, taking into consideration legal regulations, we can define the right to preemption as *a right with a temporary character, established by the law or through a convention of the parties, in which certain title holders called preemptors have the priority right to buy movables or immovables.*

The right to preemption must be viewed as a possibility conferred upon a person to purchase a good with precedence over any other buyer. This priority materializes through the exercise of the right to private property following the consent agreement of the parties, which allows the characterization of this institution as ultracontractual.

The right to preemption is provided by Articles 1730–1740 of the NCC, and its domain of application extends to all movables and immovables. Titleholders of the legal right to preemption are the following[11]:

(I) in the case of lands that belong to the forest registry in private property, these can be sold respecting, seriatim, the preemptive right of coowners or neighbors (Article 1746 of NCC); Beleiu
(II) in the case of agricultural goods, tenant farmers have the right to preemption over the rented agricultural goods (Article 1849 of NCC).[12]

Article 1732 of NCC regarding the conditions of the exercise of the right to preemption provides that the seller is obliged to immediately notify the preemptor

[10]Beleiu, Gh. 1992. The Right to Preemption Regulated by Law No 18/1991 of the Land Registry. Bucharest: *Dreptul* 12. p. 14.

[11]In addition of the new Civile Code, there are other norm acts, which admit diffrent preemption rights, like:

- preemption right of the last owner, in the situation when the working, wherefore the expropriation was made, wasn't execute, but expropriator would like to appropriate the property, according to 37 din Legea nr. 33/1994, on the expropriation to the cause of public use
- the preemption right of Romanian state, respective territorial administrativ units, at the selling of property, which are placed funeral and the military commemoration, and are in the property of individual or legal entity, according to Article 9 alin. (2) din Legea nr. 379/2003 on the system of funeral and the military commemoration
- the preemption right in the favour of coproprietor and neigbour, at the selling of fields from forestry fond private property, according to Article 45 alin. (2) from Forestry code; New Civil code, through Article 1828.

[12]According to Article 1828 of the new Civil code, introduce a newness in the lease material, namely the right of preemption of the tenant in lease. A conversation in this topic, see *Emőd Veress, Does estabilish the new Civil code a legal law of preemption for the tenant (renter) preference?* Published in Curierul Judiciar, nr. 8/2012, pp. 459–462.

regarding a contract signed with a third party. Notification can also be done by the third party. It includes the first and last name of the seller, the description of the good, the responsibilites encumbent upon him/her, the terms and conditions of the sale, as well as the place where the good is situated. The preemptor can exercise his/her right by communicating his agreement to sign a selling contract to the seller, together with the specification of the price. The right to preemption is exercised in case of movable sales within a period of 10 days at most, and in the case of immovable sales, within a period of 30 days at most. In both cases the time period is calculated starting with the preemptor's communication of the notification.

As regards the effects of the exercise of preemption (Article 1733 of the NCC), the contract of sale is considered final between the preemptor and seller under the conditions included in the contract with the the third party, and the latter contract is terminated retroactively. However, the seller is responsible to the third person for good faith for an eviction resulting from the exercise of preemption.

The NCC, inspired by French legislation, opts for the possibility of the exercise of the preemptive right following the consent agreement between the seller and the third party under the form of a retraction. The contract is signed between the owner and the third party, subsequently the title holder of the preemptive right (coowner or neighbor, in case of lands belonging to the Forest Registry); then, the tenant farmer, in case of rented agricultural goods, or the renter on signing a new lease is notified about the existence of the translative property act. These persons may exercise their rights, substituting themselves for the buyer from the initial contract, thus assuming all the rights and obligations of the third party, as in the case of a cession.[13] We have reservations about this solution chosen by the Romanian legislature. We consider that the chosen option—the exercise of the right to preemption following the finalization of legal acts—will not prove its practical utility. The procedure needed to exercise this right is much more useful and pragmatic if it is carried out before the consent agreement on a good, which serves the effectiveness of the civil sphere better.

3. Legal Forms of Property Rights The right to property is presented as pure and simple or affected by various forms.[14]

The pure and simple right to property is the right belonging to a single person and is acquired by its owner actually, surely, and irrevocably; its existence in the owner's patrimony does not depend on a future event or circumstance which could terminate it through resolution, revocation, or annulment.

The right to property affected by various modalities exists when its general characteristics are modified; its existence in the patrimony of a person is uncertain,

[13]Cf. I. Malaurie, L. Aynès, P.-Yv. Gautier, *Cours de droit civil,* t. VIII, *Les contrats spéciaux civils et commerciaux,* 14-e édition, Cujas, Paris, 2001, p. 132.

[14]C. Stătescu, C. Bârsan, *Civil Law. The General Theory of Real Rights.* University Publishing House, Bucharest, 1980, pp. 177–179; Gh. Beleiu, *Romanian Civil Law. Introduction in Romanian Civil Law, Subjects of Civil Law.* Şansa Publishing House, Bucharest, 1994, p. 154.

another person exercises his/her attributes, or it belongs evenly and at the same time to two or more subjects of the law, and each is entitled to a part of this right.

The pure and simple right to property is the norm, and the right to property affected by various forms is the exception.

Clause 555, para 2 of the NCC specifies that: *Under the law, the right to private property is susceptible to various modalities and partitions depending on the case in question.* One must note, however, that not only the right to property is susceptible to modifications, but all the other main/principal real rights.

Romanian Civil Law recognizes the following forms of property rights: (a) resolvable property (b) annulable property and (c) common property.[15] Some authors,[16] due to the common chracteristics of the resolvable and annulable properties, include both in the larger notion of *conditioned property.*

Resolvable property exists when the transfer of the right was done through a legal act affected by a resolutionary condition. It is also called revokable property. Suppose a person sells a good to another person under the condition that if he/she has a baby, that good should revert to his/her or his/her heirs' patrimony. In the example given, the acquirer is an owner under resolutionary condition, and the transmitter is an owner in suspension.

Conditional obligation is defined by Article 1399 of the NCC: *an obligation affected by condition is an obligation whose efficacy or termination depends on an uncertain future event, and the condition is resolutory when its fulfilment determines the termination of the obligation* (Article 1401, para 1 of the NCC). The fate of the right to property depends on the fulfillment or nonfulfillment of the uncertain future event. Theoretically, we are in the presence of the *pendente conditione:* the good that is the object of expropriation belongs to two owners. Therefore, the expropriator has a right to property that is subject to a suspensive condition, and the acquirer has a right to property that is subject to a resolutory condition. The acquirer's resolutory condition has the effects of a suspensive condition toward the transmitter, and vice versa. Namely, the acquirer is the actual and temporary owner; his/her right is made uncertain by the resolutory condition, and the transmitter has the possibility of becoming the owner of the property in question if the suspensive condition materializes.

Resolvable property can result from the convention of the parties; there are two cases when it results from the law. The first situation is regulated by Article 1022, paras 1–2 of the NCC: the promise of donation is revoked by right if one of the revocation cases for ingratitude appears anterior to its execution, as prescribed by Article 1023 of the NCC (if the beneficiary attempted to harm the donor, a person close to him/her, or, knowing that others intend to harm the donor, did not notify him/her; if the beneficiary is guilty of penal acts, cruelty or serious injuries to the

[15]For another perspective for the property rights in Romanian civil law, see T. Sâmbrian, *Property in the time sharing sysitem–periodic property–a new method of the property law,* in Dreptul nr. 5/1997, pp. 35–38.

[16]L. Josserand, *Cours de droit civil positiv français,* Tome prèmiere, Recueil Sirey, Paris, 1938, pp. 1009–1014.

donor; if the beneficiary unjustifiedly refuses to ensure food to the donor in need, limited to the actual worth of the donated good and considering the condition of the good at the time of donation). Similarly, the promise of donation is revoked by right when, anterior to its execution, the material situation of the promisor has deteriorated to the degree that the execution of the promise has become excessively onerous for him/her, or the promisor has become insolvent. The second situation is regulated by Article 1031 of the NCC, which stipulates that donations between married couples are revokable only during marriage, rendering uncertain the property rights of the beneficiary spouse.

Annulable property is a legal form of the right to property, which appears in the situation when the transfer of property from one person to another is done on the basis of a legal act struck down by relative (annulable) annulment. The relative annulment of the legal act is very important, that is, it should focus on the interests of the parties who signed the agreement, and therefore contain the possibility for the expressed or tacit confirmation of those who are interested to invoke annulment.

In case of relative annulment of the legal act, the action taken for its court annulment is prescribed by law (in the NCC) within the time frame of three years.

The one who acquired the right to property is in an uncertain situation until the fulfilment of the prescribed term as a successful annulment action will retroactively terminate his/her title.

We need to mention that if the annulable act is expressly confirmed by the one who could have invoked its annulability during this time period, the fragility of the act disappears, and the right to property is definitely consolidated.

These are also the two effects of annulable property.

If the nullified act is confirmed by the one entitled to an annulment action, the right is consolidated without the right to return or oppose the annulment motive to a possible forced execution. The confirmation effects do not take place in case of third parties except for universal successors or simple contract creditors.

The second effect takes place when the annulment motive is invoked and the title of the annulable property is annuled. *Common property* is considered to be the most important form of the right to property. In the case of this property, the prerogatives of common law belong to two or more titleholders together and simultaneously. According to the provisions of Article 632, para 1 of the NCC, common property is of two kinds: *(a) common property based on quota (coownership)* and *(b) common property in joint ownership.*

Common property based on quota or coownership is a form of common property where a good belongs to more titleholders simultaneously and at the same time, unfractioned in its entity. Each coowner has an ideal, abstract, mathematical share determined, which is expressed by fraction or percentage. The right of each owner meets the rights of the other owners as regards every part that comes into the make-up of the good in its whole.

The right to property in joint ownership is a form of common property in which a good belongs undividedly, indivisibly to all titleholders, who own it together. According to Article 667, joint ownership can result from the law or on the basis of a legal act.

The main characteristic of the right to common property in joint ownership is that the title holders of this right do not know either the extent of their property rights, the share they are entitled to, or the goods each of them possesses in their entity.

Periodical property was introduced into the NCC (Articles 687–692) as an absolute novelty. It is possible for the right to private property to have more titleholders, each of them successively and repetitively exercising their attribute of use over an immovable or movable, in equally or unequally determined intervals of time. This practical application generally appeared in the domain of real estate investments, especially in the case of vacation homes.

The general system of periodical property is applied obligatorily in the absence of special regulations. In other words, whenever the characteristic elements of periodical property are present, another legal system of private property cannot be chosen. This solution is provided by Article 687 of NCC, according to which *the dispositions of the present chapter (periodical property) are applied in the absence of a special regulation. Per a contrario,* if a legal derogatory regime has been established, it will be applied.

The following characteristics result from the notion of periodical property:

- the right to property belongs to many title holders;
- the attribute of use is exercised successively and repetitively by the title holders, in equally or unequally determined intervals of time;
- its objects can be any kind of movables or immovable.

According to the provisions of Article 688 of the NCC, periodical property is formed on the basis of a legal act, in which *the dispositions regarding the land registry are applied accordingly*. The legal act can be a bequest or a convention. For example: the parties agree to acquire the right to periodical property for the building of a house; the parties agree to acquire periodical property right over the purchase of a certain good; the parties agree to transform coownership into periodical property.

4. The Right to Public Property The right to public property is a property right belonging to the state or to a territorial-administrative unit over goods, which, in their nature or by law, are of public use or interest, under the condition that they be acquired through one of the ways prescribed by the law; the prerogatives of this right are exercised as public right, which is *inalienable, imprescribable and unseizable (exempt from seizure).*

The normative acts regulating the right to public property provide for the titleholders of the right in a limiting manner. Accordingly, Article 136.2 of the Constitution states that *public property is protected and guaranteed by law and belongs to the state and territorial-administrative units*. Similarly, Article 1 of Law No. 213/1998 stipulates that the right to public property belongs to the state or territorial-administrative units. Article 860, para 1 of NCC distinguishes public property goods of national, county, or local public domain. In reference to public property lands, Article 4, para 2 of Land Registry Law No. 18/1991 presribes that *the public domain can be of national interest, in which case the property, in the system of public rights, belongs to the state; or of local interest in which case the property, also in the system of public rights, belongs to the towns, townships, cities, or counties.*

One concludes from the legal texts above that the titleholders of the right to public property are:

(a) *the state*, over goods that are part of the national public domain;
(b) *territorial administrative units*—townships, towns, cities, and counties—over goods that are part of the local or county public domain and belong to territorial administrative units as legal entities of public right.

In this context, one most emphasize that no other subject of public or private right can be the titleholder of the right to property over goods that constitute the public domain. Such legal entities acquire, by law, the right to administer, use, lease, or rent the goods that are part of the public domain, which are real rights. However, these rights cannot be mistaken for the exercise of attributes of the public property right.

Article 863 of NCC principally regulates cases of acquisition of public property rights. These are:

(a) public acquisition carried out according to the law;
(b) expropriation for public utility according to the law;
(c) donation or bequest, accepted according to the law, if the good, through its nature or through the disposer's will, becomes of public use or interest;
(d) contract with a gratuitous clause, if the good, through its nature or through the acquirer's will, becomes of public use or interest;
(e) transfer of a good from the private domain of the state into its public domain, or from the private domain of a territorial-administrative unit into its public domain, according to the law;
(f) other ways established by law.

The inclusion of goods in the public domain can be accomplished through means of civil, administrative, or penal law.

It is important to note that inclusion in the public or private domain of the state or the territorial-administrative units depends on the nature, distinction, or characteristics of the goods in question.

References

Beleiu, Gh. 1992. The Right to Preemption Regulated by Law No 18/1991 of the Land Registry. Bucharest: *Dreptul* 12. 1994. *Romanian Civil Law. Introduction in Romanian Civil Law, Subjects of Civil Law*. Bucharest: Şansa.

Chelaru, E. 1998. The Right to Preemption Regulated by Law No 54/1998. Bucharest: *Dreptul* 8.

Coyrt of Justice of THE European Community. *1991*. Cause Georg Von Deetzen C. Hauptzollampt Oldenburg. 1989. *Bulletin CJCE* 18(1).

Deak, Fr. 1992. The Right to Preemption. Bucharest: *Dreptul* 7.

European Convention on Human Rights, as amended by Protocol no 11. 2001. Strasbourg: *European Treaty Series* 5.

Josserand, L. 1938. *Cours de droit civil positiv français*. Paris, Recueil Sirey: Tome premiere.

Malaurie, I.–AYNÈS, L.–GAUTIER, P.-Yv. 2001. *Cours de droit civil, Les contrats spéciaux civils et commerciaux*. Paris, Cujas: 14-e edition.

Sabau-POP, I. 2000. *Acquiring the Right to Property*. Bucharest: Accent.

Statescu, C.–BÎRSAN, C. 1980. *Civil Law. The General Theory of Real Rights*. Bucharest: Editura Universității din București.

Chapter 7
Intellectual Property in the New Civil Code of Hungary

Gábor Faludi

Abstract The new Civil Code of Hungary maintained the direct connection to the special intellectual property (IP) acts by a simple provision on the subsidiary application of the Code to all civil law matters that are not provided for in the IP acts. The new code gave up the comprehensive protection of all miscellaneous intellectual creations that do not fall within the scope of the IP acts based on well-founded arguments, and reconsidered the approach to the legal protection of know-how in light of the TRIPS Agreement. The know-how is no longer a type of intellectual creation but a subcategory of trade secrets that are, in turn, a subcategory of issues protected by personality (privacy) rights.

7.1 Introduction—the 1959 Civil Code

The new Civil Code of Hungary[1] contains just one provision that rules on the connection between the intellectual property laws and the CC. Nevertheless, it deserves a presentation. The reason is simple: a significant change happened in the theoretical approach to the relationship between IP law and the CC, which will surely have a serious impact on both jurisprudence and legal education. The practicing lawyer will however not at first sight perceive the CC to be a radical change in his or her daily routine, except in a few instances.[2] The provision to be examined reads as follows:

Intellectual Property— Abbreviated as IP.

Edited version of the presentation held at the seminar titled the "The New Civil Codes in Hungary and Romania I." on 24 May 2013, Cluj-Napoca (Kolozsvár, Klausenburg).

[1]Act V of 2013 (hereafter: CC).

[2]E.g. a miscellaneous intellectual creation ceases to be a protected subject-matter.

G. Faludi (✉)
Civil Law Department, ELTE Eötvös Loránd University, Budapest, Hungary
e-mail: ardafalu@t-online.hu

A. Menyhárd and E. Veress (eds.), *New Civil Codes in Hungary and Romania*,
Ius Gentium: Comparative Perspectives on Law and Justice 63,
DOI 10.1007/978-3-319-63327-5_7

"§ 2:55 CC [Subsidiary application]

This Act shall be applicable to subject-matters falling within the scope of this Act that are not covered by the acts on copyright and industrial property rights".

In order to give a general picture as an introduction on all relevant new features, a number of different provisions, having a direct effect on IP protection and in particular on IP contracts, have to be mentioned.

First there are the modified rules on trade secret and know-how in § 2: 47 CC, which correctly formulate know-how protection as a subtype of the protection of trade secret. This approach—being in conformity with Article 39(2) of the TRIPs Agreement[3]—replaces the traditional approach used by the 1959 Civil Code (Act IV of 1959) that regarded know-how as a type of intellectual creation, and provided for an exclusive right, without any exceptions or limitations, to prohibit all unlicensed exploitations of know-how.

The rules of §§ 6:175 and 6:176 of CC as general rules for breaches of contract provide for the title warranty and non-conformity liability that are also applicable with regard to transfer (assignment) of economic IP rights, while § 6:178 provides for title warranty and contractual liability, and is relevant for covering the remedies for defective performance of copyright, trademark, commercial name and other intellectual property licensing agreements.

A provision in § 6:331(2) CC on the definition of the lease agreement unfortunately expands the scope of rules of property lease to the temporary use of rights for consideration. The application of this rule to IP licensing agreements is dubious. The use of the adjective "dubious" is justified since the subject-matter of the IP licensing agreements is never the IP right holder's use of rights, but rather the usage of protected subject-matter (protected work in copyright licensing agreements, patented or patent-pending inventions in patent licensing agreements, registered or to-be registered signs in trademark licensing agreements, and trade names in trade name licensing agreements).

7.2 The Location and Structure of the Reference to the IP Rules in the CC

In the 1959 Civil Code, the IP rules found their place in the same chapter as the moral (personality) rights of natural persons. The provisions were placed under the title "Rights pertaining to intellectual creations". It contained an umbrella rule, "Intellectual creations shall enjoy legal protection" (§ 86(1) of the 1959 Civil Code). § 86(2) of the 1959 Civil Code referred to the list of special acts providing for the protection of copyright and industrial property. In addition, the old Code

[3]The TRIPS Agreement is the first international instrument to define and protect trade secrets against their unlawful (unlicensed) acquisition, disclosure, making public or exploitation if committed as unfair commercial behaviour.

ruled on the protection of know-how and of miscellaneous intellectual creations that did not qualify as subject–matters protected by the special copyright and industrial property acts (§ 86(3), 86(4) and 87(2) of the 1959 Civil Code). § 87(1) of the old Code provided for the subsidiary application of the sanctions for the violation of moral rights in the event of copyright or industrial property infringement. The title warranty applicable to IP assignments and licenses was provided for in the chapters on sale and purchase agreement and lease agreement and found a per analogy application. This solution resulted in the application of rules for contract types that were in no way related to the IP contracts.

The new code devotes a brief but separate part to IP protection and contains one "orphan" provision following the third part of Book 2 of the CC on moral (personality) rights. The separate part carries the title: "Copyright and industrial property rights", and the rule provides for the application of the CC to civil law subject-matters that are not covered by the copyright and industrial property acts. The rules in the CC have been furnished with auxiliary titles. This provision can be found under the title "subsidiary application".

7.3 The Neutral Title of the Provision

The title of the section, "copyright and industrial property", expresses a neutral approach by the legislator towards the perpetual debate of whether the moral or the economic aspects should play the leading role in IP protection. The Concept of the Civil Code (2003) had already laid down that it "does not wish to decide whether IP rights are of a moral or economic nature. Their dual nature is acknowledged by everyone; the scholars' views merely put the emphasis on one or the other aspect." The position taken by the Concept was preceded by a debate on the direction to be chosen.[4] In line with the Concept, the new provisions reflect that the legislator did not want to choose between the approaches of intellectual creation or intellectual property jurisprudential theory regarding copyright and industrial property rights. The CC does not take a stand on whether copyright and industrial property protects intellectual creations or intellectual property. It remains to be seen, and the solutions—if there are any, which is doubtful—might be different for the various subject-matters (e.g. trademark as compared to works or performances protected by copyright).

[4]For the introduction of the intellectual property approach: BACHER, VILMOS: A szellemi tulajdon jogi védelme és a Ptk. Polgári Jogi Kodifikáció 2000/3, 23–32., BOBROVSZKY, JENŐ: A szellemi tulajdon néhány dilemmájáról a körte és a sajt között. Libri Amicorum 17. Studia Gy. Boytha dedicata ELTE ÁJK Polgári Jogi Tanszék Budapest 2004. 33–45., FICSOR MIHÁLY ZOLTÁN: A szellemi tulajdon és a Ptk. Polgári Jogi Kodifikáció 2001/2., 27–30. For the maintenance of the intellectual creation approach: BOYTHA, GYÖRGY: A szellemi alkotások joga és az új Ptk. Polgári Jogi Kodifikáció 2000/2. 46–56, 2000/3. 13–23. For a compromise: FALUDI GÁBOR: Szerzői jog, iparvédelem és a Ptk. koncepciója. Polgári jogi kodifikáció, 2003/2. 3–14., 2003/3, 3–14.

The CC does not hesitate to use the term" intellectual property" when provides for matrimonial property,[5] and, in line with the neutral approach, the code uses the term "intellectual creation" as a result of R&D activity.[6]

There are theoretical reasons behind this neutrality. The issue of the personal or proprietary nature of legal protection has lost importance since 1977, when the 1959 Civil Code introduced the then contemporary IP reference provisions. The issue is reflected in some specific rules rather than in the general principles (e.g. legal status and the compensation of the inventor of the service invention). The relevant international treaties—in particular the TRIP- Agreement,[7] and primary EU law[8] including the Charter of Fundamental Rights[9] and the European Convention for the Protection of Human Rights (ECHR)[10] are all based on the intellectual property (in the ECHR, the general term of possessions is used) approach.

It is however true that neither the TRIPS Agreement nor EU law nor the ECHR cover the moral rights of IP right holders.

The approach of the jurisprudence has drastically changed since the 1970s. It does not deal with the philosophical or ethical roots of IP protection anymore. It rather focuses on the cost-benefit elements of IP protection. Due to the nowadays fashionable theories, new borders between exclusive rights (monopoly) and the public domain are being sought (e.g. the rationale for the public health compulsory license in patent law, new internet –tailored exceptions in copyright law, the various interpretations of the three step test provide for in the TRIPS Agreement and the 1996 WIPO "Internet treaties", the legal status of the Creative Commons license and eventual new exceptions to legalize UGC[11]).

The fundamental right to information has been extended and strengthened on and by the Internet. The constitutional roots of IP rights are measured before EU and international courts against the right to information and privacy rights.[12]

---

[5]§ 4:38(1)(c) CC: save for the royalty due during the community of property, the proprietary right of the spouse as creator of intellectual property shall be part of the spouse's separate property.

[6]§ 6:253(5) CC: the prior consent of the principal is required for the publication of the intellectual creation generated as a result of the research.

[7]Promulgated as Act IX of 1998.

[8]Article 118 of the Treaty on the Functioning of the European Union 2012/C 326/01 (TFEU).

[9]Article 17(2) of the Charter of fundamental rights of the EU (2012/C 326/02).

[10]Article 1 of the Protocol to the Convention for the Protection of Human Rights and Fundamental Freedom, promulgated as Act XXXI of 1993.

[11]User generated content, please see e.g. Assessing the economic impacts of adapting certain limitations and exceptions to copyright and related rights in the EU, Gregor Langus, Damien Neven & Gareth Shier Charles River Associates, October 2013; http://ec.europa.eu/internal_market/copyright/docs/studies/131001-study_en.pdf.

[12]E.g. EU Human Rights Guidelines on Freedom of Expression Online and Offline, Foreign Affairs Council meeting, Brussels, 12 May 2014, European Court of Human Rights: 40397/12 Fredrik NEIJ and Peter SUNDE KOLMISOPPI against Sweden—on file-sharing; 36769/08 Ashby Donald et al. against France on the freedom/copyright prohibition to post fashion photos on the internet, ECJ C-275/06, Promusicae; C-557/07 LSG, C-461/10 Bonnier on the provision of or

As a result of the development, the name IP right or intellectual creation rights is no longer important at the level of the Civil Code.

7.4 Abandonment of the Comprehensive Protection of all Intellectual Creations

The following provisions of the 1959 Civil Code have been abandoned: "Intellectual creations shall be protected under the Code" (§ 86(1) of the 1959 Civil Code); and "All intellectual creations—even if they do not qualify as subject matters of copyright or industrial property protection—shall be protected if they are useful for society and are not part of the public domain" (§ 86(4) of the 1959 Civil Code).

7.4.1 Change of the Theoretical Approach

Reasons flowing from socialist ideology justified this comprehensive protection provided by the 1959 Code. The view was stated and disseminated, even in school textbooks, that a socialist society and state ensure the complete fulfilment of one's personality, unlike the situation in capitalist countries; only the legal protection of all creation can provide the moral and economic incentive to intellectual creations and therefore all creative work shall be protected. (The philosophical roots of "Urheberrecht" in German classical philosophy were also dealt with and taught.) This approach was one of the reasons for giving up this general comprehensive protection.

7.4.2 Lack of Network of International and EU Instruments

In addition, the lack of international protection of all intellectual creations is also an argument for reconsidering this broad, borderless and unlimited in time protection. There is no specific international treaty background behind the general protection of all intellectual creations that do not qualify as copyright or industrial property subject-matters. The TRIPS Agreement defines all areas subject to IP protection, including trade secrets (know-how). TRIPS allows for a higher level of protection; as a result, the protection of intellectual creations other than those listed in the

(Footnote 12 continued)

refusal to provide data of the infringers by the intermediary service provider to the claimant in civil copyright litigations.

TRIPS Agreement could have been maintained. The TRIPS Agreement is however based on the principles of national treatment (Article 3) and most-favoured-nation treatment (Article 4). Therefore, if Hungarian law had maintained the protection of intellectual creations other than those protected by the TRIPS Agreement, this protection should then be granted to foreign right holders domiciled in a TRIPS member state as well, while Hungarian right holders would not enjoy such protection abroad.

Within the EU, the rule of non-discrimination would apply. It follows e.g. from the preliminary rulings in the Phil Collins and Cliff Richard[13] joint cases and the Tod' case,[14] that all citizens of EU (rather the EEA) Member States may rely on Article 18 of the TFEU (Article 12 of the TEC) to enforce their rights pertaining to any intellectual creation in any other member states, while the Hungarian right holders could not enforce their rights in any other Member States where such a general protection of all intellectual creations does not exist.

7.4.3 Enlargement of the Subject-Matters Eligible for IP Protection

The changes within the scope of the various types of IP protection give right to an amazing enlargement of the protected subject-matters. The enlargement of copyright protection could be observed ever since software has been a subject-matter protected by copyright. The types of works to be protected are not listed in an exhaustive, but in an exemplificative list that can at any time be interpreted broadly. Copyright in Europe also comprises the protection of non-original databases.[15] The level of the required individuality and originality has been lowered. We could learn from the Painer case[16] that also a simple portrait photo of a child (that of the later abducted Natasha Kampush) may be protected by copyright. We also learned from the Infopaq I.[17] case that eleven words of a news article may constitute an identifiable part of a work, and thereby may be protected (meaning the reproduction of this part requires a license from the right holder).

A similar enlargement of the subject matters eligible for patent protection can also be observed. Computer-based inventions (under disputed circumstances) and

[13]C-92/92, C-362/92- the performing artists of another Member State shall enjoy the same rights as the performing artists in the country of exploitation, even if such right are not afforded for foreign performing artists.

[14]C-28/04: under the general principle of non-discrimination the right of an author to claim in a Member State the copyright protection afforded by the law of that State may not be subject to a distinguishing criterion based on the country of origin of the work, where such right is not afforded to the author.

[15]96/9/EC Directive on the protection of databases.

[16]C-145/10, Eva-Maria Painer v Standard VerlagsGmbH, et al.

[17]C-5/08, Infopaq International A/S v Danske Dagblades Forening.

business methods with IT support (under similarly disputed circumstances) can be patented. Biotechnological inventions are eligible for patent protection.[18] New types of signs can be protected as trademarks, even if the registration of some of the new types (colours, tunes, touch (sense of feeling), scents, tastes, sequences of movements and holograms) seems difficult.[19]

The obvious consequence of the enlargement of the subject-matters to be protected by the "traditional" tools of copyright and industrial property is that there remains no room to protect miscellaneous intellectual creations.

The most important argument for the abrogation of the legal protection of miscellaneous intellectual creations is that the enlargement as described above takes place under controlled conditions. It means that no new monopoly is introduced without the introduction of or the possibility to introduce internal exceptions and limitations that are to guarantee the equilibrium between monopoly and public domain. A good example is the mandatory exception of temporary reproduction in EU copyright law[20] One can also think of the compulsory public health license in patent law[21] or the exception of comparative advertising in trademark law. Such internal limitations and exceptions do not exist in the protection of the miscellaneous intellectual creations. As a result, such a timeless unregistered protection that lasts until it becomes part of the public domain is uncontrolled, and does not meet the requirement of equilibrium between public domain and exclusive rights (monopolies).

7.4.4 Uncertain Court Practice

In addition, the Hungarian court practice in cases that involved the legal protection of miscellaneous intellectual creations shows that the courts were uncertain: it was extremely difficult to decide whether an idea/solution/creation met or did not meet the statutory requirements (creation + useful for society + does not belong to the public domain). The leading cases showed that the borders of the protection of miscellaneous intellectual creations were foggy. An expressive example was the

---

[18] 98/44/EC on the legal protection of biotechnological inventions.

[19] E.g. C-273/00 Sieckmann, C-49/02, Heidelberger Bauchemie GmbH: Colours or combinations of colours without contours.

[20] Article 5(1) of the so called Copyright Directive (2001/29/EC Directive: Temporary acts of reproduction referred to in Article 2, which are transient or incidental [and] an integral and essential part of a technological process and whose sole purpose is to enable: (a) a transmission in a network between third parties by an intermediary, or (b) a lawful use of a work or other subject-matter to be made, and which have no independent economic significance, shall be exempted from the reproduction right provided for in Article 2.

[21] Regulation 816/2006 on compulsory licensing of patents relating to the manufacture of pharmaceutical products for export to countries with public health problems; § 33/A of the Patent Act (Act XXXIII of 1995).

case over an idea of an employee to introduce and use by the employer the trade name "Valton" for a new champagne. First the employer rejected the idea then commenced to use the trade name "Walton". The employee stated that the employer infringed his right pertaining to the intellectual creation incorporated in his proposed trade name "Valton". The Supreme Court had to clarify that a pure idea to introduce a trade name for a new product is not eligible for the legal protection of miscellaneous intellectual creations.[22]

These reasons (4.1–4.4.) led to the abandonment of the general legal protection of all intellectual creations.

7.5 The Subsidiary Application of the CC

The starting point of the presentation was § 2:55 CC on the subsidiary application of the CC in all cases that fall within the scope of the CC and are not provided for in the specific acts on copyright and industrial property.

This brief provision implies a number of consequences. It expresses that the CC is the fundamental background to the specific acts. In other words, the introductory provisions on underlying principles shall also apply to the exercise of rights arising out of the IP acts. For example, the prohibition of the abuse of rights, the general term of culpability and the obligation to cooperate with the contracting partner all find application in the IP law via the CC.

This concise and comprehensive provision saves the listing of the various types of copyright and industrial property subject matters. Should the number types broaden or narrow, the CC may remain intact.

The CC serves as a background in civil law issues (the CC applies in cases falling within its scope only). The specific IP acts are "overloaded" with public administrative rules. It is obvious with regard to the industrial property acts, since the protection is subject to registration, and the procedure that may lead to registration is a public administrative one. However, even the Copyright Act contains a great number of public administrative provisions on the compulsory licensing of the use of orphan works, the registration and supervision of the collective management societies, on the operation of the Copyright Expert Board, etc. It goes without saying that the CC does not constitute a background in public administrative matters.

This subsidiary application of the CC is reinforced also from the aspect of the IP acts. Both the Copyright Act[23] and the Patent Act,[24] as well as the Trademark Act,[25] contain similar provisions that refer "back" to the CC. These references are

[22]BH2005. 209.

[23]§ 3 of Act LXXVI of 1999 on Copyright.

[24]§ 43/A of Act XXXIII of 1995 on the patent protection of inventions.

[25]Act XI of 1997 on the protection of trademarks and geographical indications.

in fact redundant. The general rule on the subsidiary application of the Code in civil law matters would suffice. Still, out of sheer habit and partly following the traditions, all IP acts[26] include the identical provisions that matters relating to the transfer, assignment and pledge of rights deriving from and other moral and economic issues concerning legal (i.e. copyright, patent, trademark) protection shall be governed by the CC.

In addition, the Patent and the Trademark Act contain identical references to the CC in matters of co-ownership of rights, and licensing agreements. The Patent Act provides for the application of the CC to contracts involving remuneration for service invention, and to moral rights infringement claims by the inventors. The Trademark Act rules that contesting the declaration of consent by the owner of the former trademark shall occur under the provisions of the CC on actions seeking the avoidance of a contract due to a mistake, deception or threat. Moreover, the Copyright Act provides that, in the event of infringement of moral rights, the author may demand compensation for personal injury under the CC. The redundancies as described above do not disturb the application of either the IP acts or that of the CC.

[26]The acts on the protection of design, the utility model and semiconductor chips follow the Patent Act by simple references.

Chapter 8
The New Civil Code of Romania and Its Impact on Intellectual Property

Ligia Cătuna

Abstract We hope that intellectual property enters into the great resettlement program of the Romanian legal system and receives its own code as a recognition of the importance of the field and of the necessity of unitarily bringing together all the rules that govern intellectual creation within the covers of a single regulatory book, The Intellectual Property Code of Romania. An intellectual property code has not been issued, but, in my opinion, the New Civil Code has led to a realignment of intellectual property, in the sense that it brought forth my concept according to which intellectual property is a field of civil law, in addition to other fields, such as contracts, obligations, inheritance, etc.

8.1 Introduction

8.1.1 The Structure of the Analysis

The topic addressed is very vast and may in itself be the subject of an extensive study, such as a monograph or a Ph.D. thesis. To sum up our analysis, we have tried to identify several direct implications on the social relationships governed by civil law and intellectual property law regarding the two major classical regulations: copyright and industrial property right.

8.1.2 Necessary Remarks

1. The issuance of the New Civil Code does not preclude the applicability of intellectual property laws that remain special, derogatory laws and that continue to have effect.

L. Cătuna (✉)
Ligia Catuna Law Office, Timişoara, Romania
e-mail: dr.ligia.catuna@lawoffice.ro

A. Menyhárd and E. Veress (eds.), *New Civil Codes in Hungary and Romania*,
Ius Gentium: Comparative Perspectives on Law and Justice 63,
DOI 10.1007/978-3-319-63327-5_8

2. The new general notions introduced by the New Civil Code are reflected by effect of the law, in the provisions governing intellectual property.
3. A redefinition of the notions that operate in the field of intellectual property is required.

8.1.3 Distinctions Needed Regarding the Changes to the Regulations

The New Civil Code determines a review of the intellectual property legal relationship from the perspective of non-litigious aspects, which, however, must be taken into account in case of dispute. The New Civil Code must be analysed in relation with the new Civil Procedure Code that explicitly regulates intellectual property disputes. Theorists and practitioners must conduct a proper analysis and interpretation by combining the two regulatory acts. The legal relationships which arose prior to the entry into force of the New Civil Code remain governed by the old law.

8.1.4 The Intellectual Property Legal Relationship

Under the old legislation	Under the new legislation
1. There is a clear distinction between civil law and commercial law	1. The two branches of law are unified, and a single common law regulation remains, that of civil law
2. There were two different concepts: the concept of 'civil law subject' and the concept of 'trader'	2. There is only the concept of 'professional' that covers all subjects of law both in civil and in old commercial law

8.1.5 The Subject of the Intellectual Property Legal Relationship Under the New Regulation

The holder of intellectual property rights and obligations is the legal or natural person that is subject of law, holding or not the quality of professional.

Professional is the law subject who operates a business—operating a business is the systematic exercise performed by one or more persons of an organized activity consisting in the production, management or alienation of goods or in rendering services, whether or not for financial gain—Article 3 of the New Civil Code.

8.1.6 The Subject of the Intellectual Property Legal Relationship

If the holder of the intellectual property right is a minor lacking capacity to exercise these rights, legal documents shall be concluded on his/her behalf by legal representatives—without disposal regarding the nature of the rights, estimable or not in money.

The text of the Code may negatively interfere with copyright law provisions in relation to the moral rights of deciding when, where and how the work is brought forth to the public, the name under which the work is made public, the right to withdraw the work, etc.

The right of the minor author acknowledged by the copyright law is practically limited in its exercise by the mandatory and general provisions of the civil code.

In case of litigation, court practice will decide, indicating that, in our opinion, the provisions of the special copyright law will prevail in the exercise of moral author rights.

If the author is a minor and is under guardianship, his/her goods will be under the management and care of the guardian, under the guardian's control, or under the approval of the guardianship court, respectively.

These imperative provisions of the civil code may cause practical issues in the exercise of copyright rights, which are *intuitu personae* rights.

The civil code does not expressly govern the pseudonym as an identification attribute of the individual, although it is recognized as such by the copyright law.

In case of litigation before the courts, the pseudonym should be indicated clearly as an identification attribute, although the civil code does not regulate it.

Failing to mention the pseudonym may cause problems in court practice regarding the identification of the legal relationship brought before the court of law.

Since in industrial property the notion of 'trader' has virtually disappeared, issues related to effectively proving the quality of 'professional' might arise. Proof of this quality is conditioned by the cumulation of all the attributes indicated in the definition given by law, the quality of 'professional' also entailing the person's coercion to comply with all registration formalities required by law: registration in the trade register, in the register of associations and foundations, issues related to tax provisions, fees and taxes, etc.

8.1.7 Goods Subject to Protection from the Perspective of the Civil Code in Conjunction with Intellectual Property Law

The civil code does not expressly define the movable goods but indirectly states that everything not immovable is movable.

From this perspective, intellectual goods can be included in both the fixed goods category—such as architecture works—and in the category of mobile goods (tangible or intangible assets).

There is no express reference to goods subject to intellectual property protection, but the civil code contains reference to the legal status of heirlooms—this category may also include properties protected by copyright (paintings, photographs, letters or unpublished manuscripts).

The status of heirlooms is regulated in heritage matter and it is stated that joint tenancy cannot be terminated unless by voluntary separation.

We believe that in this field the notary or the judge must simultaneously apply the special law provisions that strictly concern not only patrimony rights on these goods but also moral rights—the notary or judge shall designate an individual or a collective management organization for the correct protection of the work because the good is not just a movable but may also be an object of copyright.

8.1.8 Rights and Obligations in the Civil Code Applicable to Goods Protected by Intellectual Property Law

As a novelty, usufruct may be established on movables according to Articles 703, 704 NCC.

Any movable or immovable goods, tangible or intangible assets, including mass assets, *de facto* universalities or shares thereof can be given in usufruct.

From the above provisions it results that intellectual property may also be subject to usufruct. Although the law does not state, we consider that in the field of copyright there are no restrictions; in the case of industrial property, however, usufruct cannot be established unless the intellectual good is effectively protected, can by itself produce the effect of protection, so it was subject to registration with the State Office for Inventions and Trademarks or other body for European or international registrations recognized by law.

The legal regulation of occupation is deficient in relation to copyright in the New Civil Code.

The holder of a movable good that belongs to nobody becomes its owner by occupation from the date of entry into possession if this procedure is performed according to law.

We believe that in the case of goods which are subject to copyright, collective management organizations should manage the good and it should enter their property by analogy with the principle applied in the case of a vacant succession.

8.1.9 Provisions Relating to Contracts in the Civil Code, Applicable on Intellectual Property

Contracts which are not expressly regulated by law are subject to Articles 1166 et seq. of the New Civil Code, and to the rules applicable to the contracts regulated by the law with which there is the most resemblance.

Intellectual property law governs the contracts applicable in this field, and in our opinion, the provision in the civil code shall take effect only in the case of new intellectual goods, which cannot be subject to special rules yet and which cannot be covered by intellectual property contracts already expressly regulated by the special law.

8.1.10 Contracts in the New Civil Code and Intellectual Property Law

In the matter of purchase and sale contracts of intellectual goods, we believe that the provisions of the civil code apply in full, with no expressly derogatory regulation in special legislation on the sale of intellectual goods.

We have the same opinion in regard to exchange contracts, and partly in regard to contractor agreements if the object of the contract is the performance of intellectual works. However, a distinction must be made between the contractor agreement and the publishing contract as the latter is covered by copyright law. A distinction must also be made between a contractor agreement regarding an intellectual good and an employment agreement with an intellectual creation clause.

In the matter of company contracts governed by the New Civil Code, there is reference to the contribution to the establishment of the capital by submitting intangible assets, ignoring, however, the special provisions of intellectual property. Although the contribution of intangible assets is expressly addressed (Article 1897 NCC), the law does not mention the possibility of bringing intellectual goods as contribution, which seems to be a shortcoming of the code, especially since special laws allow this. A rigid interpretation of the code could lead to the conclusion that this is no longer possible, but we are not agreeing with this literal interpretation of the text of the code.

8.2 Procedural Aspects in Settling Disputes Under the Provisions of the Old Civil Procedure Code

Subjective rights protection in case of violation remains exclusively in the competence of the courts, civil or criminal, as appropriate, depending on the seriousness of the violation or disregard of the law, the degree of social danger, the nature of violated rights, or the type of act that violates the normal exercise of these subjective rights.

Summons in industrial property rights are exempt from court fees.[1] The provisions of Law no. 350/2007 are clear in this regard and, in our opinion, serve as amendments to Article 5 of Government Ordinance no. 146/1997 on judicial taxes.[2]

Consequently, the person who owns intellectual property and industrial property rights may file a claim in this field before the court, and the court considers to be properly invested with judging such claim without judicial taxes, as a consequence of the special rules in the field.

Regarding dispute settlement jurisdiction, given the special regulatory field of social relationships protected by the rule of law, the law has conferred jurisdiction over the settlement of intellectual property rights disputes to the tribunals.[3]

According to Article 2, Section 1 letter (e) of the 1865 Civil Procedure Code, tribunals judge in first instance the judicial claims regarding intellectual and industrial property creations.

With reference to the criterion of material jurisdiction, namely the vertical distribution of cases for settlement, it is undeniable that only tribunals are first instance courts for the settlement of intellectual property rights, copyright and industrial property rights cases.

The law allows the establishing of tribunals or panels specialized in a particular field if that field has a share in the work of the court by the specifics of cases presented to the court.[4]

Where there are no specialized intellectual property rights panels in tribunals, the question is what sections are competent to deal with two categories of disputes, i.e. copyright disputes and industrial property rights disputes.

Where there are no specialized intellectual and industrial property creation rights sections, we considered that each case has to be analysed depending on the legal basis invoked, and the cases related to intellectual creation (to be read copyright) should be distributed to the tribunal's civil section and the cases related to industrial property rights should be distributed to the former Commercial section of the tribunal.

---

[1]Article 24, para (3) of Law no. 350/2007 on utility models, entering into force on March 12, 2008.

[2]According to Article 5 of Law no. 146/1997, "summons in the field of copyright and inventor rights are charged as follows: (a) summons for the recognition of copyright and related rights, for establishing their violation and for repairing damages, including payment of copyright and amounts due for works of art, and for taking action to prevent the occurrence of imminent damages or for ensuring their reparation—39 lei; (b) summons for recognition as inventor, patent holder, holder of the rights deriving from the patent, assignment and license contracts, including patrimonial rights of the inventor—39 lei".

[3]For further information, see also *L. Dănilă Cătuna*, Consideraţii privind competenţa instanţelor de judecată în soluţionarea litigiilor de drept de proprietate intelectuală, in R.R.D.P.I. Nr. 1/2007, Bucharest, pp. 29–37.

[4]Article 37 of Law no. 304/2004.

Appreciating the nature of the dispute as civil or commercial must be made with reference to the substantive rule and the common law applicable to the special rule, which in the case of copyright is, as already shown, civil law, while in the case of industrial property rights it is commercial law.

This statement is also supported by the procedural text expressly stating that tribunals try two categories of disputes, namely trials and summons in the field of intellectual creation and industrial property trials and summons.

However, confusion may arise from the terminology used in the Civil Procedure Code, namely from the phrase *intellectual creation right*, which covers copyright. Regardless of the phrase used, however, we believe that the legislature had in mind on the one hand disputes arising in connection with intellectual creations with no applicability in industry (i.e., copyright), on the other hand disputes concerning intellectual creations with applicability in industry (i.e. industrial property right).

The fact that the High Court of Cassation and Justice settles intellectual property rights disputes in a section that also resolves civil disputes is in our opinion not a sufficient argument to justify the resolution of all intellectual property rights disputes in the first instance only by the civil section or only by the commercial section of the court, for the reasons synthetically expressed above.[5]

Therefore, the jurisdiction of tribunals includes both common law actions, actions for the realization of rights or for the establishment of rights if an injunction is not available, and any actions or summons, such as the ordering of precautionary measures when there is a risk of violating rights arising from a title of protection or from the existence of a work subject to copyright.

The legislature has provided by way of derogation the exclusive material jurisdiction to the Bucharest Tribunal for certain industrial property disputes; these cases are, however, expressly provided by law and are strictly construed.

Take as example disputes relating to the cancellation of an invention patent, a summons that, according to Article 55, para (1) of Law no. 64/1991, is judged by the Bucharest Tribunal, the cancellation of the application for the registration of a design or model, or summons for compulsory invention licenses, which, according to Article 46 of Law no. 64/1991, are also the sole responsibility of the Bucharest Tribunal, or appeals against decisions of the OSIM[6] Contestation Committee in applications for the registration of an industrial design or model, against decisions of the OSIM Contestation Committee in variety patents, etc.

Disputes regarding the quality of breeder, variety patent holders or those regarding other rights arising from the variety patent including patrimonial rights of the breeder in the assignment or license contract or those related to the noncompliance with Article 38, para (1) and Article 39 of Law no. 255/1998 are the

[5]For further information and additional arguments, see also L. Dănilă Cătuna, Considerații privind competența instanțelor de judecată în soluționarea litigiilor de drept de proprietate intelectuală, ibid., pp. 29–36.

[6]State Office for Inventions and Trademarks.

responsibility of tribunals as first instance courts, according to the Civil Procedure Code.

Regarding disputes generated by a registered design or model, the special law contains some special procedural provisions.[7]

The Bucharest Tribunal has exclusive jurisdiction over disputes covering community designs and models for which Regulation no. 6/2002/EC confers jurisdiction on community designs and models to tribunals under Article 80, para (1) of the Regulation,[8] remedies promoted against decisions of the OSIM Examination Committee regarding the registration of a design or model.

According to common law, disputes on **the authorship of the design or model**, on the quality of the holder of the registration certificate, on the patrimonial rights arising from assignment or license contracts for designs or models fall within the jurisdiction of courts.[9]

The owner of a registered design or model may request the court to order precautionary measures when there is a risk of infringement of a registered design or model and if the violation is likely to cause irreparable harm or if there is a risk of destruction of evidence.

To order the precautionary measures, there are general procedure provisions representing the common law. In taking precautionary measures ordered by the court, the plaintiff may request a guarantee sufficient to prevent abuse.

The court may require the plaintiff to provide any evidence that he/she has in order to prove that he/she is the holder of the violated right or whose violation is inevitable.

If the evidence supporting the plaintiff's claims is under the control of the defendant, the court may order that evidence to be produced by the defendant, guaranteeing the confidentiality of information according to the law.

The court may order that the author of the rights violations resulting from a registration certificate provide immediate information on the origin and distribution channels of counterfeit goods, and information on the identity of the manufacturer or dealer, provided that such measure is not excessive in relation to the severity of harm to the right's holder.

At the request of the court, OSIM is obliged to submit the papers, documents and information necessary for trying the presented case.

In all disputes relating to designs and models, citation of holders is mandatory.[10] This means that citation is mandatory even in cases where a presidential ordinance is promoted, the text of the special law derogating from the provisions of the Civil Procedure Code. Also, consequently, for all presidential ordinances that deal with registered designs and models, the promotional period of remedies will run from delivery, and they will be always given summoning the parties.

---

[7]Article 53 and 56 of Law no. 129/1992.

[8]Article 47 of Law no. 129/1992.

[9]Article 43 of Law no. 129/1992.

[10]Article 56, para (2) of Law no. 129/1992.

8.3 Particular Aspects of Establishing the Procedural Framework in Intellectual Property Disputes

8.3.1 The Pseudonym, a Procedural Identification Attribute[11]

The legal framework regarding the certification and protection of copyrights is represented by the provisions of Law no. 8/1996, and for the violation, disregard or harm to these rights the legal instrument that determines when, if and how they can be restored to their normal exercise—if necessary by court decision—is represented by the Civil Procedure Code and the Criminal Procedure Code, respectively.

In the case of a legal action, the rigors of the Civil Procedure Code require the plaintiff to indicate all the elements of the civil action in the summons, all data necessary for the court to be properly notified, and the procedural framework to be fair and well defined.

The plaintiff has to identify him or herself according to Article 112 of the 1865 Civil Procedure Code by surname and name, domicile, and establish precisely that he or she is the holder of the violated subjective right.

According to Article 112, Section 1 of the 1865 Civil Procedure Code,[12] "a summons shall include: the surname and name, the domicile or residence of the parties, for legal persons their name and headquarters, and, as appropriate, the registration number with the trade register or the registration number with the register of legal persons, the tax code and the bank account". The imperative corroboration required by the legislature in the same article with the provisions of Article 82 of the current Civil Procedure Code complements the formal framework of the summons in that "any summons before the courts must be made in writing and include the indication of the court, the surname and name, domicile or residence of the parties (…)".[13]

Under the provisions of the New Civil Procedure Code (Article 194), the summons shall include the surname and name, domicile or residence of the parties or, for legal persons, their name and headquarters. The summons shall also include

---

[11]For further information, see also *L. Dănilă Cătuna*, Pseudonimul—atribut de identificare procesuală, in R.R.D.P.I., no. 4/2010, pp. 18–24.

[12]Section 1 of Article 112 is reproduced as amended by Article I, Section 11 of Law no. 202/2010. Prior to the issue of the Small Reform Law, the text of the Code stipulated the following: "A summons shall include: 1. The name, the domicile or residence of the parties, for legal persons their name and headquarters, and, as appropriate, the registration number with the trade register or the registration number with the register of legal persons, the tax code and the bank account. If the plaintiff resides abroad, he/she will also indicate an address for service in Romania where all communications regarding the trial shall be sent".

[13]From our point of view, the specification regarding the surname and the name is a tautology, as long as, from a strictly legal point of view, a person's name as attribute of identification refers to both the surname and the name. For further information, see *G. Boroi*, Drept civil. Partea generală. Persoanele, ed. a III-a, Ed. Hamangiu, Bucharest, 2008, p. 418.

the personal identification number or, as appropriate, the unique registration code or the tax ID code, the registration number with the trade register or the registration number with the register of legal persons and the bank account of the plaintiff, the same being applicable to the defendant, if the parties possess or have been attributed with these identifiers according to the law, to the extent that they are known to the plaintiff.

Therefore, the Civil Procedure Code is actually requiring the irrefutable identification of the parties in a civil trial. The requirement is natural because there is need to correctly identify the holders of the right, the procedural obligations in relation to the holders of the rights and the obligations of material law legal relationships to be decided.

We believe that the identification of the natural person in certain disputes generated by branches of law whose specificity is undeniable must be further achieved, including identification attributes expressly provided in the text of the substantive law.

It is the case of some material law legal relationships governed by the Law on copyright and related rights, namely of legal relationships in which the author of the work understands to identify him or herself by a pseudonym.

Our legal literature contains the statement according to which identifying a natural person means individualizing the natural person in legal relationships.[14]

The same author points out that the individualization of the natural person in legal relationships is a complex institution and only part of this institution belongs to civil law, namely the part composed of civil legal rules governing the means of individualization of natural persons in civil legal relationships.[15]

Under civil law, common law, the natural person is identified by surname and name.

The legal definition of the identification attributes of a natural person subject to the law as represented by surname and name does not exist. But it is widely recognized that the right to a name is a non-patrimonial, personal, moral right.

Pseudonyms are also a means of identification. Just as in the case of names, there is no legal definition of pseudonyms.

There are, however, some references to the recognition of the existence of the institution of the pseudonym in the Law on copyright and related rights. By analysing them we can conclude that the right to a pseudonym is part of the right of authorship of the work, and that its legal nature is that of a non-patrimonial, personal, moral right.

If the name is the identification attribute of the natural person consisting in person's subjective right to be individualized in the family and society through set words, we can define the pseudonym *mutatis mutandis* as any author's right to be individualized, based solely on his expressly expressed will, in the family and society, through other different names and/or compounds with his civil identification name as the creator of intellectual property.

---

[14] *G. Boroi*, op. cit., p. 414.

[15] Idem.

Procedurally, the New Civil Procedure Code rules on the requirements for summons relating to civil trial parties in Article 194, stating: "the summons shall include: the surname and name, domicile or residence of the parties or, for legal persons their name and headquarters. The summons shall also include the personal identification number or, as appropriate, the unique registration code or the tax ID code, the registration number with the trade register or the registration number with the register of legal persons and the bank account of the plaintiff, the same being applicable to the defendant, if the parties possess or have been attributed with these identifiers according to the law, to the extent that they are known to the plaintiff. If the plaintiff resides abroad, he/she will also indicate an address for service in Romania where all communications regarding the trial shall be sent."

Apparently the text of the law is all encompassing. In reality, the Code does not make any references to any other possible identifications.

However, in terms of intellectual property law, we believe that the text is improvable regarding the identification attributes of the parties in the trial—natural persons. We believe that a complete text of the law from this perspective should also include the pseudonym as mandatory to be mentioned in cases where it should be invoked in relation to the specifics of the case to be decided.

The analysis was determined as shown above by the incidence in the case of rights conferred by Law no. 8/1996, namely the right of authorship which includes the right to decide under what name will the work be brought to the public.

Synthetically, this means that the author can decide alone and freely if his/her work is made public under his/her real name or a pseudonym.

According to the Law on copyright and related rights, the author can also be identified by a pseudonym.

The pseudonym is not defined by the Law on copyright and related rights.

However, references to the legal possibility to use a pseudonym and its recognition as an identification attribute of the author of the work exist in the law.

A distinct legal regime as moral right expressly stipulated by law does not exist for pseudonyms, as it is left to practitioners to use the normative texts fairly in recognizing and protecting the rights of authors who use a pseudonym in the exercise of their rights of authorship of the work.

So the legislature says that the person under whose name the work was first brought to public knowledge is only presumed to be the author until proven otherwise. When the work was made public in an anonymous way or under a pseudonym that does not allow the identification of the author, the copyright shall be exercised by the natural or legal person that makes it public with the author's consent, as long as the latter does not disclose his/her identity.[16]

The duration of patrimonial rights on works made public legally under a pseudonym or without indicating the author starts from the date of their disclosure to the public and lasts for 70 years. Where the author's identity is made public before the deadline or the pseudonym adopted by the author leaves no doubt

---

[16]Article 4 of Law no. 8/1996.

regarding the identity of the author, the provisions of Article 25, para (1) of Law no. 8/1996 apply, which provide that the rights stipulated in Articles 13 and 21 of Law. 8/1996 last throughout the author's lifetime, and after his/her death are transmitted by inheritance according to civil law for a period of 70 years, regardless of the date on which the work was legally made public. If there are no heirs, the exercise of rights falls within the collective management body authorized by the author during his/her lifetime, or, in the absence of an authorization, to the collective management body with the largest number of members in that creative field.[17]

In connection with works of art, the law also recognizes the use of pseudonyms as possible, stating explicitly that a contract for the reproduction of a work of art must contain information enabling the identification of the work, that reproductions shall not be sold without the copyright holder's approval of the copy that was submitted for review, that all copies shall bear the name or pseudonym of the author or any other agreed sign to allow his/her identification.[18]

With respect to performers, they also have the explicitly stipulated moral right to claim that their name or pseudonyms be shown or communicated in every show and in every use of its recording.[19]

This listing ends the series of legal provisions on the pseudonym. What can we conclude from the above? That the pseudonym is expressly recognized by the legislature, it is assimilated as a legal identification attribute that must be observed, being opposable *erga omnes*, and the person using it benefits from all legal rights and obligations derived from the quality of author of a work made public pseudonymously.

We are concerned with two issues relating to the legal status of the pseudonym. Since the law does not stipulate so, no formalities need be carried out to choose and use a pseudonym, the public circuit of the pseudonym being inevitably tied to the circuit of the work it accompanies.

Evidence of the link between work, author and pseudonym are not expressly provided by law, and therefore we can only relate to the evidentiary common law regime. If we consider pseudonyms as an attribute of personal identification, we believe that a specific administrative award procedure should be carried out. In this situation, the only way to prove pseudonyms would be by a pseudonym award document, which would go beyond the legal framework and naturalness of all the attributes of a creative act. Therefore, we do not believe this to be the case.

The pseudonym, its designation and appropriation by the author constitutes, nevertheless, a unilateral act of will that, by derogation from the evidentiary rules of legal documents, we believe should be provable by any evidence.

The existence of a pseudonym can be problematic in practice if pseudonymous works made public are questioned, and the author is not known.

---

[17]Article 26 of Law no. 8/1996 read in conjunction with Article 25 of the same law.

[18]Article 83, para, (1)–(3) of Law no. 8/1996.

[19]Article 96 letter (c) of Law no. 8/1996.

We are referring to cases where it is necessary to prove the identity of the person identified by a surname and name to be the same with the person who uses or has used a pseudonym.

Therefore, returning to the requirement of the Civil Procedure Code on the identification of parties in a trial by surname and name, we consider that in the matter of intellectual property disputes, summons should be individualized also by indicating a pseudonym if the dispute is related to works made public pseudonymously.

We believe that the same statement should be made in succession matters. The notary succession procedure started relating to a deceased person's succession whose work has been made public under a pseudonym can raise the same issues of proof of identity as those between *de cuius* and the author individualized by a pseudonym.

We believe, however, that the procedural legitimacy of an author who made his/her work public under a pseudonym must be established only in case of disputes relating to that identity and that proof may be made by any means.

In case the summons requests the protection of moral rights derived from making public a/some work(s) pseudonymously, we consider that, mandatorily and additionally to the mandatory requirements of the Civil Procedure Code, the summons must identify the plaintiff not only by surname and name, but also by pseudonym in all cases where the disputed state is generated by legal copyright relationships where at least one of the subjects is individualized by pseudonym.

In conclusion, we believe that, on the one hand, pseudonyms should be explicitly regulated as identification attributes of the author, and, on the other hand, that the Civil Procedure Code is deficient in the procedural identification of the author individualized by a pseudonym. The very correlation between the holder of the right to action and the holder of the subjective right violated justify its active procedural quality. And if the holder of the violated subjective right is indeed individualized in the legal substantive right relationship by a pseudonym, we consider it to be normal to preserve his/her identification by pseudonym in the possible procedural framework as well.

Our proposal derives both from the many cases when authors resort to pseudonyms, on the one hand, and, on the other hand, from the fact that the legislature must also look down on full norming in all areas of law, therefore including the procedural aspects related to the branch of copyright and intellectual property rights.

8.4 The Provisional Measures Procedure in the Matter of Intellectual Property Rights in the New Civil Procedure Code

8.4.1 Overview

The text of the New Civil Procedure Code, which entered into force in Romania on February 15, 2013, completing the new legislative framework initiated by the Civil

Code which has been applied for two years now, brings a large number of innovations and new procedural institutions.[20]

Among the special procedures covered by the text of the New Civil Procedure Code we find a procedure specifically dedicated to protecting intellectual property rights by procedural means.

Chapter IV, Title IV, Book VI of the New Civil Procedure Code is dedicated to the newly introduced procedure.

The advent of this new procedure in a unitary regulation in a separate section of the Civil Procedure Code cannot, however, be construed as a novelty in the provisional protection of intellectual property rights, which may be protected by way of presidential ordinance and under the influence of the old Procedure Code. But we cannot not welcome the initiative of the legislator to create a special, separate procedure on the provisional protection of these categories of civil subjective rights derived from intellectual creation, which, by this new institution, confirms yet again, if needed, the importance of intellectual creation and its protection through civil trial instruments.

Below we summarize the provisions dedicated by the legislature to the institution of provisional measures in the matter of intellectual property rights, followed later by other reflections to try to analyse in more detail the specific issues and potential theoretical problems that can arise from the analysed text.

8.4.2 The Concept of Intellectual Property Rights and Procedural Provisional Measures in the Field of Intellectual Property Rights. Relevant Provisions. Provisional Measures that May Be Ordered by the Court in the Field of Intellectual Property Rights

Although the new text of the Civil Code does not specifically regulate intellectual property rights, the substantial matter of the intellectual property right is generously covered by provisions under special laws, and the importance of protecting subjective intellectual property rights cannot be contested in the current context where the production of intellectual property is part of everyday life.

The New Civil Procedure Code expressly states that these intellectual property rights may be protected not only by way of common procedural law, but also by taking provisional measures in this matter, devoting an entire chapter to the special procedure that applies if provisional measures are requested and are necessary.

---

[20]Law no. 134/2010 on the Civil Procedure Code, republished (Official Gazette no. 545 of August 3, 2012).

To implement the special procedure established by the New Civil Procedure Code ('NCPC'), one must not ignore, but rather must absolutely refer to the notions of substantive law, namely to the branch of intellectual property rights.

Therefore, when talking about the new relevant provisions of the procedural institution to which we refer, we must specify that the relevant provisions are found both in the text of special laws governing copyright and industrial property rights, and in the provisions of Articles 977–978 NCPC.

Intellectual property rights include all subjective rights related to the intellectual creation process in the field of copyright and industrial property rights, with patrimonial and/or moral content.

Provisional measures that may be taken by the court are determined by the existence of illegal actions, actual or imminent, which, provided that they meet the conditions expressly required by law for this new procedure, allow the court to order especially:

(a) The prohibition of violation or temporary cessation of action;
(b) The taking of necessary measures to preserve evidence.[21]

For damages by means of written or audio-visual media, the court may not terminate the detrimental action provisionally unless the damages caused to the plaintiff are serious, the action is clearly justified under Article 75 NCC, and the measure taken by the court does not appear to be disproportionate to the damages caused. The provisions of Article 253, para (2) NCC remain applicable.[22]

8.4.3 The Jurisdiction of the Court

The court having jurisdiction to resolve cases requesting provisional measures on the protection of intellectual property rights is determined according to the general rules of establishing the material and territorial jurisdiction from the common law procedure.

Apparently, the only competent court would be the local court, but if the patrimonial rights derived from the intellectual property right required to be protected by provisional measures exceed the limit of 200,000 lei, we consider that the local court will have the jurisdiction to resolve these cases in the first instance, because the tribunal is also the court of first instance to judge a main summons based on common law and derived from the same rights with regard to which the provisional measures are requested.

The jurisdiction of the court is checked by default, based on the documents submitted by the plaintiff in the original petition.

[21]Article 978, para (2) letters (a) and (b) of the NCPC.

[22]Article 978, para (3) of the NCPC.

It is not mandatory to have a common law dispute pending at the time the summons for provisional measures was filed, but the court's jurisdiction is nevertheless determined by reference to the value of the petition.

If the summons for provisional measures aims to protect both the moral and the patrimonial rights, the court's jurisdiction is also determined in the light of Article 99, para (1) NCPC, which expressly provides that if plaintiff informs the court with several heads of claim founded on different facts or causes, jurisdiction is set in relation to the value or, as appropriate, to the nature or objective of each claim. If one of the heads of claim falls within the jurisdiction of another court, the notified court shall order severance and shall decline its jurisdiction accordingly.[23]

Where several main heads of claim based on a common title or having the same or even different, but closely connected cause, these were to be decided by a single summons, the court who has jurisdiction to resolve them is determined taking into account that claim that attracts the jurisdiction of the higher court.[24]

8.4.4 The Summons for Provisional Measures

The specifics of the summons application for provisional measures in the field of intellectual property rights is generated by the active procedural quality of the person generating such a summons.

The law recognizes this right for the holder of intellectual property rights.

From this perspective, we must distinguish two cases, depending on the type of intellectual property right owned by the plaintiff.

If the rightful holder of an intellectual property right is in the field of copyright, as expressly regulated by the provisions of Law no. 8/1996 as supplemented and amended, the proof of copyright in the patrimony of the material law subject is unconditioned by the existence of a prior recognition or enrolment in a register procedure (except as provided by law, cases which are strictly interpreted). Under the law, the author quality of the law matter is born with the creation of the work.

However, if the plaintiff relies on the protection and adoption of provisional measures on industrial property rights, his/her active procedural quality must be verified through the evidence attesting the enrolment, namely the registration with OSIM, and the issuance by this institution of the protection title, its validity, the object being protected in relation to the object of the summons.

Thus, we see that in this special procedure the plaintiff is implicitly required to prove all this evidence on his/her active procedural quality, taking into account the specifics of social relationships protected by the copyright rule or the industrial property rule.

---

[23]Article 99, para (1) of the NCPC.

[24]Article 99, para (2) of the NCPC.

The Civil Procedure Code itself conditionally states provisional measures using the wording: if the plaintiff credibly proves that his/her intellectual property rights are subject of an unlawful action, actual or imminent.

If the protection object is a joint, collective work, the plaintiff's procedural steps right has to be verified in relation to the provisional measures requested, especially if the procedural stance of defendant/defendants is held by the co-authors of the intellectual property work requiring action. Obviously, this is not necessary in the case of an active dispute consortium.

The summons based on this special procedure can also be introduced prior to the beginning of the common law dispute which has the aim of unravelling the merits.

The procedural condition for the admissibility of this type of summons is that the plaintiff, or plaintiffs, must also file the merits by the deadline set by the court.[25] Failure to meet this condition draws in case of a favourable resolution of a summons for precautionary measures the automatic termination of the effect of the provisional measures taken.[26]

This provision actually provides a balance in disputes between parties, preventing abuse of law by the plaintiff.

By the provisional measures taken by the court, the plaintiff is satisfied in its interest, without having determined to promote a dispute on the merits, as it is protected as a result of the provisional measures.

Ordering the plaintiff to start a common law dispute based on the right is ultimately a measure of procedural fairness and assurance of the safety of the civil circuit.[27]

The defendant subjected to provisional measures may find him or herself blocked by the institution of these measures in terms of conducting normal legal relationships, without there actually being a decision on the merits, thus being deprived of access to justice by the court's decision on the merits.

However, once the plaintiff's obligation to assume the conduct of a dispute amid the legal relationship referred to the court is established, the risk of abuse of rights disappears and the right delivery by the court requirement is ensured, the court not being able to do this on its own as it is bound by the principle of availability.

Obviously, the obligation established by law to start the merits in a certain period is only for the plaintiff of the summons for provisional measures.

The law does not prohibit the initiation of the dispute on the merits to be made by the defendant him or herself in a matter referring to provisional measures.[28]

We believe that in this situation, although pending before the court there is a trial aimed at the merits, the provisional measures ordered by the court in the special procedure will cease at the deadline set by the judge or by law, because the requirement for filing a summons aimed at the merits is the exclusive right of the plaintiff whose summons of provisional measures has been granted.

---

[25]Article 978, para (4) of the NCPC.

[26]Article 978, para (6) of the NCPC.

[27]Article 978, paras (4) and (6) of the NCPC.

[28]Article 978, para (6) of the NCPC.

Otherwise, the action starting a common law dispute generated by the defendant from the matter which dealt with taking the provision measures would create an obvious procedural imbalance for the latter, the plaintiff being in the position of indirectly creating the possibility of law abuse.

8.4.5 Judging the Summons for Provisional Measures

The properly notified court, in terms of material and territorial jurisdiction, proceeds to the resolution of the summons for provisional measures.

The procedure is also correlated with the specific provisions of the presidential ordinance, stating that the court is required to verify beyond the fulfilment of the procedural law relationship (capacity, quality, right, interest, question) the existence of an illegal action, actual or imminent.

The conditions laid down by the legislature regarding the admissibility of the summons need to be met cumulatively. It is enough for a current unlawful action or imminent unlawful action to exist and this action to likely cause a damage difficult to repair to the plaintiff for the latter to be able to turn to the special procedure established by the New Civil Procedure Code.[29]

The unlawfulness of the action subject to the censorship of the court must be examined also in the light of the illegal nature specific to copyright, industrial property right, respectively, being known that the specificity of the intellectual property right relationship materializes by exemptions from the common law civil legal relationship.

The court is also required to verify whether the defendant's action is likely to cause injuries to the plaintiff that are difficult to repair.

Evidence on these circumstances can be achieved by any means of proof, as we are being faced with proving an actual situation.

The court must proceed differently if the summons for provisional measures is filed before or after the merits.

If the summons is made before the merits, the judge verifying the evidence finds that the summons has to be accepted, with the resolution of all issues, will also state a deadline, not exceeding 30 days of taking such measure, within which the plaintiff must file the action on the merits.

Failure to meet the deadline set by the court rightfully entails the termination of the provisional measures imposed by the court.[30]

If at the date the summons for provisional measures there is a pending case on the merits of the intellectual right, and if the court accepts the summons, it will not be required to state the above.

---

[29]Article 978, para (1) of the NCPC.

[30]Article 978 para (6) of the NCPC.

In both cases, if the measures sought are likely to cause damage to the other party, the court may order the plaintiff to give a bail in the amount fixed by itself, under the penalty of the automatic termination of the measure ordered.[31]

If the bail set is arranged in the procedure for provisional measures prior to the filing of the common law action on the merits, the bail also automatically ceases with the deadline set by the court for filing the common law summons.

8.4.6 Judgment. Types of Provisional Measures That Can Be Taken by the Court. Effects. Remedies

The court notified on a summons for provisional measures in the matter of intellectual property rights may accept or reject this summons.

Acceptance of the summons leads to the institution of one of the following measures:

- prohibition of the current or imminent illegal action;
- prohibition of the current or imminent illegal action provisional termination;
- taking steps to preserve evidence.

In case of damages by means of written or audio-visual media, the court may not terminate the detrimental action provisionally unless the damages caused to the plaintiff are serious, the action is clearly justified, and the measure taken by the court does not appear to be disproportionate to the damages caused.

Although the legislature does not expressly state what serious damages to the plaintiff means, depending on the actual case the judge must determine the impact of these measures on the plaintiff also in relation to the nature of the right that is at issue, namely whether it is a moral right or a property right. From this perspective, it should be mandatory for a judge to correlate the general civil protection of those rights both in terms of civil law and in light of the special law on intellectual property and its derogatory rules. In other words, we consider that the court must correlate the actual situation of the case submitted for trial with the general context of the principles and rules of substantive law.

The procedure is subject to judgment rules specific to the presidential ordinance procedure. Thus, to trial the summons, the citing of the parties shall be made in accordance with the rules laid down for urgent trials. The trial may be judged without citing the parties. In case of extreme urgency, the judgment can be given on the same day, the court being able to decide on the required measure based on the summons and documents submitted, without the conclusions of the parties. Judgment is made urgently and with priority, evidence on whose management requires a longer time not being admissible. Provisions on the trial investigation are not applicable.[32]

[31] Article 978, para (5) of the NCPC.

[32] Article 978 of the NCPC.

In our opinion, this provision that applies *mutatis mutandis* starting with the presidential ordinance to the provisional measures procedure in the matter of intellectual property rights can lead to a hasty judgment, especially since the specifics of the damage caused in the field of intellectual property may involve producing even more evidentiary through the court.

This is especially the case when trying the summons must be made urgently and with priority, no evidence on whose management requires a longer time being admissible (for example, a judicial expertise to state the damage).

Where the merits filed by the plaintiff are dismissed as unfounded, the court may at the request of the interested party compel the plaintiff to repair the damages caused by the provisional measures.[33]

That is not the case permitted by law where the summons is rejected on an exception, as prescribed or illegal.

The solution proposed by the legislature may seem unfair, but given that the law expressly provides for the possibility of recovering the possible damage only if the action is dismissed as unfounded, we do not see another solution possible.

If the merits were dismissed as unfounded, and a summons is made by the interested party with the repair of the damages caused by the provisional measures, the court may still reject this summons for the reparation of damages if it finds that the plaintiff in the provisional measures summons was not at fault or had a slight fault, depending on the actual circumstances of the case. Another possible solution to this situation of lack of fault or slight fault is to diminish by judgment the reduction of the amount the defendant is required to pay.

If the opposing party does not request damages, the court shall order the release of bail, at the request of the plaintiff, by a judgment passed with citing the parties.

The summons shall be dealt with under the provisions of the presidential ordinance which applies accordingly. If the court finds that the measures are likely to cause damage to the opposing party, the court may order the plaintiff to give a bail in the amount fixed by itself, under the penalty of automatic termination of the measure ordered.[34]

If the opposing party does not request damages, the court shall order the release of bail, at the request of the plaintiff, by a judgment passed with citing the parties. The summons shall be dealt with under the provisions of the presidential ordinance which applies accordingly. If the defendant opposes to the bail release, the court will set a deadline for filling the merits, which may not be longer than 30 days from the decision, under the penalty of automatic termination of the seizure measure of the amount secured by the bail.[35]

The 30 days deadline is, in our opinion, a limitation period.

Since this special procedure is expressly subject to the provisions of the presidential ordinance, the judgment is subject to remedies specific to the presidential

[33]Article 978, para (7) of the NCPC.

[34]Article 978, para (5) of the NCPC.

[35]Article 978, para (8) of the NCPC.

ordinance procedure. Delivery may be delayed 24 hours at most, and the motivation shall be done within 48 hours from delivery.

The remedy is an appeal; the appeal, if specifically requested, may allow a possible summons to suspend the provisional measures pending the resolution of the remedy.

The judgment in summons dealing with provisional measures in the matter of intellectual property rights has no effect of a *res judicata*.

Moreover, if the deadlines specified by the court or the Civil Procedure Code are not met, the measures ordered by the court become obsolete, lose their effects, and their eventual judicial enforcement, if occurred, gives rise to the right to initiate the return of execution.

If judicial enforcement was not completed by the deadline mentioned in the previous paragraph, in our opinion, this is the case where judicial enforcement must stop, even if this is not expressly provided among the termination of judicial enforcement cases referred to in the New Code. In our opinion, judicial enforcement should cease automatically, without following the procedure to abolish the writ of execution represented by the decision ordering the provisional measures.

Clearly, although the drafting of text for these matters is limited to a total of only two articles, in reality, they represent an entire chapter of the Code, which will certainly lead to many interpretations and discussions in the literature and in court practice.

8.4.7 Precautionary Measures and Evidence in the Protection of New Plant Varieties

Disputes about the quality of breeder, variety patent holder or those regarding other rights arising from the variety patent, including patrimonial rights of the breeder in the assignment or license contract or those related to the noncompliance with Article 37, para (1) and Article 38 of Law no. 255/1998 are the responsibility of tribunals.[36]

Causes may be subject to criminal and/or civil law disputes.

Apart from the provisions of the civil procedure law representing common law, in the field of new varieties of plants protection, the legislature lays down special provisions.

A violation summons is initiated only after the publication of the variety patent. If a license has been granted and there are no other provisions in the contract, the licensee may file a violation summons only with the consent of the variety patent holder. The holder of an exclusive license may file a violation summons if he/she has notified the holder of the variety patent and the latter has not acted in the timeframe requested by the licensee. When a violation summons was started by the

[36]Article 42 of Law no. 255/1998, republished.

variety patent holder, the licensee can constitute the civil party for reparation of the damages.[37]

The variety patent holder may ask the court:

- to order precautionary measures when there is a risk of violation of rights arising from the variety patent and if such violation is likely to cause an irreparable damage and there is a risk of destruction of evidence;
- to order immediately after the investigation measures on the cessation of acts of violation of the rights arising from the variety patent, committed by a third person when introducing in civil circulation important goods, that involve an infringement of such rights;
- to order the confiscation or destruction of propagating material referred to in Article 43, para (2) of Law no. 255/1998.

The measures mentioned above are subject to the application of the Civil Procedure Code.

The court shall order the infringer of rights arising from the variety patent to notify the holder of the identity of others who participated in the production and distribution of the propagating material referred to in Article 43 para (2) of Law no. 255/1998.

When ordering precautionary measures, the court may require the plaintiff to pay bail in the amount fixed by itself.

The court may require the plaintiff to furnish any evidence available to prove that he or she is the holder of the right that has been violated or whose violation is inevitable.

If the evidence supporting the plaintiff's claims are under the control of the defendant, the court may order that evidence be produced by the defendant, guaranteeing the confidentiality of information, according to the law.[38]

8.5 Instead of Conclusions

Observing the principle of good faith and the respect for the rule of law, I believe that the issuance of the New Civil Code has an impact on intellectual property, meaning that, in my opinion, we can no longer speak of a separate legal branch, but only of a civil law field, whether we like it or not.

The monistic theory adopted by the lawmaker prevents even nostalgics from maintaining the old mentality of several branches of law as there is no family law or commercial law, and I think we cannot say that there is a distinct branch of intellectual property law. However, we can state that currently intellectual property

[37]Article 44 of Law no. 255/1998, republished.

[38]Article 45, para (6) of Law no. 255/1998, republished.

represents in the new regulation a field of civil law—with both its components, that is copyright and industrial property law.

Now more than ever, it is necessary to draw up a code of intellectual property covering all aspects which are currently in various regulatory acts, from the New Civil Code to laws, government decisions, emergency ordinances, government ordinances.

I believe that applying the New Civil Code will lead to an increase in the number of legal issues that will require not only their practical clarification by concrete case solutions, but the clarification of the issues in theory especially.

Chapter 9
Some Structural Questions on the Relationship Between Contractual and Extracontractual Liability in the New Hungarian Civil Code

Ádám Fuglinszky

Abstract The new Hungarian Civil Code turns the contractual liability regime upside down. First, the fault based liability for breach of (onerous) contracts has been replaced by a strict liability according to Article 79 CISG. Second, the foreseeability limitation on consequential damages and loss of profit has been implemented in line with Article 74 CISG. Third, the new regime has been topped by the exclusion of parallel damage claims in tort (if the breach of contract qualifies simultaneously as wrongful or tortious conduct), i.e. Non-Cumul, the French approach of an exclusionary relationship between contract and tort, has been introduced. This Chapter reports briefly on all three pillars of the reform but focuses primarily on the third one. Besides the reasons for Non-Cumul, its outcome in the new Hungarian Civil Code, as well as its effects and side-effects, will be analysed. Beyond some general questions at a structural level on the relationship between contractual and extracontractual liability, the predictable difficulties of distinction and qualification and also the inequitable differences between the damage claims asserted by a party to the contract and by third parties are dealt with.

This chapter was presented at the conference "New Civil Codes in Hungary and Romania II" held on 20th September 2013 at the Eötvös Loránd University, Faculty of Law. Unless specified otherwise, the English translations are those of the author's.

Á. Fuglinszky (✉)
Civil Law Department, ELTE Eötvös Loránd University, Budapest, Hungary
e-mail: fuglinszky@ajk.elte.hu

A. Menyhárd and E. Veress (eds.), *New Civil Codes in Hungary and Romania*, Ius Gentium: Comparative Perspectives on Law and Justice 63,
DOI 10.1007/978-3-319-63327-5_9

9.1 Introductory Remarks

As Prof. Lajos Vékás, president of the Codification Committee notes, the new Hungarian Civil Code[1] does not follow any foreign pattern exclusively, but the drafting was preceded by substantial comparative analyses on several questions and the committee drew upon many highly qualified achievements of recent codifications (such as the Burgerlijk Wetboek of the Netherlands or the Code Civil du Québec) and even more so of acknowledged model laws (e.g. The Principles of International Commercial Contracts, 2010; The Principles of European Contract Law, 1999, 2002; The Draft Common Frame of Reference—Principles of European Law).[2] This chapter is about a subject of the new Hungarian contract law which is based, by and large, on legal transplants. The reform of contractual liability will be tackled in a nutshell, with special regard to the relationship between contractual and extracontractual liability in the new Civil Code.

9.2 The Reform of Contractual Liability in the New Hungarian Civil Code in a Nutshell

The reform of contractual liability in the new code is based on three pillars.[3] These are as follows: the introduction of strict liability for breach of onerous contract; the implementation of the so called foreseeability clause or limitation on damages in line with Article 74 CISG; and finally the exclusion of parallel damage claims in tort in cases of breach of contract.

9.2.1 Strict Liability for Breach of Onerous Contracts

The first pillar is the introduction of *a strict (risk-based) liability for the breach of onerous contracts*, similar to Article 79, para 1 CISG, Article 8:108, para 1 PECL and Article III.—3:104, paras 1 and 2 DCFR. In the old civil code,[4] it was regulated

---

[1]The New Civil Code was enacted in February 2013 as Act No. V/2013 (henceforth referred to as the HCC or new code). The new Civil Code entered into force on 15th March 2014.

[2]Vékás 2013, p. 20.

[3]On the first two pillars, see generally Vékás 2010 and Fuglinszky 2015.

[4]Act No. IV/1959, henceforth referred to as HCC of 1959 or old code.

as a fault based liability; however, fault was presumed by law.[5] The liability for breach of gratuitous contracts remains a fault-based liability in the new code.

According to Section 6:142 HCC

> A person who causes damage to the other party in breach of the contract shall be liable for such damage. They shall be relieved of liability if they are able to prove that the breach was due to an impediment beyond their control and not foreseeable at the time of conclusion of the contract and they could not reasonably be expected to avoid it or to overcome the loss.

This is the strict liability regime which replaces the fault-based liability (with presumed fault) of the old code. As Vékás underlines, under true market economy conditions, contractual liability must reflect the fact that there was a foregoing and willing undertaking of an obligation between the parties and, even more so, that the aim of contract law is to secure a fair allocation of risks. Hence, exculpation from liability cannot depend on the mere efforts, even less on subjective-personal characteristics of the party in breach, i.e. on a subsequent (moral) evaluation of human conduct; especially not if the personal behaviour is hidden behind the acts of organisations (for example, of companies). Vékás adds that the Hungarian judiciary preferred such a rigorous interpretation of the "activity required generally in the given situation" (i.e. fault), even under the old code, that exculpation from liability in the event of breach of a contract was hardly ever possible, unless some kind of inevitable event could be proven.[6] This statement seems to be confirmed also from a different perspective. In a comprehensive analysis of the Common European Sales Law, German law professors pointed out that the two competing approaches (the fault-based liability in the German law and that of Article 79 CISG) lead to rather similar results in practice. They found the only difference between the two was in the liability of a seller who had not been able to inspect the goods for hidden defects. (He could exculpate himself if a fault-based liability was to apply but not under a strict liability regime as indicated in Article 79 CISG.)[7] The three requirements as specified above have to be met cumulatively in order for someone to be exculpated from liability; the burden of proof lies with the party in breach.

[5]Cf. Section 318, para 1 HCC of 1959 "The provisions of tort liability shall be applied to liability for breach of contract and to the extent of indemnification, with the difference that such indemnification may not be reduced, unless otherwise prescribed by legal regulation." with reference to the general rule of extracontractual liability, Section 339, para 1 HCC of 1959 "A person who causes damage to another person in violation of the law shall be liable for such damage. He shall be relieved of liability if he is able to prove that he has acted in a manner that can generally be expected in the given situation." (Translation of the ComplexJogtár online, WoltersKluwer group.).

[6]Vékás 2010, 97–98.

[7]Eidenmüller et al. 2012, 339.

9.2.2 Implementation of the Foreseeability Limitation Similar to Article 74 CISG

The second pillar is the implementation of a *foreseeability clause,* similar to Article 74 CISG, Article 9:503 PECL and Article III.—3:703 DCFR. There is no such explicit limitation on the extent of damages or compensation in the old code.[8]

Under Section 6:143, para 1 HCC, the loss occurred in the contractual item (or service) itself must be (fully) compensated for. (This is called the sticking, adhesive or direct damage.) There is neither foreseeability nor any other limit on the amount of this head of damages. According to para 2

> Other pecuniary losses beyond the contractual item and the loss of profit must be compensated for to such an extent as the other party proves that the loss was foreseeable as a possible consequence of the breach at the time of conclusion of the contract.

The foreseeability limitation does not apply in cases of intentional breach (para 3). If the breach itself was intentional, all damages disregarding their foreseeability must be compensated for, even if causing losses was not covered by the intent of the party in breach (but the breach itself was). The exception provision in para 3 shows that the legal transplant is surely not a comprehensive one, because the exemptive treatment of intentional breach of contract and the extension of liability beyond foreseeability in this case prevents the adaptation of the common law concept of efficient breach.[9]

The reason behind the implementation of the foreseeability clause is the legislator's aim to give preference to the risk allocation idea and, within this frame, to attune and to balance the assumed risks connected to the contract (the risk of paying damages in the event of breach of contract among them) with the contractual price, in other words, to preserve the contractual equilibrium. This explains why the reference point of foreseeability is fixed at the time the contract was concluded. The conclusion of the contract is the very last moment when the parties can adjust the price to the foreseeable financial consequences of the assumed risks, among them that of breach of contract, as may be the case. Thus, this is the last moment when, if they gain knowledge of some additional risks, they can still decide not to enter into contract, to increase the price, to insure themself or just to conclude the contract

---

[8]The foreseeability rule is not completely unknown to the Hungarian lawyers, as Hungary joined the CISG. Moreover, according to para 18 of the so called Law Decree No. 8 of 1978 on the Application of the Civil Code of the Republic of Hungary Regarding External Economic Relations, "A person who caused damages is liable for such damages which arise directly out of his conduct and which could be foreseen as a possible consequence at the time the contract was made." (Translation of the ComplexJogtár online, WoltersKluwer group.) Thus, foreseeability formed already an organic part of the Hungarian civil law, at least concerning export-import contracts.

[9]The same stands true for Article 1150 of the French Code Civil. According to Article III-3:703 DCFR (and 9:503 PECL) besides intentional breach, foreseeability is also switched off if the breach was grossly negligent.

despite the additional risks.[10] Making the party liable for all losses beyond the foreseeable consequences of their breach at the time of conclusion of the contract would spoil the fair and just risk allocation, i.e. the balance between risks and price desired by the legislator (as he decided to implement the strict liability combined with the foreseeability clause). If the party gets to know some additional risks afterwards, i.e. after the conclusion of the contract, they do not have any further opportunity to adjust the price to these additional risks. These thoughts are very well embedded in the law & economics approach. Liability law should create incentives to take the potential costs of actions into account. The "foreseeable probability of injury, combined with its foreseeable costs is to be weighed against the costs of avoiding them". Where the latter is less than the former then liability should be imposed, because this is the efficient level of deterrence. In this view, foreseeability of the injury is inevitable for calibrating the appropriate level of liability.[11]

According to Vékás, the foreseeability clause is a much better, more predictable method of finding reasonable limits to damage claims entirely lacking merit than to disallow the claim due to lack of proper evidence or to break or cut the causal chain artificially, as these methods had been practiced by the Hungarian courts so far. The latter method is criticised by Vékás as an obscure rationale, mixing various factors such as the remoteness of damages, the meaningless distinction between direct and indirect damages, etc. He praises the foreseeability clause again for its flexibility,[12] since it does shape a fair compromise between flexibility and fairness on the one hand, and predictability of law on the other. The foreseeability is a time-tested, successful legal means excluding liability for unusual, irregular and therefore incalculable damages.[13] The burden of proof lies with the other party (which suffered the loss), thus they have to prove that the party in breach foresaw or should have foreseen the harmful consequences.[14]

9.2.3 Non-Cumul: The Exclusion of Parallel Damage Claims in Tort (An Overview)

Last but not least, the Hungarian version of "*Non-Cumul*" must be mentioned as the third pillar of the reform. Where there is a contractual relationship between the plaintiff and the defendant, *parallel damage claims in extracontractual liability are excluded*, in contrast with German law for example, where there the principle of the

---

[10]McDowell 1985–1986, 302–303.

[11]Cf. the comprehensive analysis (from tort of negligence's point of view) of Cardi 2004–2005, 954–956.

[12]Vékás 2010, 99–100; Reasons 2013, § 6:143, Chap. 7. c.

[13]Vékás 2010, 100.

[14]Vékás 2010, 101–102.

free choice between the contractual and extracontractual claim (*freie Ansrpuchskonkurrenz*) applies: the plaintiff can generally decide for an extracontractual claim if this seems to be more favourable for them (provided the requirements of the extracontractual liability are fulfilled). The Hungarian standpoint on the basis of the old code was not an unambiguous one: there was no answer in the old code, neither for Cumul, nor for Non-Cumul. Due to the similarities between contractual and extracontractual liability in the old code, the issue was not of such great significance. For a passenger transport contract, however, extracontractual liability was regarded as a special rule and this was preferred to contractual liability, because the former was (and still is) constructed as a strict liability if the injuries were caused by a dangerous operation or extra-hazardous activity (and driving a car, bus, etc. is considered as to be a dangerous activity), while contractual liability in the old code was a fault-based liability with presumed fault. Apart from this distinction, one could start generally from a free choice between contractual and extracontractual liability.[15]

9.3 Non-Cumul, Exclusion of Parallel Damage Claims in Extracontractual Liability (A Detailed Analysis)

9.3.1 *Cumul or Non-Cumul: That Is the Question—Some General Thoughts*

There are four theoretical models on the relationship between contract and tort; first and foremost of contractual and extracontractual liability, if the wrongful conduct qualifies both as breach of contract and as tortious conduct the same time. The first possibility is to restrict the liability to the contract; the second is to allow the injured party the option to choose either type of liability; the third variation is to allow them to rely on both types simultaneously, choosing from each the particular rules most favourable to the case; and finally to restrict the action exclusively to tort.[16] The first option is followed by French law, even if there are several exceptions from the rule; and the second model is adopted generally in common law (complicated however by the privity of contract doctrine and its exceptions) and in German law. Since the Hungarian legislator has recently introduced Non-Cumul, i.e. the restriction of liability to the contractual regime, particular attention is going to be given to this option here.

The first question to answer is what the reasons are for restricting liability to the contract, i.e. exclusion of the parallel claims in extracontractual liability. As a matter of principle, this doctrine aims at the protection of the contract, contractual equilibrium (if one wants: the adjustment of risk and price) and the binding force of

[15] Fuglinszky 2011, 1262–1263.

[16] Hilley 1956, 135.

contractual agreements (the exclusion and limitation clauses among them), because the contractual will is deemed to be the source of liability and it fixes the measures of this liability. If there was no doctrinal iron curtain between the two fields of liability then all contractual particularities, for example the limitations of liability, could be evaded, which would require the contracting party to assume burdens (of being sued in tort), which they did not contemplate at all when entering into contract. They might find themself burdened with liability that they had not even suspected of existing.[17]

Whether the lawmaker or the judge faces a real danger of eliminating the contractual liability regime depends on some general characteristics of the legal system in question and on the differences of contractual and extracontractual liability. (If there is convergence between the two, in other words, they are kept as close to each other as possible, the choice between Cumul and Non-Cumul, i.e. drawing a borderline between the two liability regimes is not an issue any more; the need ceases to exist for such a rule.[18]) Since French law is the most cited example in the academic literature, some possible differences between contractual and extracontractual liability are illustrated by reference to this legal system. The differences cover the standard of care required, the differing measures of damages, the variances in the length of prescription, etc. In French law, foreseeability applies to contractual liability only, not in tort. Limitations of liability are allowed in contract but such clauses referring to tort are generally void. The required standard of conduct varies according to the type of contract but not in tort. The burden of proof lies with the defendant in contract law matters; they can exculpate themself if they can prove a fortuitous event (*cas fortuit*) or the fault of the other party. By contrast, the fault of the defendant must be proven by the plaintiff in tort. Prescription is much longer in tort law (30 years) than in contract law.[19]

The more differences (with several solutions favourable to the plaintiff) and the wider the scope of extracontractual liability, the bigger the danger of evading contractual liability.[20] (Even the exclusionary and limitation clauses of international treaties could be evaded by extracontractual claims, unless the treaty itself excludes any recourse to the national extracontractual liability regime.) Bypassing it by means of extracontractual liability can be justified however if there are no appropriate rules limiting the possibility of the contractual exclusion and limitation of liability in the legal system in question.[21] If such rules exist and they work properly

[17]Hilley 1956, 119, 124, 144, 146–147; Hutschinson and Van Heerden 1997, 109–111.

[18]Garoupa and Ligüerre 2011, 318.

[19]Hilley 1956, 124–130, see also Viney 1993–1994, 819 with reference to burden of proof, foreseeability, limitation clauses, prescription and jurisdiction. Regarding the DCFR, the plaintiff is generally allowed to choose liability in tort. However tort law does not apply in so far as its application would contradict the purpose of other private law rules such as foreseeability. If this is the case, the contract rule takes priority. Cf. Article VI-1:103(c) and Lando 2009, 636–637, 639.

[20]Garoupa and Ligüerre 2011, 316; Schlechtriem 1972, 437.

[21]Cf. Van Rossum 1995, 544, 548.

(for example, invalidity due to violation of good morals or to unfair commercial terms) and they also provide an adequate level of protection against erosion of contractual liability if there is an inequality of bargaining power (as in consumer contracts), there is no justification for the evasion of contractual liability on that account. Non-Cumul has been also praised from the law & economics point of view; first, because the possibility that breach of contract could generate a tort claim undermines efficient breach; second, potential tort claim could deter the conclusion of contract or increase negotiation costs to overcome potential future tort claims. It is therefore advised to allow parallel tort claims only in very exceptional circumstances, for example if the contractual regime is unable to internalize some losses of the non-performance due to externalities or the existence of serious asymmetries of information.[22]

In the following subchapter, attention will be given to why the Hungarian lawmaker decided for Non-Cumul. The analysis is restricted to the exclusion of parallel claims in tort in case of breach of contract; all questions on the relationship between contractual and extracontractual liability can most certainly not be dealt with here. In comparison with French law, the Hungarian legislator did not leave the development of a structural doctrine on the relationship between contractual and extracontractual liability to case law; the new Civil Code provides explicitly for Non-Cumul. Having learnt from the difficulties of and experiences in distinguishing between breach of contract and extracontractual wrongful conduct in other legal systems, the lawmaker tried to provide a rule in order to facilitate this distinction and hereby the classification of various occurrences of harms as contractual or extracontractual. This is namely a preliminary question which shows at which point Non-Cumul intervenes.

9.3.2 *Non-Cumul in the New Hungarian Civil Code*

Section 6:145 HCC has the title "Exclusion of parallel damage claims". The text itself does not sound unambiguously like an exclusion because it says

> The creditor can enforce his or her damage claim against the debtor according to the rules on damages caused by the breach of contract, even if the loss establishes the extracontractual liability of the debtor as well.

Despite the impression that it seems to be about granting permission, both the title and the Statement of Reasons of the new code make it clear that the claimant is

---

[22]Garoupa and Ligüerre 2011, 317; Ogus 2004, 399–400. As to the negotiation costs: if parallel claims are allowed, the legal system in question must provide an answer to whether a contractual exclusion or limitation of liability extends to the extracontractual claims automatically or only if the parties also extended the scope of the limitation to these claims. Non-Cumul is thus not the exclusive method of preventing the evasion of contractual limitation and exclusionary clauses.

divested of the possibility to claim in tort if the losses occurred in consequence of a breach of contract. To our understanding, Section 6:145 HCC is a mandatory rule, thus it cannot be set aside by the mutual consent of the parties, since this is one of the core structural rules and principles of our new liability law.[23]

The biggest challenge if such a rule applies is the distinction between breach of contract and a "simple" tortious act of the defendant. An "iron-clad separation" does not exist between the two[24] and the boundaries can be manipulated[25] by the court in order to reach allegedly fair decisions. Some courts try to identify an "independent actionable wrong" (*selbtständiges besonderes Ereignis*) or an "unlawful act arisen independently of the violation of the contractual obligation" to facilitate the distinction. The tort law bypass is permitted sometimes to avoid the application of undesirable rules by requalification or simply redefinition of the wrongful conduct.[26] Hilley prefers an approach ensuing from the contract: the judge shall check whether there is a specific contractual duty or at least an implied duty, which has been infringed; otherwise the tort law remedy applies.[27] Some scholars propose to consider policy aspects straightforwardly and to balance pros and cons: if voluntariness (and contractual equilibrium) is more important, the act should be considered as breach of contract; if, by contrast, general policy considerations reflected by the tort law are paramount then tort law prevails for the wrongful act in question.[28] Viney refers to French law and to the law of Québec and draws attention to some accessory duties which, though being covered by the contract, (such as duty of care, duty of information, duty to warn, duty of loyalty and to act in good

[23]In this regard very convincing Pusztahelyi 2016, 71–72.

[24]Hilley 1956, 120.

[25]Whittaker 1995, 336.

[26]Cf. Van Rossum with examples from the French, German and Dutch law; Van Rossum 1995, 546, 553, 557.

[27]Hilley 1956, 130.

[28]McDowell 1985–1986, 311; Hilley 1956, 141–142 refers similarly to the abuse of rights as a relay from contractual to the delictual track in French law. The subsumption of architect's, builder's, attorney's and doctor's liability under professional fault (*faute professionelle*), which is part of the tort law regime, can be also traced back to policy considerations aimed at the equalisation of the information asymmetry between the professional and the consumer, cf. Van Rossum 1995, 549; however these policy considerations have been replaced by special rules on some contracts of the kind, particularly if residential property is concerned; as to the English and French law on this matter cf. 546, 550. In Hungary, according to Section 8, para 20 of Act No. CCLII/2013 on the amendment of specific acts related to the new Civil Code's coming into force, Section 244, para 2 of Act No. CLIV/1997 on health services has been amended and, according to the amended text, extracontractual liability is to apply to medical malpractice, which is a fault based liability even in the new HCC. As such, doctors' professional liability is subsumed expressly under the extracontractual regime. The goal of the special rule in Hungary is exactly the opposite to that in French law. In French law, the professional fault (*faute professionelle*) aims at a stricter liability than the contractual regime. The Hungarian derogation aims at the detachment of the doctor's liability from the strict contractual liability regime in order to arrive at the less severe fault-based extracontractual liability, because the latter fits better to the doctor's activity within the context of a best effort contract (*obligation de moyens*).

faith, etc.) are—as she continues—nothing else but the contractual translations of general standards of conduct which should apply to everybody, regardless of whether there is contract between them. Though these general duties got redied in the contract according to the purpose and other features of that particular agreement, they are—so Viney—still Janus-faced or double-track duties.[29] They might be particularly extradited to uncertainties of qualification.

The Hungarian legislator also recognised that the exclusion of parallel claims in tort can induce difficulties in distinction between obvious breach of contracts and other damaging occurrences or "accidents" related to the contract but not having the clear character of a breach of it. For instance, if the painter or a mechanic carrying out repairs in a house breaks a valuable Ming vase, is it still a breach of contract, connected compulsorily and exclusively to the contractual liability regime, or does it qualify instead as an independent actionable wrong giving rise to an autonomous damage claim in tort, after all? In order to avoid such harsh issues of distinction, the legislator supplemented the above described "Non-Cumul" rule with an additional interpretive rule (Section 6:146 HCC) which assigns (pecuniary) damage claims for all losses occurred *in the course of the performance of the contract* compulsorily to the contractual liability regime. Since damages occurred "in the course of the performance" is a much wider notion than damages "caused by the breach of contract", there is no distinction issue in the above mentioned example: the "accidental destruction" of the Ming vase and all similar losses entitle the creditor to claim damages in contract only, but not in tort. Although these losses did not occur in consequence of the breach (because there was no breach at all in the example[30]), they did however occur during or in the course of the performance of the contract. According to the legislator's intentions, the contractual liability regime extends both to the interest of performance (expectation interest, *Erfüllungsinteresse*) and to the interest of protection (of the creditor's goods, reliance interest, *Schutzinteresse*,); these two interests of the creditor should not be subject to different liability regimes.[31] This view attracts support in the law & economics approach: it is sound to extend the contractual regime to those wrongful conducts which are tortious in nature but in fact are the by-products of the contract in order to subject them to the mutual consent test and to decrease negotiation costs by closing all gates towards tort actions.[32]

The Statement of Reasons of the new code explains the legislator's decision for Non-Cumul with the introduction of the strict liability for breach of contracts; in

---

[29]Viney 1993–1994, 824–826; she proposes to allow the choice concerning these duties on a case by case basis if this does not infringe the autonomy of the contract.

[30]It goes far beyond the aim of this chapter to substantiate, for example, the German approach on accessory or secondary obligations depending on whether they are related to the performance of contractual services or not (*leistungsbezogene Nebenpflichten*, *nichtleistungsbezogene Nebenpflichten*). In this respect, breaking the vase or of the window could qualify as the breach of an accessory obligation not related to the contractual services.

[31]Reasons 2013, § 6:146, Chap. 9.

[32]Garoupa and Ligüerre 2011, 317.

other words, if there is a no-fault liability, the claimant is even better protected than if they would claim in tort and so it does not make sense "to lift the issue out of its natural context, which is the contractual relationship".[33] Is it the real reason for the new rules? Why does the introduction of Non-Cumul make sense in the Hungarian liability law? Why should the contractual liability regime be protected against parallel claims of tort if the former became a strict liability and the latter remained generally a fault-based liability regime (which is thus less favourable to the victim) with the exception of liability for dangerous activities, which is also a no-fault liability (thus, at least as favourable but seemingly not more favourable to the victim). The answer is far not obvious. At first glance, the extracontractual bypass does not benefit at all: the requirements on standards of conduct are equally severe or even stricter in contractual liability. There is a foreseeability limitation, both in the contractual and extracontractual liability regime, even if there are slight differences in this regard. The possibilities on exclusion or limitation of liability are word for word the same in both regimes.[34] Even the prescription times correspond: the general five years' prescription applies. (A special prescription of three years applies with regard to the extracontractual liability for dangerous activities, thus if the breach of contract occurred due to an activity which can be classified as dangerous and the three years of prescription have expired, a contractual damage claim is the only route for recovery and so the contractual route seems to be more favourable from the victim's point of view also in this respect). Liability is presumed in both regimes, therefore there is no difference in the burden of proof. According to Section 6:144, para 2 HCC, damages to pay as a result of breach of contract cannot be reduced on the basis of equity, as they theoretically can be in tort law. This is however an additional difference that favours contractual liability and so contractual equilibrium is not endangered by this rule either. If there are so many contraindications or at least factors that show that there are no incentives in the system to evade contractual liability (and to opt for tort) at all; to the contrary: the contractual regime seems to be obviously more favourable to the injured party, then what is the Non-Cumul in the new Civil Code good for?

There seem to be two reasons that explain the legislator's definite standpoint and decision for the "Non-Cumul" principle. The first is the insistence on the just and fair risk allocation as a main goal of the new rules on liability, i.e. on the balance of price and assumed risks, fixed in time at the conclusion of the contract, first and foremost by the foreseeability rule. The *point of reference of the foreseeability is that of the conclusion of the contract.* All possible losses, which become or should have become known to the party in breach at a later date, are not relevant, therefore they are not covered by the foreseeability and consequently not by the liability of the party in breach either. If these latter losses were also covered, the contractual adjustment of risks and price would tumble down. Although there is a foreseeability limitation included in the extracontractual liability regime of the new Civil Code too

[33]Reasons 2013, § 6:145, Chap. 8.

[34]Cf. Section 6:152 HCC in contractual and Section 6:526 HCC in extracontractual liability.

(Section 6:521 HCC), it is however without a reference to the point in time when exactly the foreseeability "gets fixed". This allows the interpretation (moreover, this seems to be the most plausible interpretation) that all possible losses which were foreseeable at the time the wrongful conduct was performed, are covered by (extracontractual) liability. If the parallel claim in tort were allowed, there would be no solution to secure the balance and the contractual risk allocation. Thus, if a parallel claim in tort were allowed, the plaintiff could claim all losses foreseeable at the time of the breach of contract (as the breach of contract would be regarded as the wrongful conduct in the sense of the extracontractual claim), and so, potentially, losses far beyond those foreseeable at the time of conclusion of the contract. That's the one sound reason for the exclusionary rule of Section 6:145 HCC, even if this cannot be found explicitly among the official Statement of Reasons of the Act.

The other reason is linked to the *distinction* between *direct* (*adhesive, sticking*) *damages* and *consequential damages* (damages in the contractual item itself) in the event of defective performance. According to Section 6:174, para 2 of the new code, the creditor can claim direct damages only if the *special prescription times* provided for by the code for defective performance had not yet elapsed and they could not get the defective performance remedied by specific performance (repair or replacement). The special prescription time is one year for a non-consumer contract, two years for consumer contracts, thus significantly shorter than the general prescription time (applicable also to damage claims) which expires in five years. (Nevertheless a five year prescription period applies even to direct damages, if the contractual object is an immovable, so there is no difference in the latter case.) All in all, the creditor could evade these shorter prescription times and also their duty to claim specific performance first; in other words, they could, by choosing extracontractual liability, evade the right of the defendant to remedy the defect in kind before being obliged to pay damages, i.e. to remedy it in terms of money. The legislator wanted to close this back door. These two seem to be the real explanations for introducing the "Non-Cumul" principle.

The question is, however, whether this advantage or function is worth accepting, despite all the side-effects and dysfunctions eventually caused by the rule. One question of fairness arises at structural level: why should the plaintiff be worse off for the simple reason that they entered into contract with the person who displayed the wrongful (and damaging) conduct when compared to someone else (suffering the same harm) who was not in any prenegotiated relation with the defendant?[35] Regarding the strict liability for breach of contracts, exactly the opposite logic applies: the liability regime should be more severe towards the party who wilfully assumed the risks and therefore could prepare themself to perform as per contract and to avoid all harmful consequences. The contractual equilibrium [in other words, the theoretical possibility at least to adjust the contractual price to the (foreseeable)

[35]Hilley 1956, 120–121 asks the same question from the defendant's point of view with reference to the pluralist approach arguing for the free choice of the plaintiff: there is no reason to treat somebody who breached the contract more favourably than a third party who is not contractually bound to anything.

risks] seems to be preferred to the concern mentioned above. That inconsistency is tacitly approved as the price for the paradigmatic change to a contractual liability regime based on the law & economics approach that is aimed at the adjustment of price and risk. Hence, this is not a question of legal doctrine but of policy.

9.3.3 Issues of Distinction

Due to the aforementioned, all losses occurring *in the course of the performance of the contract* underlie the contractual liability regime in the new Hungarian civil code. The legislator did not succeed in eliminating the problems of distinction and classification by the additional interpretive rule, but these have indeed been reduced and shifted to more marginal and rarely occurring combinations of facts and circumstances. The expression "in the course of the performance" must still be subject to interpretation. In our understanding, all losses, the occurrence of which was made possible by the performance [i.e. by the existence of the contractual relationship between the parties, thus which would not have been occurred but for the (performance of the) contract] are covered. This is the case, for example, if the contractor harms the plants while installing the sprinkler system in the garden; the painter breaks the window while setting up in the flat; the clothing of the passenger becomes dirty or torn while travelling in the taxi; the carrier's lorry breaks down the fence while loading up at the plant of its party to the contract; the tenant's dog eats the landlady's chickens;[36] the employer's car explodes through a fire that broke out in the course of restoration works performed by the contractor[37] etc. The same stands true for damages occurring in the course of performance through personal injury, for example loss of income due to injuries caused by outdated drugs; the tenant falls down the unrepaired stairs; the elevator crashes down with the tenant; the buyer seriously burns when glue bought from the seller catches fire, etc.[38] Interpreting Section 6:146 HCC, the contractual liability shall also cover the losses which occurred as later consequences of an activity performed in the course of the performance of the contract.

Hence, if there is a contractual relation between the parties, it is hardly ever possible to claim in tort, although not unimaginable. A damage claim in tort cannot be excluded if the wrongful conduct is in no manner connected with and entirely unrelated to the contract. Having Litvinoff's example in mind, after entering a lease contract and far away from the leased premises, one of the parties accidentally runs over the other with his car.[39]

---

[36]For these and more example cf. Eörsi 1962, 191 *et seq.*

[37]Viney 1993–1994, 821 with reference to the qualification difficulties in French law.

[38]For these and more example cf. Litvinoff 1999, 4, 19, 20.

[39]Litvinoff 1999, pp. 16–18.

One does not need too vivid an imagination to find borderline cases where a distinction can still be difficult. Let's change Litvinoff's example a little bit: which regime applies if the contractual parties wanted to meet or already met at a particular place—even if far from the premises—in order to pay and receive the rent, and the running over happened just before or after this meeting? Similarly, did the loss occur in the course of the performance of the contract if the claimant had brought the car to the garage and the garage manager had offered to give him a lift for free to his home and, in the course of this accessory courtesy offered by the garage manager free of charge, an accident happened? Thus, some distinction difficulties will not be spared to the courts, even if not in that amount and significance as the case would be without the additional rule in Section 6:146 HCC. Also, if Non-Cumul applies in a legal system, it is sound to facilitate its application by such an additional interpretive rule.

9.3.4 Extracontractual Claims Not Covered by the "Non-Cumul"

The "Non-Cumul" rule excludes extracontractual claims only with regard to the contractual parties themselves and so it does not apply if *third parties* are (also) affected by the breach of contract. If the legal system in question allows a direct claim against the (*vicarious*) *agent* (*subcontractor*) of the debtor beside the contractual claim against the debtor itself, the direct claim against the agent in tort is not excluded by "Non-Cumul".

If there are relational losses suffered by the *dependants*, family members of the surviving or even deceased party to the contract (for example loss of maintenance or the non-pecuniary aspect as *solatium doloris*), the damage claims of the relatives—as far as recognised by law—can be enforced (only) on the basis of extracontractual liability (since there is no contract between them and the person doing harm to the primary victim).

In the Hungarian law an (extracontractual) strict liability applies to extra hazardous (dangerous) activities. The operator of these activities (in whose interest the activity is carried out) "shall be relieved of liability by proving that the loss was due to an unavoidable cause that fell outside the scope of their activity."[40] If the performance of the contract qualifies as an *extra-hazardous activity* too and the *party to the contract was different from the person of the operator*, an extracontractual claim against the operator is not excluded, either. For example if somebody is given a lift (which is a contract according to Hungarian law be it onerous or gratuitous), and the party to the contract offering the lift is not the operator of the activity (for example, the car is a rented one or it is a company car), and the driver causes an accident in which the claimant is injured, there is a contractual claim

[40]Cf. Sections 6:535 and 6:536 HCC, translated by Prof. Attila Menyhárd.

against the driver (unless they acted as the agent of the operator) and a parallel claim in tort against the operator, and the two are considered to have caused the damage as multiple accountable defendants.[41] (The claimant can finally be compensated only once but they can choose between the two or sue both of them, as the two are jointly and severally liable. The questions on the interpretation of the notion of "operator", on the outcome of the process with the parallel claims and on the recourse claims between the driver and the operator in the end go far beyond the aim of this chapter.)

A kind of parallel (extracontractual) claim by mandatory rules is imaginable, even *between the contractual parties*. In such an unlikely case, if the consumer concludes a contract directly with the producer or quasi producer as per product liability legislation, the "Non-Cumul" rule cannot exclude their claim due to the special rules on *product liability* (now in Sections 6:550-6:559 HCC), because they represent the implementation of Council Directive 85/374/EEC of 25 July 1985 on the approximation of the laws, regulations and administrative provisions of the Member States concerning liability for defective products. Putting the implementing rules aside would infringe European Law.[42]

The most serious point of criticism by Viney on the double-track character of liability regimes and on Non-Cumul is that third persons' extracontractual claims for suffering harms as a result of the breach of contract between the parties do not underlie either contractual exclusions and limitations or the shorter prescription times of contractual liability. Additionally, the foreseeability limitation does not apply to them, at least in French law.[43] Therefore she proposes that these contractual rules be extended to the (extracontractual claims) of third parties, particularly with regard to the chain of *subcontractors*.[44] These concerns are crucial also to the Hungarian liability rule to some extent. Although foreseeability applies in both regimes, the time of reference of the foreseeability is different: the time of conclusion of the contract for contractual claims and most probably the time of performing the wrongful conduct from a tort claim's point of view. Thus, more can be foreseeable towards a third party than to the party to the contract, because all facts and circumstances the party became or should have become aware of after concluding the contract up to the time of breach (which can qualify simultaneously as a tort toward a third party) are relevant and included in their liability in tort toward third parties but not in their liability towards the other party to the contract. If the party to the contract dies as a consequence of the breach, the annuity of their *dependents* is to be paid regardless of foreseeability due to the special rule of Section 6:529, para 1 HCC, thus the foreseeability does not play a role in this

[41]This case is also mentioned by Vékás 2013, § 6:145, 609.

[42]Cf. the following cases on the exclusionary nature of the harmonised product liability law: C-52/00 Commission v France, C-154/00 Commission v Greece, C-183/00 María Victoria González Sanchez v Medicina Asturiana SA. With the same conclusion Pusztahelyi 2016, p. 12.

[43]Viney 1993–1994, 823–824.

[44]Viney 1993–1994, 825–826.

latter respect. The different time of reference concerning foreseeability certainly matters if the plaintiff sues both the party to the contract for breach of contract and the subcontractor in extracontractual liability (if the two claims are based on the same factual situation). There is no explicit rule on this issue in the Hungarian Civil Code, hence the following solutions are worth consideration. Either the court does not approve the direct extracontractual claim against the subcontractor or makes it conditional on further requirements, such as the conduct of the subcontractor must turn out to be an independent wrong, a qualified wrong or an additional wrongful act beyond the simple inappropriate performance. This solution sounds quite artificial and affected, introducing vague categories and additional problems of qualification and distinction. The second way would be to extend the contractual limitations of liability and also the time of conclusion of the contract as the point of reference of foreseeability to extracontractual claims towards the subcontractor. This could work after careful consideration in well-justified cases by analogy; however, Hungarian courts are rather reluctant to apply analogy in fear of being overturned by court of appeals on the grounds of alleged *contra legem* interpretation. The third option is to accept the above described inconsistency as the price of the new structure of liability regimes, which involves (one hopes) several advantages in other contexts. The inconsistency could be balanced and mitigated by the consideration of the fact that the subcontractor acted within the frame of a contract between them and a party to the contract, and therefore the standards of conduct to be expected from them were shaped also by this contract. This must be taken into account, even regarding the extracontractual claim against them, while deciding on fault.

9.3.5 "Side Effects" and Other Consequences of "Non-Cumul"

There are certainly effects that the legislator might not have considered or at least which seem to be somewhat underestimated. First of all, by closing the gate between contract and tort, the weight and importance of *exclusionary* and *limitation clauses* in contract increases significantly. (Liability can be excluded or restricted except regarding personal injuries or damages caused intentionally according to Section 6:152 HCC.) The prescription period can be shortened by mutual agreement too (Section 6:22, para 3 HCC). A harsh limitation clause combined with another clause on shortening the prescription significantly can completely hollow out the liability of the party *per se* or to diminish it to a symbolic one entirely lacking content. Thus, the role of other institutions and rules of contract law which are devoted to preventing the abuse of market power—for example, invalidity due to infringement of good morals or to unfair commercial terms—will increase enormously in significance, as there is definitely no emergency exit via parallel tort claims. Furthermore, there are several particular statutes and international treaties which exclude or limit liability or damage claims (postal services, international transport contracts): practitioners must bear in mind that there are no extracontractual detours any more, not even in the lack of explicit exclusionary provisions in the treaties themselves.

Next, the following gap in the law illustrates some possible consequences of the new rules. Giving somebody a lift for free—taking a hitchhiker—is a gratuitous contract as laid down in Hungarian law. With a gratuitous contract, there is no liability for breach of the contract without fault. Hence if the driver causes an accident but they are not at fault, there is no damage claim on the passenger's side. There is a tort claim—as seen above—against the "operator" of the car as a source of an extra-hazardous activity, but not even this special extracontractual liability rule applies if the party to the contract offering the free ride and the operator were the same person. Thus, there is a possible combination of facts and circumstances where there the victims of car accidents remain without any (legal) coverage, if there was no other car involved in the accident and the driver (who was the operator himself) was not at fault in causing the accident. The fault-based (contractual) liability for the breach of gratuitous contracts squeezes out the strict liability for operating a car as performing a "dangerous activity" in tort. It might happen that the legislator recognizes this gap and tries to fill it with a special rule requalifying the operation of a car as always performing an extra-hazardous activity (as it was and still is according to Hungarian law), hence redirecting it in all cases very consistently to the domain of tort law,[45] despite the fact that there might be a contract in the background, the outcome could be a different and a more justifiable one. But this solution—as with every medicine—would have considerable side-effects too. First, the fragmentation of law: some situations wherein a car would be involved would be subsumed under the extracontractual (strict) liability for extra-hazardous activities. Other dangerous activities, by contrast, would be deemed as contractual if carried out within the frame of a contract, thus fault-based liability would apply if the contracts were gratuitous ones. This solution would treat like cases differently.[46]

---

[45]Such an attempt can be discerned from the Statement of Reasons on Section 121 of Act No. CCXXXVI/2013 on the amendment of specific financial acts related to EU law harmonization; see also the Statement of Reasons at page 74 of the Draft Act T/13082. It is prefaced by the statement (with reference to the amendment of Act No. LXII/2009 on Compulsory Third-Party Vehicle Insurance), that "The injuries caused by the operation of a motor vehicle qualify as losses caused by an extracontractual conduct." However, is a sentence *obiter dictum* in the reasoning of an act with a completely different subject sufficient to break through the Non-Cumul principle provided for by the new Civil Code? Such solutions are definitely the sources of legal uncertainty, which is why they should be repudiated.

[46]Viney 1993–1994, 821 analyses a French case wherein the plaintiff was injured by a chainsaw while helping his brother. Using a chainsaw qualifies certainly as a dangerous activity according to Hungarian law, thus surely the strict extracontractual liability applies if a third party (a bystander or passer-by) is injured by the chainsaw. If a gratuitous service was provided to the injured person, fault-based liability for the breach of a gratuitous contract would apply without any possibility to choose tort law. I do not see any reason to treat alike cases differently. Although one could give an explanation with reference to the increased frequency with which a car is used and can cause an accident if one wanted; i.e. de facto more people use cars than chainsaws, thus the chance of being

In comparison with this way, it seems to be even better to outsource all harms that occurred in car accidents and to bring them under a no-fault plan maintained by social security or private insurance companies. As another conceivable solution, rethinking the notion and boarders of the contract comes to one's mind, taking into consideration that giving a lift—or providing any other service—for free is not necessarily a binding contract at all, but only a non-binding courtesy outside the law of obligations, similar to the German "*Gefälligkeitsverhältnis*".[47] This target-oriented adaptation of the consideration doctrine would be on the one hand antagonistic to the logic and doctrinal content of the Hungarian law of contracts in their current state where gratuitous contracts are seen and deemed to be contracts too. On the other hand, this solution resulted in another contradiction in providing a higher standard of protection for those who are given a lift for free than for those who conclude a contract with due consideration, i.e. pay the market price, because the former could rely on the strict liability in tort for dangerous activities while the latter could not, and as we will elaborate on in the next paragraph, the strict liability in tort for dangerous activities seems to be even more severe than the strict liability for losses caused by the breach of (onerous) contracts. Finally, the Hungarian courts detected this issue, too. The Civil Law Department of the Szeged Regional Court of Appeal passed an Opinion (which is not formally binding upon the lower courts, will however generally be followed by them), whereby Sections 6:145-6:146 HCC do not even apply to injuries suffered during free car drives or similar accidents, because the liability for the breach of gratuitous contracts in Sections 6:147 HCC can be found only after the respective rules.[48] To our understanding this is obviously a *contra legem* approach and the reasoning is not very convincing with reference to the order of the rules within the Code.

Last but not least, some cases, which were solved by the strict (extracontractual) liability for extra hazardous (dangerous) activities according to Section 345 of the old Code (as with driving a car), now belong to the scope of contractual liability according to Sections 6:145 and 6:142 of the new Code. In these cases, the injuries were caused by an extra hazardous activity (operation), however also in the course of the performance of a contractual service. For example, coming flying out of a waterslide or from a summer toboggan run were seen as being injured through an extra hazardous operation, and the operator of these kind of facilities was held liable

(Footnote 46 continued)

injured by a car or a car accident is bigger than being cut by a chainsaw. This would however be a policy rationale which might be reflected by the argumentation quoted above in footnote No. 45.

[47]This was an option based on the thoughts of my colleague Prof. Attila Menyhárd (not yet published).

[48]Cf. Opinion No. 2/2016. (XI.24.) of the Civil Law Department of the Szeged Regional Court of Appeal (Szegedi Ítélőtábla), explained by Kemenes 2017, 7, 10. The Court and the cited author refer to the Reasons referred to above in note 45 too. In order to avoid the contradiction tackled by us above, the Szeged Regional Court of Appeal takes the view that there is no significant difference between the strict liability in tort for dangerous activities on the one hand and the strict liability for losses caused by the breach of (onerous) contracts on the other.

for the injuries suffered on the basis of extracontractual (strict) liability as described above, irrespective of the contractual nature of the parties′ relationship. According to this rule, an operator could be only relieved of liability by proving that the injury was due to an unavoidable event that fell outside or was beyond the scope of his (extra dangerous) activity. From now on, these waterslide, summer toboggan and similar cases will underlie only and exclusively contractual liability due to the Non-Cumul principle (Section 6:145). However, there is a difference in the exculpation prerequisites between the two liability regimes. While in the event of breach of a contract, "an impediment beyond the control" of the party in breach suffices (provided it was unforeseeable and the party could not be reasonably expected to avoid it), according to Section 6:142 HCC, an unavoidable event "beyond the scope" of the dangerous activity is required to be relieved of strict liability in tort. The two formulations: "beyond control" and "beyond the scope of activity" do not necessarily mean the same. Exculpation can be easier if only the former is required. There are many occasions, which are beyond the control of the operator but not beyond the scope of the extra hazardous activity in question. It must be highlighted that the group of cases in question includes very common contractual situations beyond the world of leisure parks too: travelling by taxi, coach and train can be cited as very frequent examples in everyday life. These cases fell under the strict liability in tort for dangerous activities while the former Civil Code was in force. Now the "beyond control" test seems to have replaced the "beyond the scope of activity" test. It does not necessarily mean the same whether we measure and qualify, for example a technical defect in a car or the driver's health issue using the "beyond control" or the "beyond the scope of activity" tool and benchmark. The question whether exculpation would succeed more often in this case group must be answered by the courts through interpretation of the exculpation prerequisites. There is no unity in the academic scholarship in this regard, either. While Kemenes takes the view that those two benchmarks cannot be different, they must mean the same unless car, train, and coach accident victims suffer a significant decrease of legal protection;[49] by contrast, Pusztahelyi represents a different understanding and emphasises that two different notions cannot have the same meaning.[50] We follow the second view and propose a structural *de lege ferenda* solution below.

9.4 Summary

As comparative experience shows, whether the rule may be *Cumul* or *Non-Cumul* (i.e. free choice between contractual and extracontractual liability or, to the contrary, exclusion of parallel claims in tort if there is a contract between the parties), there are always exceptions that weaken the rule. Surprisingly however, the same

[49]Kemenes 2017, p. 4.

[50]Pusztahelyi 2016, pp. 73–74.

policy considerations might hide behind the rule and the exception too. The one liability regime is harsher than the other. Prescription times are shorter (or longer) in the one than in the other. The range or scope of damages to be compensated is wider in the one than in the other. As such, it is influenced mostly by the historical factors of the particular legal system whether Cumul or Non-Cumul prevails as the rule, which is then mellowed by many policy exceptions.

The legislator should opt for the solution whereby the fewest exceptions are needed. Exceptions evoke issues of distinction and increase transactional costs. *Non-Cumul* seems to be a *sound choice* if the protection of the contractual equilibrium is emphasised; extracontractual liability has a wide range and broad scope (as in French or Hungarian law) and there are many substantial differences between the two liability regimes, which are more favourable to those who suffered losses and/or injuries and therefore it should be a concern that claimants would try to evade the contractual liability by the delictual bypass.

There are however not too many differences between contractual and extracontractual liability in the Hungarian civil law. Even those that are present plead for the choice of the contractual liability and definitely not for the extracontractual regime. The risk of evasion of the contractual rules is not that blatant. Nevertheless the Hungarian legislator decided for Non-Cumul in order to prevent two malfunctions. The first possible risk is the *evasion of the shorter prescription times* of damage claims for *direct* (*sticking*) *damages*; i.e. for damages in the contractual item itself, which can be or could have been remedied by specific performance. The second risk is the different *temporal points of reference of foreseeability* in the two liability regimes. In the contractual regime, the time of the conclusion of the contract counts; by contrast, the time of performing the wrongful conduct matters in extracontractual liability. Claiming in tort instead of in contract could lead to the inclusion of all the additional risks into the scope of liability that became foreseeable after the conclusion up to the breach of the contract (as the latter can be seen and qualified also as tortious conduct). The delictual bypass would eliminate the contractual adjustment of price and risk.

Non-Cumul itself is predestined to evoke issues of qualification and distinction. Distinctions are drawn frequently arbitrarily in order to achieve policy targets. It is sound to enact an interpretive rule beside Non-Cumul, as the Hungarian legislator did; whereby contractual liability is extended to all losses suffered *in the course of the performance*, i.e. not just expectation interest but also reliance interest is covered by contractual liability. The interpretive rule cannot prevent all issues of distinction but there will be definitely fewer borderline cases due to this extension.

The construct chosen by the Hungarian legislator is not free from side-effects either. The following difficulties can be envisaged. First, if a breach of contract—most frequently defective performance—results in harms both to the person or assets of a party to the contract and to the person or goods of *third parties*, the time of reference of foreseeability will not be the same. The same stands true if the party to the contract sues both their contracting partner for breach of contract and simultaneously the subcontractor of the party in tort.

Second, *lacunae* will emerge in case of *gratuitous contracts*. If a gratuitous contract is breached, there is no liability without fault. Hence, if the victim is given a lift for free and the driver (who is the owner of the car) faints (without any fault, just by a quirk of fate), the victim will not be covered at all. (Liability insurance does not apply in the absence of liability either.) To sue the owner and operator of a dangerous activity in extracontractual strict liability is barred by Non-Cumul. If, however, the driver cannot be considered the operator of the dangerous activity (because they are not the owner of the car), there is doubtless a valid claim against the operator in tort. There is no real satisfying solution for this concern. The notion of contract could be eventually reconsidered and might undergo a restriction to onerous contracts, in other words to contracts with due consideration. This would be however antagonistic to the logic and doctrinal content of the Hungarian law of contracts and resulted in a higher standard of legal protection for those who are given a lift for free than for those who pay for the taxi, coach or train ticket due to the differences between the strict liability in tort for dangerous activities and the strict liability for losses caused by the breach of (onerous) contracts in the new Civil Code. Enacting a special rule—most probably assigning these and similar situations to extracontractual liability—would lead to the fragmentation of civil law in this field. If there were special regulations for car accidents, why not enact another for other kind of accidents? (For example, if the losses occur in the course of a benevolent action to help my neighbour in his garden with my chainsaw?) In that comparison, even the complete outsourcing of car accidents into a no-fault insurance scheme sounds more convincing.

If the Hungarian legislator or the courts had followed, for example, the German case law in regarding the "free ride" or hitchhiking as a non-binding agreement of courtesy, i.e. as not a contract, in order to switch off the Non-Cumul barrier, that would result again in replacing the fault-based liability by the strict liability for dangerous activities in tort. In this case, however, the level of protection of passengers being transported free of charge would be higher that for onerous passenger transport contracts such as travelling by taxi or train, because the exemption from liability would be possible only if the accident were caused by an inevitable event *beyond the dangerous activity* and not "just" *beyond control.*

Finally, in the so-called waterslide or summer toboggan run case group, wherein the injuries were caused in the course of the performance of a contractual service, contractual liability applies due to the contractual nature of the parties′ relationship, despite the fact that performing such services also qualifies as an extra hazardous or dangerous activity in tort. Due to the Non-Cumul principle, contractual liability supersedes the special (and strict) extracontractual liability for dangerous activities. Consequently, it will suffice again to be relieved of liability for an unforeseeable event "beyond the control" of the party in breach (of the provider of the service) instead of an unavoidable event "beyond the scope of the dangerous activity" as was the applicable rule so far to these cases. The interpretation of the rule by the courts, whether exculpation would really be easier from now on, remains to be seen.

One Hungarian scholar, Kemenes, proposes to solve this problem by putting an equal sign between these two different legal notions,[51] i.e. the two benchmarks should merge and resolve into one another. As pointed out earlier, this issue is definitely not a theoretical one, because travelling by taxi, local bus or coach or by the train also qualifies as a contractual relationship and the passenger has to pay the contractual price (thus the contract is an onerous one whereto the strict liability for losses caused by the breach of contract applies, irrespective of the fact that an accident could also qualify as wrongful conduct that underlies strict liability in tort for dangerous activities).

To summarise, the introduction of the Non-Cumul principle seems to have generated more difficulties than it solved. As we made clear earlier, we do not support the introduction of legislative exceptions from the rule eroding the Non-Cumul principle. Instead, the legislator should consider whether the goals targeted by Non-Cumul can be achieved through other "smoother" ways and means. Two goals were identified above: first, preservation of the point of reference of the foreseeability limitation exactly at the time of the conclusion of the contract; second: protection of the order of remedies in cases of defective performance, i.e. that specific performance goes first and the same time not to allow the claimants to bypass the shorter prescription by opting for damage claims in tort. The same goals could be achieved without Non-Cumul too. We propose that the legislator should consider repealing the Non-Cumul principle. At the same time, the legislator should consider the following amendments: first the introduction of special provisions that extend the effect of the contractual limitation and exclusion clauses to extracontractual claims[52] (the limits of contractual freedom in this regard are exactly the same anyway in Section 6:521 for contracts and in Section 6:526 for torts);[53] second, to make it clear that if the claimant and the defendant have a contractual relationship then the contractual foreseeability clause applies, i.e. the reference point of foreseeability becomes fixed at the very time when the contract was concluded, even if the claimant refers to extracontractual liability for the losses suffered due to the breach of contract;[54] and finally, third, that the order of remedies and the special prescription apply even if the creditor claims compensation for the so-called direct damages in tort instead of contractual liability.

[51]Kemenes 2017, 4 cf. however the opposite view of Pusztahelyi 2016, pp. 73–74.

[52]Limitation and exclusion clauses should definitely be under judicial control by invalidity rules (violation of good morals or unfair commercial terms).

[53]Similarly Pusztahelyi 2016, pp. 77–78. She considers other alternatives, for example to keep the Non-Cumul principle but to reshape it as a default rule or to keep it but make a general exception for personal injuries.

[54]Pusztahelyi 2016, p. 77 considers this too and remarks that there is another difference between the two foreseeability clauses. As far as the contractual foreseeability rule is concerned, intentional breach of the contract sets foreseeability aside and the party in breach is liable for all losses irrespective of their foreseeability; while there is no such "cancel button" for deliberate wrongfulness among the rules of extracontractual liability and she is right in this respect too and so this should be considered indeed.

References

Cardi, W. Jonathan. 2004–2005. Reconstructing Foreseeability. *Boston College Law Review* 46:921–988.

Eidenmüller, Horst, Jansen, Nils, Kieninger, Eva-Maria, Wagner, Gerhard, and Zimmermann, Reinhard. 2012. The Proposal for a Regulation on a Common European Sales Law: Deficits of the Most Recent Textual Layer of European Contract Law. *Edinburgh Law Review* 16: 301–357.

Eörsi Gyula. 1962. *Elhatárolási problémák az anyagi felelősség körében* [Problems of Distinction in Material Liability]. Budapest: Közgazdasági és Jogi Könyvkiadó.

Fuglinszky Ádám. 2011. 339. §. In *A Polgári Törvénykönyvről szóló 1959. évi IV. törvény magyarázata, II. kötet* [Commentary on Act No. IV/1959 on the Civil Code, Vol. 2], ed. András Osztovits, 1261–1278. Budapest: Opten.

Fuglinszky Ádám. 2015. The Reform of Contractual Liability in the New Hungarian Civil Code: Strict Liability and Foreseeability Clause as Legal Transplants. *Rabels Zeitschrift für Ausländisches und Internationales Privatrecht* 79:72–116.

Garoupa, Nuno, and Ligüerre, Carlos Gómez. 2011. The Syndrome of the Efficiency of the Common Law. *Boston University International Law Journal* 29:287–335.

Hilley, E. Byron. 1956. The Interrelationship of Tort and Contract in French Law. *Journal of Public Law* 5:116–147.

Hutchinson, Dale, and Van Heerden, Belinda. 1997. The tort/contract divide seen from the South African perspective. *Acta Juridica* 1997:97–120.

Kemenes István. 2017. A kontraktuális kártérítés egyes kérdései [Some Questions on Contractual Liability]. *Magyar Jog LXIV*/1:1–10.

Lando, Ole. 2009. Foreseeability and Remoteness of Damages in Contract in the DCFR. *European Review of Private Law* 4:619–639.

Litvinoff, Saul. 1999. Contract, Delict, Morals and Law. *Loyola Law Review* 45:1–54.

McDowell, Banks. 1985–1986. Foreseeability in Contract and Tort: the Problems of Responsibility and Remoteness. *Case Western Reserve Law Review* 36:286–325.

N.N. 2013. Reasons to Act No. V./2013 on the Civil Code (referred to as Reasons), available a.o. in Complex online law (Member of the Wolteres Kluwer group).

Ogus, Antony. 2004. What Legal Scholars Can Learn from Law and Economics. *Chicago-Kent Law Review* 79:383–401.

Pusztahelyi Réka. 2016. Igényhalmazatok a szerződésszegési jogkövetkezmények rendszerében, különös tekintettel a Ptk. 6:145. §-ára [Cumulated Claims in the System of the Breach of the Contract's Consequences, with Special Regard to Section 6:145 HCC]. *Pro Futuro* 5/2:60–78.

Schlechtriem, Peter. 1972. *Vertragsordnung und außervertragliche Haftung*. Frankfurt am Main: Alfred Metzner.

van Rossum, Madeleine. 1995. Concurrency of Contractual and Delictual Liability in a European Perspective. *European Review of Private Law* 4:539–559.

Vékás Lajos (ed.). 2013. *A polgári Törvénykönyv magyarázatokkal* [The Civil Code with Commentaries]. Budapest: Complex.

Vékás Lajos. 2010. About Contract Law in the New Hungarian Civil Code. *European Review of Contract Law* 6:1:95–102.

Viney, Geneviéve. 1993–1994. Pour une interpretation modérée et raisonnée du refus d'option entre responsabilité contractuelle et responasbilité délictuelle (article 1458, deuxième aliéna du *Code Civil du Québec*). *McGill Law Journal* 39:813–827.

Whittaker, Simon. 1995. Privity of Contract and the Law of Tort: the French Experience. *Oxford Journal of Legal Studies* 15:327–370.

Chapter 10
New Particular Agreements in the New Hungarian Civil Code

Balázs Tőkey

Abstract The new Hungarian Civil Code incorporates some new particular agreements in Book 6 (Law of Obligations) Part 3 (Particular Agreements). This article reports on four of these newly incorporated particular agreements: the intermediary agreement, the (bank) guarantee, the health insurance contract and trusts. The new Hungarian Civil Code re-implements the private law rules of Council Directive 86/653/EEC among the norms of the commercial agency agreement, which is a special intermediary agreement. According to the new regulations, the (bank) guarantee is a collateral contract and not just a collateral commitment for securing contracts as it was before. The structure of the regulation of insurance agreements has been reviewed by the legislator and the health insurance contract is regulated in a separate chapter after the chapter on indemnity insurance and the chapter on insurance of fixed sums. Trusts, which were previously unknown in Hungarian law, have been incorporated by the new Hungarian Civil Code to offer a new option for property management but they can help to realise other economic or legal aims, too.

The new Hungarian Civil Code (Act V of 2013 on the Civil Code, hereinafter the NHCC)[1] is built on the first Hungarian Civil Code (Act IV of 1959 on the Civil Code of the Republic of Hungary, hereinafter the HCC of 1959). However, the NHCC has brought several important changes, one of which is the introduction of some new particular agreements in the Book 6 (Law of Obligations). We would like to give a short overview and interpretation of the regulation of some new particular agreements in this paper.

[1]The NHCC entered into force on 15th March, 2014.

B. Tőkey (✉)
Civil Law Department, ELTE Eötvös Loránd University, Budapest, Hungary
e-mail: tokeybalazs@gmail.com

A. Menyhárd and E. Veress (eds.), *New Civil Codes in Hungary and Romania*,
Ius Gentium: Comparative Perspectives on Law and Justice 63,
DOI 10.1007/978-3-319-63327-5_10

10.1 Classification of the New Particular Agreements in the NHCC

First we have to give a brief explanation of what we mean under the expression "new particular agreement or contract". Of course those specific contracts that had already been regulated in detail in the HCC of 1959 are not "new". All the other particular contracts, which can be found in Book 6 (Part 3 Particular Agreements) of the NHCC, can be regarded as new contracts. In our opinion, we can classify these agreements according to the nature of their novelty.

The first group covers the agreements which were not regulated by the HCC of 1959 but had already been regulated by another act, e.g. the commercial agency contract (Act CXVII of 2000 on the Commercial Representation Contracts of Self-employed Commercial Agents, hereinafter referred to as Act CXVII of 2000) and residential leases (Act LXXVIII of 1993 on the Leasing of Residential Property and Premises and on Some Regulations on their Alienation). The second category is a really special case: Section 249 of the HCC of 1959 defines bank guarantee as a collateral commitment for securing contracts without regulating it in detail. The NHCC defines the guarantee as a contract with detailed norms (in Book 6, Part 3, among the particular agreements). The next group is the biggest one: it contains particular agreements, which have not been regulated by act before the NHCC, but have been used in practice: e.g. franchise, factoring and financial leasing. The fourth and last group comprises just one particular contract, which has neither been regulated by act nor has been used in the practice before: this is the trust. We cannot interpret all these new contracts of the NHCC in one article; therefore we will just give a short presentation of one contract from each of the above categories.

10.2 Intermediary Agreement

We have chosen the intermediary agreement from the first group. The NHCC implements Council Directive of 18 December 1986 (86/653/EEC) on the coordination of the laws of the Member State relating to self-employed commercial agents (hereinafter the Directive) among the norms of intermediary agreements. Although the Directive had already been implemented in Hungary by Act CXVII of 2000, we can find important differences between how it was implemented by Act CXVII of 2000 and by the NHCC. In the following we will focus on these differences.

Act CXVII of 2000 implemented both the private and public law norms of the Directive. The NHCC implements just the private law norms of the Directive, but not all of them. It implements just the private law provisions that are sufficiently abstract (Vékás 2013, 777–778). The NHCC does not implement those private law regulations of the Directive that are consistent with the general norms of the NHCC: for example, the norms regulating the obligations of the agent are not implemented because these obligations ensue from the general contract obligations of the NHCC

(Vékás 2013, 783). All other norms of the Directive were to be implemented by other acts (Vékás 2013, 778), because Act CXVII of 2000 was repealed when the NHCC entered into force.[2]

A further innovation of the NHCC is that it not only regulates commercial agency agreements, but also all intermediary agreements (of course, the subject of Act CXVII of 2000 was just commercial agency). We can see the difference between an intermediary agreement and a commercial agency agreement if we examine the definitions of these agreements.

Section 6:288 NHCC defines an intermediary agreement:

> According to an intermediary agreement, the agent shall pursue activities which facilitate the conclusion of a contract between the principal and a third party; the principal shall pay remuneration.

Section 6:293. Para 1 defines a commercial agency agreement:

> According to a commercial agency agreement, the self-employed agent, who has continuous authority, shall negotiate the conclusion of a contract between the principal and a third party, or shall negotiate and conclude a contract in the name of the principal; the principal shall pay remuneration.

The NHCC makes it clear that, according to both the intermediary agreement and the commercial agency agreement, the agent shall negotiate the conclusion of a contract between the principal and third party. However, a commercial agency agreement is a special intermediary agreement: if the agent has continuous authority to negotiate between the principal and the third party then it is not just an intermediary agreement, but a commercial agency agreement. Continuous authority is a necessary term of a commercial agency agreement. For example, a real estate agency is generally engaged via an intermediary agreement and normally not a commercial agency agreement because the agent does not have continuous authority.[3]

Furthermore, the NHCC expands the subject of intermediation. According to the Directive the subject of intermediation is the sale or the purchase of goods.[4] Act CXVII of 2000 also defined this subject as the sale or the purchase of goods,[5] but as the Section 1, paras 5 and 6 said:

> Unless prescribed in specific other legislation to the contrary, this Act shall apply *mutatis mutandis* to the commercial agency contracts of self-employed agents when negotiating for services, intangible assets or securities in the commodity exchange or the commodity market. Within the meaning of this Act, any property that can be taken into possession shall be treated as goods.[6]

[2]Section 67 of the Act CLXXVII of 2013 on the Transitional and Authorizing Provisions Connected to the Promulgation of the Act V of 2013 on the Civil Code.

[3]The Supreme Court of Hungary had the same conclusion in judgement 2/2005 PJE: Act CXVII of 2000 is not applicable to real estate agencies because of the lack of continuous authority.

[4]See Article 1 of the Directive.

[5]Section 1, para 2.

[6]Translation of the ComplexJogtár online, WoltersKluwer group.

The NHCC goes even further: the agent may negotiate any contract.[7] We have to mention that numerous Hungarian acts contain special rules about those commercial agencies, the subject of which is not the sale or the purchase of goods but other services (e.g. on insurance mediation, Act LXXXVIII of 2014 on the Insurance Business). The NHCC—as with Act CXVII of 2000—shall apply as a subsidiary act if the subject of the commercial agency is not the sale or the purchase of goods but another service and this agency is regulated by another special act.[8]

According to the NHCC, an intermediary agreement is a special mandate or agency.[9] There are some opinions expressed in the Hungarian legal literature that an intermediary agreement is closer to a service provision contract than to a mandate, because normally the only form of remuneration is the commission on commercial transactions concluded during the period covered by the intermediary agreement. The NHCC represents the opposite view: an intermediary contract is a special mandate because the failure of the result is not considered to be a breach of contract (Vékás 2013, p. 778).

The NHCC contains just a few rules for intermediary agreements because—as mentioned before—the regulations governing mandates must apply to intermediary agreements. We would like to mention just the most important ones.

The first rule after the definition is Section 6:289, which settles the question of the right of representation:

> Unless prescribed in another part of this act to the contrary, the agent is not entitled to conclude the contract mediated by him in the name of the principal or to accept consideration for the mediated contract.

The meaning of this norm is clear: the agent is not entitled to represent the principal. Of course this is not a mandatory rule; the parties can entitle the agent to represent the principal by mutual agreement.

The NHCC also prescribes that the agent shall be entitled to remuneration on mediated contracts concluded after the intermediary contract has terminated.[10] It is questionable how this rule should be interpreted, whether the agent is entitled to remuneration if the offer by the third party to conclude the contract is made before the intermediary contract has terminated or if it can be done later, too. The juridical practice interpreted the HCC of 1959, which does not contain this special norm, in such way that a (real estate) agent is not entitled to remuneration if the offer by the third party to conclude the contract is made after the intermediary contract has terminated.[11] However, we can imagine that this practice will be changed because of this rule. We have to mention in connection with the remuneration that most

[7]See Section 6:288 and 6:293. para 1.

[8]But these special acts contains just a few private law rules, most of their norms are public law rules.

[9]"Unless otherwise provided by this Chapter—the regulations governing mandate must apply to intermediary agreement." See Sections 6:292.

[10]See Section 6:291 Para 2.

[11]See judgement BH2011.251 of the Hungarian Supreme Court.

rules of the Directive governing remuneration are not implemented by NHCC but by Government Decree 65/2014 (III. 13.) on the Right of the Agent to Commission Based on a Commercial Agency Agreement.

As we wrote before, the general norms of an intermediary agreement shall also apply to a commercial agency agreement, but the NHCC also contains special rules governing commercial agency agreements. Most of them concern the implementation of the Directive. In some cases the Directive does not give an obligatory rule but offers several options for regulation to the member states. We will show in the following section which options were chosen by the Hungarian legislator.

The written form of a commercial agency agreement is not prescribed by the NHCC,[12] but Section 6:293, para 4 states:

> If the agreement is made in writing, each party is entitled to receive from the other a copy of the contract and its amendments on request. Any agreement contrary to the provision and the disclaimer of this right shall be null and void.

Although this is a mandatory rule, in our opinion the implementation of this norm by the NHCC is however incorrect. According to the Directive[13] the parties shall also be entitled to receive a signed written document in default of a transcribed agreement, but this rule is missing from the NHCC.

Section 6:297 of the NHCC governs termination:

> (1) Where an agency contract is concluded for an indefinite period then either party may terminate it by giving notice. The period of notice shall be one month for the first year of the contract, two months for the second year commenced, and three months for the third year commenced and subsequent years. Shorter periods of notice shall be null and void.

According to Article 15 3. of the Directive:

> Member States may fix the period of notice at four months for the fourth year of the contract, five months for the fifth year and six months for the sixth and subsequent years. They may decide that the parties may not agree to shorter periods.

However, the NHCC does not exercise this option.

The Directive offers two alternatives to the member states on how to regulate the settlement after the termination of the commercial agency agreement: the agents shall be entitled to be indemnified or compensated for damage.[14] The lawmakers chose the same option for the NHCC as Act CXVII of 2000, opting for indemnity, because the regulations in the Directive governing the compensation for damage are less compatible with Hungarian private law. For example, the loss of profit or the possibility to amortise the costs and expenses as a consequence of a legitimate termination of a contract cannot be regarded as damage demanding compensation,

---

[12]Act CXVII of 2000 prescribed the written form for all commercial agency agreements in Section 4, which has been a mandatory rule.

[13]See Article 13.

[14]See Articles 17 and 18.

because these are just risk and both parties shall bear their own risks according to Hungarian private law (Molnár 2009, p. 36).

The regulation of the commercial agency agreement by the NHCC also governs questions which are not regulated by the Directive, for example the representation of the principal by the agent. According to the NHCC,[15] the agent is entitled to represent the principal only if there is a mutual agreement. However, in that case, if the agent is entitled to represent the principal, he or she is not entitled to amend the contract, to receive money or to set a due date for payment. Of course these norms are not mandatory; the parties are free to define the governing rules of representation.[16]

10.3 (Bank) Guarantee

As mentioned before, the HCC of 1959 defines bank guarantee as a collateral commitment for securing contracts among the general rules of contracts. The NHCC expands the rules of the particular agreements (Book 6, Part 3) with the chapter on collateral contracts (no. LXI), which contains surety and guarantee. The relevant provision of the former HCC of 1959 is just one sentence (the definition of the guarantee); therefore the regulations in the NHCC are based on international models (Vékás 2013, p. 879): e.g. Principles of European Law Personal Security (PEL Pers. Sec.); Uniform Rules for Demand Guarantees (URDG 758) of the ICC; the United Nations Convention on Independent Guarantees and Stand-by Letters of Credit; and the International Standby Practices (ISP98).

Despite the change in the placement of guarantee in the NHCC, the guarantee does not have to be a contract. As the appropriate definition in the Section 6:431 of the NHCC sets out:

> The guarantee agreement or declaration is a commitment by the guarantor to pay an amount to the beneficiary under specific terms. The agreement and the declaration must be made in writing.

The definition also makes it clear that any person and not just a bank, is entitled to be a guarantor.[17] However, something is missing from this definition: it does not distinguish a guarantee from a letter of credit, because it does not say anything about the aim of the guarantee. The letter of credit is a payment method but the guarantee serves as collateral. Unfortunately this difference does not come to light in the definition of guarantee.

[15]Section 6:294.

[16]Act CXVII of 2000 contains different regulations. For example, according to Section 3 Para 1 of Act CXVII of 2000, if the agent is entitled to represent the principal then he or she is entitled to accept the consideration due (receive the purchase price).

[17]However, the NHCC contains a special norm in Section 6:438: if the guarantor is a consumer, his or her guarantee must be regarded as a contingent surety agreement.

The most important norm of the guarantee is that one prescribing the independence of undertaking: the commitment of the guarantor is independent from the obligation which is secured by the guarantee. The guarantor is not entitled to enforce the objections based on the secured obligation. It does not influence the independence of the guarantee if its text refers to the secured obligation in general.[18] However, the NHCC contains some exceptions:[19] in the event of manifestly abusive or fraudulent demands, the guarantor is not obliged to make payment or he or she is entitled to reclaim the amount paid earlier. The NHCC does not define what a manifestly abusive or fraudulent demand is, but gives some examples:

- any document has been falsified;
- the underlying obligation has been fulfilled or the beneficiary is not entitled to receive the amount assigned by the demand for any other reason;
- fulfilment of the underlying obligation has been prevented by the wilful misconduct of the beneficiary;
- the underlying obligation has been declared invalid by a court, unless the undertaking indicates that such contingency falls within the risk to be covered by the undertaking.

Most of these examples are also known in international practice,[20] but we can also find terms that can be somewhat problematic to apply: for example, it is not really clear which reasons can be referred to by the guarantor if he or she states that the beneficiary is not entitled to receive the amount assigned by the demand "for any other reason". One of the commentaries (Wellmann 2013, p. 334) of the NHCC states that the correct interpretation of this term shall be that the guarantor may refer to a manifestly abusive or fraudulent demand only where it is obvious also to the beneficiary that he or she is not entitled to demand the guarantee. However, if there is a dispute between the beneficiary and the debtor, the guarantor is not entitled to withhold payment. In our opinion, the interpretation of this objection by the legal practice has to be as narrow as possible because otherwise the independence of the undertaking will not have any meaning.

According to the NHCC, the beneficiary's right to demand payment may be transferred only if it is authorized by the guarantor but he or she is entitled to designate the person to whom the guarantor shall pay and the right to demand payment shall devolve to the successor of the beneficiary.[21] The commentaries represent controversial opinions on the question of what succession means in this norm. According to one of them (Vékás 2013, pp. 895–896) the NHCC refers just to the legal succession; the other one (Wellmann 2013, p. 334) explains that if the beneficiary, as the creditor, assigns his or her claim to another person, the assignee

[18]Section 6:432.

[19]Section 6:436.

[20]E.g. see Article 19 of United Nations Convention on Independent Guarantees and Stand-by Letters of Credit http://www.uncitral.org/pdf/english/texts/payments/guarantees/guarantees.pdf.

[21]Sections 6:433 and 6:434.

shall be entitled to demand payment, because he is the special successor to the beneficiary. The fact that the former versions[22] of the NHCC used the expression "legal succession" but the final version of the NHCC just contains the expression "succession", which confirms the second interpretation, that succession shall be understood as both legal and special succession.

After the presentation of the most important rules of the NHCC, we will show some points that are missing from the governing regulation of (bank) guarantees. The NHCC does not deal with so-called "extend or pay" demands: these entitle the beneficiary to state that he or she accepts the extension of the guarantee in place of the payment. If the guarantor receives an "extend or pay" demand, he or she has two options: he or she will either extend the guarantee or pay the amount assigned by the demand. Of course, the parties can agree on an "extend or pay" demand without the governing regulation of the NHCC, and it is a useful term because it can help to avoid the enforcement of the guarantee, which is the interest of all parties (Vékás 2013, pp. 896–897). However, in our opinion, it would facilitate the spread of "extend or pay" demands if the NHCC regulated this issue.

The NHCC does not regulate how many times the beneficiary can demand payment up to the limit of the undertaking, either. It is also not clear whether, if the parties agree that the beneficiary is entitled to demand payment just once, he or she is entitled to demand payment a second time if the first demand was incorrect. According to one of the commentaries (Vékás 2013, p. 897) Article 17 of URDG 758 shall be followed in these questions: the beneficiary shall be entitled to demand payment several times, up to the limit of the undertaking, and an incorrect demand must not be regarded as a demand unless otherwise prescribed in the guarantee. However, we are not sure that the Hungarian legal practice will also follow the rules of the URDG on these questions.

In our opinion the most serious gap in the regulation is that the NHCC does not deal with the examination of the documents before payment.[23] It remains open to question who must bear the consequences if the guarantor fulfils the payment in when he could have rejected the demand. Is the debtor of the secured obligation entitled to enforce a claim against the guarantor or can he just sue the beneficiary?

10.4 Health Insurance Contract

Health insurance contracts have not been regulated in Hungarian Law before the NHCC, but it was not unknown in practice. The NHCC reviewed the structure of the regulation of insurance agreements which had to be taken into consideration at

[22]See Section 5:407 in Vékás 2010, p. 1044 and the Section 5:392, para 2 of the Act CXX of 2009.

[23]We do not know why the NHCC does not follow the international models which regulate this question; see e.g. Article 16 of United Nations Convention on Independent Guarantees and Stand-by Letters of Credit.

the time of incorporating health insurance contracts. The NHCC distinguishes the indemnity insurance and the insurances of fixed sums.[24] However, the health insurance contracts can be concluded as indemnity insurance or insurance of fixed sums, too. Health insurance contracts—as the only particular type of insurance—are therefore regulated in a separate chapter, after the chapter on indemnity insurance and the chapter on insurance of fixed sums.

The NHCC defines a health insurance contract as a commitment of the insurer to perform the service specified in the contract in the event the insured being ill.[25] The coverage of the health insurance contract can be very diverse (e.g. it can be an indemnity or a fixed sum; we can distinguish between reimbursement services and the in kind services, etc.); therefore the definition does not try to specify the insurer's services. The word "illness", which is used by the definition, shall be interpreted as the deterioration of health.[26] The expression "in the event of the insured being ill" does not mean that the insured event is the illness: the insurer does not perform the service automatically if there is illness: e.g. the insurer shall perform the service if the illness has already been diagnosed by a doctor or in the event a medical treatment. Moreover, illness in not a necessary condition for the service of the insurer, as the second sentence of the definition states that the insurer can perform its service to healthy insured people (e.g. services related to pregnancy).

The norms of the health insurance contract are mandatory in that the parties shall not deviate from the provisions of the chapter concerned to the disadvantage of the policyholder, the insured or the beneficiary if the policyholder is a consumer. Theoretically, the parties may deviate from this provisions to the disadvantage of the client if the policyholder is not a consumer but it is not practicable in most cases, because this insurance relationship also affects personality (inherent) rights: for example, it would be nonsense if the insured was obliged to preserve his or her status after the occurrence of the insured event. In our opinion, the NHCC had to follow international practice[27] in this question: the norms of the health insurance contract are mandatory in favour of the client, irrespective fact whether the policyholder is a consumer or not.

[24]"Indemnity insurance" means insurance under which the insurer is obliged to indemnify against loss (suffered on the occurrence of an insured event) in the manner and to the extent specified in the contract, or to perform another service. "Insurance of fixed sums" means insurance under which the insurer is obliged to pay a fixed sum of money (on the occurrence of an insured event). See Section 6:439, para 2.

[25]Section 6:487, Sentence 1.

[26]The Spanish act on insurance contract (Ley 50/1980, de 8 de octubre, de Contrato de Seguro) uses also the word "illness" and the commentaries say that it means deterioration of health, see Badillo Arias 2011, p. 1637.

[27]E.g. the German act on insurance contract (Versicherungsvertragsgesetz, VVG), the Austrian act on insurance contract (Versicherungsvertragsgesetz, VersVG) or the Spanish act on insurance contract.

The regulation of the health insurance contract is based on referring rules. However, the structure and the content of these norms are somewhat problematic. We would just like to give some examples.

According to the NHCC, some norms from life insurance shall apply to all health insurance, but the general rules of insurance of fixed sums should not. This means, for example, that the rules of multiple insurance shall not apply to health insurance concluded as insurance of fixed sums, either. However, if we see the function of the norms of multiple insurance, we can easily understand that it should apply to all insurance of fixed sums (also for health insurance concluded as insurance of fixed sums) and we do not understand why this referring rule is missing.

According to the NHCC, the referred norms of the indemnity insurance shall apply only to health insurance concluded as indemnity insurance. This provision is controversial because the norms of indemnity insurance shall apply to accident insurance but not to health insurance concluded as insurance of fixed sums, even though there is no significant difference between these insurance agreements in this respect.

We just mention that there are not only references which are missing (e.g. the norms of multiple insurance) but the NHCC also contains unnecessary references (e.g. norms of group insurance, because these rules are general insurance norms which shall apply to all particular insurance contracts without any referring norm). In our opinion, these examples show us that the chosen method of dividing the particular insurance policies[28] (indemnity insurance and insurance of fixed sums) by the NHCC has several disadvantages, which led to these inconsistencies in the regulations.

Of course the NHCC does not govern the health insurance using just referring rules but it also contains a few special norms. We will present some of them in the following.

The NHCC entitles the insured to refuse medical treatment and this must not be regarded as a breach of the obligation to mitigate damages. It means that the risk pool has to bear the costs but we are not sure that this is a fair solution. We do not see why the insured does not have to take the consequences if he or she makes an illogical decision.

The NHCC also contains some special norms about the waiting period: e.g. the insured shall be entitled to include the expired waiting period of their former health insurance contract in the new health insurance contract. The application of this norm will be problematic because the services of the health insurance providers can be quite different: we do not know whether we have to pay attention to what services the former and the new contract offer, and if the answer is yes, we do not know how similar the services have to be.

[28]See e.g. the VVG, the VersVG or the Spanish act on insurance contracts. These acts distinguish the indemnity insurance and the insurance of a person.

The application of norms governing increased risks is restricted in the NHCC, but it does not deal with the problem of how to control the increase of risk in the whole pool. It would be a fundamental question, because health insurance is a long-term agreement; it endures for decades, while changes in the conditions can be unpredictable and significant (e.g. the costs of medical treatments).[29]

Last, we would like to mention that the insurer has no right to voluntary termination. It would be an important rule to protect the interest of the client: in the event of termination, an older patient with a poor health status might not find a new health insurance policy with the same contractual conditions. However, this norm has no sense without the rule of "lifetime cover", which is missing from the NHCC. It is important to note that health insurance contracts are typically fixed term agreements for one year in Hungarian practice. Hence, if the insurer wants to terminate a contract (e.g. because the client makes him lose money), they has nothing more to do but just refuse to renew the contract at the end of the period of insurance.

10.5 Trust

Trusts—as a particular agreement—had been unknown in Hungarian law before the NHCC. The legislator introduced this new particular agreement because it wanted to offer a new option for property management. There are several other models of for separating the owner's position and the professional manager of the assets (e.g. the business association or the foundation), which are essential elements of the economy, and the trust shall complete these models (Vékás 2013, pp. 793–794). However, trusts are applicable in other fields of Hungarian law, too (Illés 2011, pp. 552–556). The main reason for the introduction of trusts by the NHCC is that it is assumed that trusts can increase the competitiveness of the Hungarian economy, and this will be more attractive for capital and investments.

There is no internationally accepted model for and definition of trusts (Vékás 2013, p. 794). We can say that the Hungarian model is closer to the common law trust than to the German "Treuhand" or the French "fiducie" (Wellmann 2013, p. 157). If we see the classification of trusts in common law then Hungarian trusts can be described as express[30] trusts (Sándor, 2013).

The legislator had to take several issues into consideration while developing the governing regulations. First we would like to mention the principal-agent problem (Casadesus-Masanell and Spulber 2005, p. 46):

---

[29]See e.g. the VVG and the VersVG. These acts contain a detailed regulation about the insurer's rights on unilateral amendment of the contract. See Langheid and Wandt 2009, § 203 and Fenyves, Kronsteiner and Schauer 1998, § 178 f.

[30]"An express declaration of trust is a manifestation of the settlor's consent to the creation of the equitable interests. Express trusts arise because the settlor wants them to arise". See Birks 2000, p. 280.

What drives principals to rely on agents, and agents to act in the interest of principals?

How can the agents be motivated to act in the best interest of the principal instead of their own interests? Second, the regulations must find a balance between the interests of the settlor's creditors and the beneficiaries. Third, the legislator needs to find the most flexible regulatory regime possible in order to create a really multifunctional model.

According to the concept of the Hungarian trust, this new agreement is based on the transfer of property (Vékás 2013, p. 794). The trustee will become the owner of the settlor's specified assets in order to manage them in favour of the beneficiary.[31] Thc trust is an oncrous[32] contract in written form (the trust cannot be created without the acceptance of the foundation by the trustee). The trust is not regulated as a property transfer agreement, but it is a special form of mandate (agency): the regulations governing mandates shall apply as appropriate to trusts.[33] It is not clear in all cases whether the norms of mandate are applicable or not. For example, Section 6:326 contains special norms and cases for termination of trust, but it is not unequivocal whether Section 6:278 Para 4 which prescribes that inter alia the exclusion of the right of termination shall be null and void in case of mandate is applicable for the trust or not.

In the following, we will present just the most important elements of the detailed regulation of trusts (or fiduciary asset management contracts). First, it should be mentioned that the trust automatically terminates after 50 years, but of course it can also be founded for a shorter time. The NHCC contains a similar solution to the usufruct of legal persons.[34] The aim of the legislator is the same, to avoid the property from falling out of the control of the "original owner" for an unlimited time.

In our opinion, one of the key points of the regulations is the strict sequestration of the properties: the trustee shall separate the trust properties from each other and from his or her own property.[35] Neither the creditors of the settlor nor the creditors of the trustee[36] are entitled to claim the trust property.

We have to mention that the trust could be abused because of this strict sequestration of the properties. However, the regulation of the NHCC aims to avoid it: for example, if the trust can be regarded as an agreement to draw off funds ("Actio pauliana") the creditors of the settlor are entitled to refer to it (Vékás 2013, p. 795). Beside the general rules of contracts, the chapter on trust also contains some tools: e.g. the NHCC prescribes that the trustee cannot be the only beneficiary.[37]

[31]Section 6:310, para 1.

[32]The gratuitous form is exceptional.

[33]See Section 6:330.

[34]Section 5:147, para 5.

[35]Section 6:312.

[36]Section 6:313.

[37]Section 6:311, para 4.

It can appear controversial that the trust is a special agency but neither the settlor nor the beneficiary is entitled to give instructions to the trustee.[38] However, this is a necessary norm, because the interest of the settlor and the beneficiary or the interest of several beneficiaries can be conflicting[39] and the trustee is entitled to decide freely about the trust properties and he or she has his/her own liability (Vékás 2013, p. 794). This liability is a special contractual liability: the trustee shall act in a commercially reasonable manner.[40] If he does not breach this commitment then he/she is not liable to the settlor or the beneficiary for the loss of trust property. If the trustee undertakes a commitment to a third person on the trust property then he or she has a "cum viribus" liability. However, if the third person does not know and did not have to know that the commitment was undertaken by a trustee on the trust property then the trustee is liable with his or her own property, too.[41]

After the presentation of the most important rules of the NHCC about trusts, we would like to emphasise that there are several questions concerning trusts which are not regulated by the NHCC. First we have to mention Act XV of 2014 on the Trustees and Regulation of Trust Activities. According to Section 3 of this Act, the business of trust on a commercial scale may be performed only if in possession of the relevant authorisation from the Hungarian National Bank. According to Sections 19 and 20, the business of trust on a non-commercial scale may be performed without an authorisation, but the trustee shall notify the Hungarian National Bank of his or her business, attaching the fiduciary asset management contract. As such, who can be a trustee and the business of the trustees are quite strictly regulated.

The other crucial question about trusts is their tax regulation. The trusts could not be viable without special tax norms, because they would be too expensive if the general tax regulations were applicable. The Hungarian tax regulations (e.g. Act XCIII of 1990 on Duties; Act CXVII of 1995 on Personal Income Tax and Act CXXVII of 2007 on Value Added Tax) therefore contain some special rules on trusts, for example, according to Sections 17/D of Act XCIII of 1990 on Duties, the financial gains acquired by a person or organisation notified to the state tax authority as a trustee (fiduciary) under a trust (fiduciary asset management contract) shall not be subject to gift duty, including if acquired by way of succession of the trustee (fiduciary), but excluding if the trustee (fiduciary) is named as beneficiary. If the assets managed in a trust fund and their proceeds are acquired by the beneficiary then it shall be construed for dutiable purposes as if the beneficiary acquired the trust fund and its proceeds directly from the settlor (principal). If the contract between the settlor (principal) and the beneficiary was concluded with regard to an onerous contract then, upon the acquisition of the trust fund and its proceeds,

---

[38]Section 6:316.

[39]If they had the right to give instructions to the trustee then their instructions could be open to dispute because of their conflict of interest and this situation must be avoided.

[40]Section 6:317.

[41]Section 6:323.

the beneficiary shall be liable to pay duty on the transfer of property for consideration, in accordance with the provisions of the Act XCIII of 1990 on Duties relating to duty on transfer of property for consideration.

Finally, we have to admit that we cannot evaluate what role will be played by trusts in Hungarian law and the economy. The trust is a brand new legal institution; neither transaction experience nor the judicial practice is present. However, according to the records of the Hungarian National Bank, four companies have already received authorisation to perform trust business on a commercial scale. It means that trusts have already become a living legal institution in the Hungarian legal system.

References

Badillo Arias JA (ed) (2011) Ley de Contrato de Seguro [Act on Insurance Contract]. Aranzadi, Cizur Menor (Navarra)

Birks P (ed) (2002) English Private Law, Volume I. Oxford University Press, Oxford

Casadesus-Masanell R, Spulber DF (2005) Trust and Incentives in Agency. Southern California Interdisciplinary Law Journal 15(1):45–104

Fenyves A, Kronsteiner F, Schauer M (eds) (1998) VersVG-Novellen—Versicherungsvertragsgesetz Die Novellen '92, '94 und '96 [VersVG Amendments—Act on Insurance Contract Amendment of '92, '94 and '96]. Springer, Vienna

Illés I (2011) Mire jó a bizalmi vagyonkezelés? [What Does the Trust Serve for?]. Jogtudományi Közlöny (66)11:550–556

Langheid T, Wandt M (eds) (2009) Münchener Kommentar zum Versicherungsvertragsgesetz, Band 3 [Munich Commentary of the Act on Insurance Contract, Volume 3]. C.H. Beck, Munich

Molnár H (2009) Gondolatok a kereskedelmi ügynökök kompenzációs jogáról a Lonsdale ügy kapcsán [Thoughts on the commission agent's right for compensation in connection with the Lonsdale case]. Themis 22–40

Sándor I (2013) Gondolatok a bizalmi vagyonkezelés szabályozásáról az új Ptk.-ban [Thoughts about the Regulation of the Trust in the New HCC] http://ptk2013.hu/szakcikkek/sandor-istvan-gondolatok-a-bizalmi-vagyonkezeles-szabalyozasarol-az-uj-ptk-ban/2355 Accessed 18 November 2013

Vékás L (ed) (2010) Szakértői Javaslat az új Polgári Törvénykönyv tervezetéhez [Expert Proposal to the Project of the New Civil Code]. Complex, Budapest

Vékás L (ed) (2013) A Polgári Törvénykönyv magyarázatokkal [The Civil Code with Commentaries]. Complex, Budapest

Wellmann Gy (ed) (2013) Polgári Jog Kötelmi Jog Harmadik, Negyedik, Ötödik és Hatodik Rész—Az új Ptk. magyarázata VI/VI. [Civil Law Law of Obligations Part 3, 4, 5 and 6—The Commentary of the New HCC 6/6]. hvgorac, Budapest

Chapter 11
Unforeseeable Changes in Circumstances in Contracts in the New Romanian Civil Code

Johanna Szekrényes

Abstract The new Romanian Civil Code regulates the legal institution of unforeseeability, aiming to resolve situations in which one of the contractual subjects faces disproportionate and impossible burdens in his/her contractual legal relationship du to unforeseeable changes of circumstances intervened after the conclusion of the contract. With the entry into force of this code, the institution of unforeseeability enjoys explicit regulation, and as such, it becomes compulsory in the judicial practice. This, however, was not always the case: the legal institution known as the principle unforeseeability had existed before the entry into force of the new Civil Code, but only on a theoretical level, and in this respect, case law was not coherent. The present study offers a retrospect of the case law, with a special regard to the acceptance or rejection of this principle in the different judicial decisions.

11.1 Introduction

> There are unpredictable factors and events in every profession, and as a consequence, every professional, regardless of competence, skill, and experience, can face unexpected, unpredictable situations during exercising their profession.[1]

As a result of the negative impacts caused by the (first) economic crisis of the 21st century, starting in 2008, there was need to revitalize the economic and legal systems. The economic crisis posed a challenge to science, which was supposed to find the most suitable solutions for the application of basic scientific institutions. In terms of justice and the legal system, the legislature had to adapt the legislation to the new economic, social and political situation. Contracts are seen as an essential

[1]Costin, M. N.; Deleanu, S.: *Dreptul comerţului internaţional.* Vol. II. Partea specială, Ed. Lumina Lex, Bucureşti, 1995, p. 134.

J. Szekrényes (✉)
Cluj-Napoca (Kolozsvár/Klausenburg), Romania
e-mail: jogtanacs@reformatus.ro

A. Menyhárd and E. Veress (eds.), *New Civil Codes in Hungary and Romania*, Ius Gentium: Comparative Perspectives on Law and Justice 63,
DOI 10.1007/978-3-319-63327-5_11

part of civic and economic activity, with a theoretical and a practical role from both the legal and economic point of view, and as such, the new provisions formulated in this area are of a particular importance.

After long and thorough negotiations regarding the terms and clauses of any concluded contract, the contracting parties naturally expect that everything they had stipulated and agreed upon is respected, and as such, every party abides by their part in performing contractual obligations. The question arises: what happens if during the execution of the agreement such economic, financial, social or natural circumstances supervene, that could not be foreseen when the contract was concluded and that cause imbalance in contractual relationships, thereby the fulfilment of contractual obligations becomes too burdensome for one of the contracting parties?

The present study aims to present the possibilities and solutions the contracting parties may make use of when such unforeseen events occur in order to reduce excessively burdensome obligations and losses, as well as to renegotiate the contract. The objective of the theory of unforeseeability is to find viable solutions in cases when after the conclusion of the contract significant changes occur in the circumstances affecting any of the parties which result in contractual imbalance. This theory is actually a tool to harmonize the legal and economic challenges of the 21st century as well.

The new Romanian Civil Code regulates the legal institution of unforeseeability,[2] aiming to resolve situations in which one of the contractual subjects faces disproportionate and impossible burdens in his/her contractual legal relationship. With the entry into force of this code, the institution of unforeseeability enjoys explicit regulation, and as such, it becomes compulsory. This, however, was not always the case: the legal institution known as the principle unforeseeability had existed before the entry into force of the new Civil Code, but only on a theoretical level (the old Civil Code did not regulate it, although there

---

[2]The new Civil Code, Article 1271. **Unforeseeability.**

1. The parties must fulfil their contractual obligations even if these obligations become more burdensome for one of the parties than at the conclusion of the contract.
2. The judicial authorities have the possibility to intervene in a contract in the case when as the result of a substantial change in circumstances, execution becomes excessively burdensome and as a result the debtor's obligation to execute would obviously be unjust. They can order the following:
   (a) to adapt the contract in such a way that the contractual losses and benefits resulting from the change in the initial conditions are divided equally between the parties;
   (b) the termination of the contract at a specified time and in a specified manner.
3. The provisions of para (2) can be applied only if the following conditions are met:
   (a) the changes in conditions occurred after the conclusion of the contract;
   (b) the changes in conditions could not have been foreseen at the conclusion of the contract;
   (c) the party suffering the damage does not have to bear the risk of these changes;
   (d) the party suffering the damage will try within reasonable time and in good faith to renegotiate and adapt the contract to the new conditions.

were laws that tried to enforce it[3]), and in this respect, case law was not coherent. The present study offers a historical analysis of the case law, with a special regard to the acceptance or rejection of this principle in the different judicial decisions.

11.2 The Principle of *clausula rebus sic stantibus* as the Basis of the Principle of Unforeseeability Short History of the Principle

Contracts must fulfil the principle of the *pacta sunt servanda*, used and expected since as early as the Middle Ages regarding contractual loyalty. Nevertheless, the different judicial systems have made and make breaching this principle possible through contractual agreements, legislative provisions (risks, breach of contract penalties) or through institutions developed by science and practice. The tools of the different judicial systems to loosen or remit the obligations of the party who does not (because he/she cannot) keep his/her obligations, have changed from time to time, and they still do. Most legal systems (both from the synchronic and diachronic point of view) recognizes in some form, even if only as a covert possibility (tacit—developed by science and case law), the effects of essential changes in circumstances, that influence contractual obligations. The principle of *clausula rebus sic stanibus* was a principle brought to life by the Pandectists against the main principle of Roman law and medieval canon law, *pacta sunt servanda*; according to it, the performance of contracts may be refused due to subsequent consequences.[4]

The principle of the *clausula rebus sic stanibus* first appeared in Roman law, but only on the theoretical level. It was not officially recognized, only later was this idea presently considered to be an axiom pronounced, using Roman law. Nevertheless, we come across it in the works of Cicero, the famous lawyer and orator, as well as Seneca, Nero's infamous advisor. In his work *De officiis* created in 44 BC, Cicero points out that promises need not be kept if they cause more harm to the one who makes them than benefit to the one the promise is made to.[5]

According to the most prominent representative of canon law, Thomas Aquinas, the precursor of the principle of unforeseeability: "the one who promises

[3]Paragraph (3) of Article 43 of Law No. 8 of 1996 on Copyright and Neighbouring Rights (Published in the "Monitorul Oficial"—Official Gazette of Romania Part I, No. 60/March 26, 1996), para (2) of Article 60 of the Government Ordinance 42/1997 on civil navigation (Published in the Official Gazette of Romania Part I, No. 221/August 29, 1997), Article 14 of law No. 195/2001 on Volunteering. (Republished in the Official Gazette of Romania Part I, No. 276/April 25, 2006).

[4]Földi A, Hamza G.: *A római jog története és Institúciói*. Nemzeti Tankönyvkiadó, Budapest, 1996, p. 585.

[5]Lukács, N.: *A clausula rebus sic stantibus elv az ókori és középkori jogtudomány tükrében*—article. Iustum Aequum Salutare. XI.2015.1. p. 241. http://ias.jak.ppke.hu/hir/ias/20151sz/12.pdf [Last accessed on March 20, 2017].

something, if he/she intends to keep the promise, does not lie as he/she does not speak against his/her thoughts, but if he/she does not do as promised, he/she is unfaithful. The person can still be exonerated if the conditions change."[6]

The principle was generally known since the 14th century, but its first thorough theoretical exposition, however, was performed in the 15th century. The person who created the dogmatic foundation and taxonomic position of the rule was Andreas Alciatus, a humanist jurist. Alciatus made a distinction between unilateral and bilateral manifestations of will, however he identified several options for withdrawal and revocation.[7] Referring to certain general principles (fairness), Grotius looks for and finds arguments to settle changes in the contract's truth: we can say that in his conception the delicate balance between contractual limitations and contractual fairness is restored. He however breaks with the arguments of his predecessors, being the first to put the theory of the *clausula* on objective grounds. This is why he is considered the forerunner of doctrines developed in the 19th and 20th centuries propagating and varying objective[8] theories.

The concept, the *clausula rebus sic stantibus* was not originally part of the French Code Civile. French private law only knew of *imprévision* as an excuse for non-performance in the case of government contracts, which is the result of unforeseeable and unavoidable events. According to French law, unforeseen contractual risk meant the termination of the contract.[9]

The BGB (the German Civil Code) of 1900 did not contain the principle of the *clausula.* In the 19th century Bernard Windscheid, the famous lawyer spoke out in favour of the application of the *clausula.* The "Wegfall der Geschäftsgrundlage"-rule says that uncontrollable changes that lead to fundamental imbalances in contracts and therefore to a disproportionate burden to one of the parties, justify the termination of the contract. The BGB also applied this principle.[10]

The Italians—probably due to canon law—introduced the principle very soon. The codification solution was not followed by Spanish and Latin-American law.[11]

[6]Zamşa, C. E.: *Teoria impreviziunii. Studiu de doctrină şi jurisprudenţă.* Editura Hamangiu, Bucharest, 2006, p. 8.

[7]Lukács, N., *op. cit.*, p. 243.

[8]The *clausula*, understood objectively and having a non-contractual position, offers an opportunity for the party negatively affected by the changes in the circumstances to ask for the modification of the contract or the termination of its legal effect. According to some objective theories, it would be contrary to the principle of good faith if the contracting party would be expected to bear the additional burdens and performance difficulties arising from changes in circumstances by himself/herself. Source: http://jog.unideb.hu/documents/tanszekek/jogtorteneti/romai-jogi-anyagok/2012/ohmaganjog7-12.pdf. [Last accessed on: March 20, 2017].

[9]Zamşa, C. E., *op. cit.*, p. 53.

[10]Dobrev, D.: *Impreviziunea, o cutie a Pandorei în Noul Cod Civil?*, in: *Noul Cod Civil al României, Comentarii*, 2nd edition, Editura Universul Juridic, Bucharest, 2011, p. 213.

[11]Zamşa, C.E., *op. cit.*, pp. 317−322.

11.3 Area of Application of the Legal Institution of Unforeseeability

According to the doctrine, the definition of contractual unforeseeability is the following: the damage that one of the parties suffers during the performance of the contract, due to the lack of balance between service and value, usually caused by the economic situation and financial fluctuation.[12] According to this definition, contractual unforeseeability mostly occurs in economic and financial areas.[13]

The range of contract types is narrow, as we cannot use this principle with every single contract. Taking into consideration the conditions that need to be met,[14] we can state that only those contracts can be discussed in the case of which obligations have a financial value, and their execution does not coincide with the date of the conclusion of the contract. Thus, the law is applied in the case of continuously executed contracts, or that of *uno ictu*-type legal transactions with deadlines. In both cases it is important that the deadline is relatively long as this ensures the real possibility of the changes in contractual balance starting with the date of the conclusion of the contract.[15]

11.4 Unforeseen Changes of Circumstances in the Case Law

For a long period of time, legislation, case law and doctrine remained true to the theory of stability of contracts, even in cases when in the period between the conclusion of the contract and its execution such unforeseeable circumstanced occurred, that caused imbalance in the contract. The profound economic changes following the two World Wars, as well as the ones occurring today used to and still need certain contracts to be reviewed by the contracting parties or by judicial authorities. Before the entry into force of the new CC, although the principle was not explicitly regulated, there was judicial case law that took into account its effectiveness in ruling. Such rulings constitute the main source for the current regulation. The past elements of continuity that represent the basis of the present

---

[12]Pop, L.: *Tratat de drept civil, Obligațiile,* II. Vol., *Contractul*. Editura Universul Juridic, Bucharest, 2009, p. 534.

[13]Pătru, R. S.: *Teoria impreviziunii din perspectiva dimensiunii economice și juridice a analizei contractului.* Juridical Tribune, Volume 1, Issue 1, June 2011. Link: http://www.tribunajuridica.eu/arhiva/An1v1/nr1/art%207.pdf [Last accessed on: March 20, 2017].

[14]Based on Article 1271 of the new Civil Code, the conditions of fundamental changes in circumstances are the following: they occurred after the conclusion of the contract, they were not reasonably foreseeable at the conclusion of the contract, the damaged party does not have to carry the risks of these changes.

[15]Anton, G.: *Teoria impreviziunii în dreptul român și dreptul comparat*, Dreptul, nr. 7/2000, p. 27.

regulation can be best observed by analysing case law, together with the monitoring of the existing differences.

11.5 The Acceptance and Rejection of the Principle of Unforeseeability Between the Two World Wars

In the case of the Romanian legal system, the application of the principle of unforeseeability first happened after the First World War as a contrast to contracts concluded before 1919, where—due to the economic situation—execution became obviously more burdensome for one of the parties. The first legal case in the decision of which this principle was used was the Lascăr Catargiu *vs.* Bercovici Bank case.[16]

Lascăr Catargiu bought 250 shares for 180,000 Lei, the sum being transferred by the Bercovici Bank to the Romanian Credit Bank. In 1919, Lascăr Catargiu orders his bank to sell his shares kept as antichresis. The bank asks for the value of the shares in Francs and not in Lei saying that the account was opened in that particular currency. It is important to emphasize that due to the economic situation of those times, the difference between Franks and Lei had increased seven fold. Lascăr Catargiu sued the Bercovici Bank, requesting to be able to pay the shares in Lei since the stocks were paid in Lei in 1912.

In its resolution made on May 11, 1920, the Commercial department no. 1. of the Ilfov court of justice accepted the request of the applicant concluding that: "when extraordinary events occur that upset the balance of the contract by creating excessive advances to one of the parties, while the other is substantially aggrieved, the obligant can be absolved if the change in conditions was unforeseeable at the conclusion of the agreement."

In the case of bilateral agreements, the parties—with their own interests in mind—create mutual benefits and disadvantages, and their calculations are based on known and predictable conditions that prevail at the conclusion of the contract. As a consequence, the parties conclude the contract with the tacit acceptance of the *clausula rebus sic stantibus* (the clause referring to the present state of things).[17] The principle of the *rebus sic stantibus* refers to to the will of the parties in the sense that the contract needs to be interpreted in such a way that the will of the parties prevails. According to this, in the case of every contract, the existence of a clause needs to be assumed, according to which the obligations of the parties remain unchanged until the circumstances prevailing at the conclusion of the legal transaction remain unchanged. The radical changes in conditions cause changes in

[16]Zamşa, C.E, *op. cit.*, pp. 231–234.

[17]Beleiu, Gh.: *Teoria impreviziunii – rebus sic stantibus – în dreptul civil român*. Dreptul, 10–11/1993, p. 34.

obligations as well.[18] In this sense, the binding force of the contracts is subject to the principle of *rebus sic stantibus*,[19] and the existence of the clause referring to the present state of things is self-evident,[20] the parties tacitly accepting it.[21] In the above mentioned case this concept was applied.

Referring to the *rebus sic stantibus clausula* and Article 970 of the old CC, the court approved the applicant's request to pay in Lei instead of Belgian Francs.

According to the approach rejecting the principle of unforeseeability, some provisions of the old Civil Code refute the previous argument, stating that the tacit acceptance of the *clausula rebus sic stantibus* does not correspond to reality, as in order to gain a profit, both parties want to create and ensure a stable situation for themselves at the time of the conclusion of the contract. Therefore there is no evidence of the parties having tacitly agreed upon concluding the contract in such a way that it is subsequently adapted to the current conditions. The *rebus sic stantibus* clause can be interpreted only in accordance with the will of one of the parties (in this case, that of the debtor), in contrast, the existence of such a clause does not suit the will of the other party (the creditor.) According to Article 977,[22] the clause does not hold, as in interpreting a contract it is not sufficient to merely refer to the will of one of the parties; the contract needs to be interpreted as the common intention of the parties.

In the following case[23] we can observe how two completely contradictory principles come together: Article 969 of the old CC[24] and the principle of unforeseeability. The Mehedinți court of law applied the principle of unforeseeability in the case of a delivery contract. Due to the increase in the value of British Pounds, the supplier did not execute contractual obligations because of the rise in cotton prices. For this reason, the customer requested the execution of the contract and refused to pay for the delivered goods until the arrival of the full load.

Taking into account Article 969 of the CC, the court ruled: the agreements have binding force in cases when circumstances that were foreseeable at the conclusion of the contract arise. However, in situations when the changes in circumstances cannot be foreseen and the balance of economic relations is radically altered as the result of war, it is indisputable that the principle of unforeseeability can be applied,

[18]Chelaru, E.: *Forța obligatorie a contractului, teoria impreviziunii și competența în materie a instanțelor judecătorești.* Dreptul, 9/2003, p. 50.

[19]The principle of the *pacta sunt servanda* is valid only until the circumstances are not fundamentally changed.

[20]The old Civil Code, Article 981. The usual clauses within a contract are self-evident even if they are not included in the contract.

[21]Beleiu, Gh., *op. cit.*, p. 32.

[22]The contracts need to be interpreted according to the common intention of the parties rather than according to the literal meaning of expressions.

[23]Trib. Mehedinți, s. II., Pandectele Române, 1926, part III. p. 136. *in* Zamșa, C. E.: *Teoria impreviziunii. Studiu de doctrină și jurisprudență.* Editura Hamangiu, Bucharest, 2006, pp. 231–234.

[24]Agreements between contracting parties have legal force. These can be withdrawn by mutual consent or if permitted by law.

since if the defendant had foreseen the great differences between British Pounds and Lei that occurred in 1914, or the degree of depreciation of the latter, he would have not concluded the contract. In this case the *rebus sic stantibus* clause was applied instead of the binding force of contracts, and the court ruled in favour of the termination of the contract.

In the previous decision we could see that the binding force of the contracts and the principle of unforeseeability can in fact coexist. The ruling in the next case demonstrates the contrary. In its Decision of 1921,[25] the Bucharest Court of Appeal rejected the application of the principle of unforeseeability on the grounds that contractual binding force stipulated by Article 969 was already completely inconsistent with the principle of rebus sic stantibus. In its reference to comparative law, the ruling also stated that the principle of unforeseeability was not regulated in the Napoleonic Code (which also serves as inspiration for the Romanian CC). In this case the rejection of the principle was thus supported by the lack of regulation by the Napoleonic Code.

11.6 The Application of the Principle of Unforeseeability in the 20th Century

The case law of the period between 1989 rejected the application of the principle of unforeseeability, as the phenomenon of inflation was not considered a threat of uncertainty. By contrast, since 1990, inflation has become a serious and permanent risk factor. In such an environment the debates about the principle of unforeseeability were reignited, and as a result, it became possible for contracts to be reviewed in courts of law. The permanent depreciation of money compels the legal system to recognize the right of judges to review contracts in the case of unforeseeable changes in circumstances, which result in the bringing of an action that re-evaluates loans and debts, especially financial obligations.[26]

Romanian civil judicial authorities—especially in the case of rent contracts (accepting the requests regarding the increase of rent)—apply the principle of unforeseeability. The Supreme Court also applied the principle in the case of a rental contract concluded in 1990.[27] In this case the applicant let out an apartment to the defendant for 5 years. In the contract concluded on December 31, 1990, the parties agreed upon a 1441.20 Lei monthly rent. Invoking price liberalisation[28] after

[25]Decision no. 33/1921., C. Hamangiu, *Codul civil adnotat.* Ed. All Beck, Bucharest, 1999, p. 468.

[26]Munteanu, C.; Ungureanu, O.: *Reflecții privind moneda în dreptul privat.* Revista de drept privat, 2/2010, p. 218.

[27]Curtea Supremă de Justiție, Secțiile unite, Dec. 21/1994. Dreptul, 12/1994, p. 59.

[28]Financial Times Lexicon: To allow prices to move according to market forces. Link: http://lexicon.ft.com/Term?term=price-liberalisation [Last accessed on: March 20, 2017].

the conclusion of the contract, as well as the rate of inflation, the applicant requested an increase in the rent, even in the absence of such a clause. The principle of fairness[29] also played an important role in making a decision, as it was considered the legal basis of unforeseeability. According to the judicial authority, there was no legal basis to reject the applicant's request, the *per a contrario* approved it.

The ones who refute the principle—invoking the binding force of the contracts—would have rejected the request of the applicant; from this point of view the request does not stand.

Thus, in the process of ruling, emphasis falls on the application of Article 970—which confirms the acceptance of the applicant's request—not on the lack of legal basis by which the application could be dismissed. In this contractual relationship, the extra burden is the intended upkeep of the rented apartment, which belongs to the obligations of the applicant.[30]

We see a new approach here, according to which the execution of the contract became too burdensome for the applicant due to the lack of profit.[31, 32] Since 1990 was a transition period between the old and the new economic systems, it is no question that the parties could not have foreseen the possibility of the unpredictable fluctuations in the inflation rate. However, if the contract was concluded a few years later, when inflation was considered to be a general phenomenon, the fact that the decrease of the value of money was not predictable or foreseeable would have not been grounded enough. If this was the case, the principle could not be applied due to the fact that the condition of unforeseeability would not be met. After an expertise, the Supreme Court recommended the amendment of the contract to establish the actual value of the rent. It was also considered that in cases when the defendant does not comply with the decision and does not pay the newly set rent, the contract can be terminated by the court ordered to retry the case in first instance.[33]

Regarding the issue of rent adaptation, the Bucharest Court of Appeal proceeded similarly to the previous decision in two other cases,[34] invoking the same legal bases[35]: in the first case it ordered the termination of the contract, while in the second the increase of the rent. With the occurrence of new, unforeseeable circumstances—in the above cases, inflation—the agreement became unfair for the landlord, and thus the demand for the increase of the rent was well-founded in order

[29]Article 970, para (2): Not only the express obligations must be performed; the agreement can implement the execution of every consequence that is required by fairness, custom or law according to the nature of the obligation.

[30]Old Civil Code, Article 1420, para (2): The lessor, due to the nature of the contract, without the need for any other clauses, is required to perform the intended maintenance of the rented object.

[31]The balance between the rent and the consideration would be altered as the landlord could not perform the intended maintenance of the apartment from the price of the rent.

[32]Zamşa, C. E. *op.cit.*, p. 240.

[33]Chelaru, E., *op. cit.*, p. 58.

[34]Decizia nr. 96/1994, Decizia nr. 412/1994, published in M. Tăbăraş: *Răspunderea contractuală. Daune-interese. Culegerea de practică judiciară*, Ed. All Beck, Bucharest, 2005, pp. 21–24.

[35]The old Civil Code, Articles 970 and 977.

to re-balance the contract. Refusing to pay the increased rent means bad faith in the execution of the lessee's obligations, which is contrary with the stipulations of Article 970.

11.7 The Relationship Between the Unforeseeable Circumstances and the Principle of Unforeseeability

The old and the new Civil Code does not include any provisions which would prevent or prohibit the parties from adding a clause to their contract, with the help of which they ensure themselves for the possibility of changes in circumstances. In this case we talk about the clause of unforeseeable circumstances, which is usually applied in the case of international commercial agreements; nevertheless nothing in the Romanian legal system is stopping the parties from including clauses based on contractual freedom, to ensure the mechanisms of adaptation in new situations arising during the execution of the contract. Based on such a clause, the parties can renegotiate the contract between themselves, however, if they cannot reach an agreement, the contract can be adapted by a court of law.[36]

We differentiate two types of unforeseeability clauses in practice: clauses that make the automatic adaptation of the contract possible, and—in case of changes in circumstances—clauses stipulating the renegotiation of the contract.[37] Both are aimed to prevent the upsetting of the synallagmatic contractual relationship as a result of changes in circumstances occurring during the execution of the contract.

The indexing clause (clauza de indexare) belongs to the former. Its aim is to preserve the balance between services by eliminating the difficulties caused by price fluctuation. By indexing we understand the relationship and mutual interdependence between economic values.[38] The clause ensures that based on the reference point chosen by the parties—may it be the exchange rate, the value of precious metals, etc.—the prices stipulated in the contract change. The clause acts immediately, automatically rebalancing financial services.[39] The following simple example illustrates the operation of the clause. The price of the contract at the time of the conclusion was 1000 Euro at the Euro/Lei exchange rate (1 Euro = 3.2 Lei). Due to the automatic clause, if the exchange rate changed, for example to 4 Lei/Euro, the price would be 900 Euros.[40] We can see that without the intervention of the parties, based on the fluctuations in the Euro/Lei exchange rate, the old price is replaced by the new one, without any actions.

---

[36]Lisievici, A.: *Clauza de impreviziune.* Dreptul, 6/2010, p. 103.

[37]Anton, G., *op. cit.*, p. 32.

[38]Bobaşu, C. M.: *Consideraţii privind teoria impreviziunii.* Dreptul, 3/2006, p. 29.

[39]Pop, L.; Popa, I. F.; Vidu, S. T.: Tratat *elementar de drept civil. Obligaţiile conform noului Cod Civil.* Editura Universul Juridic, Bucharest, 2012, p. 155.

[40]Lisievici, A., *op. cit.*, p. 108.

The other type of clauses available for the parties to prevent the effects of unforeseeable changes in circumstances is the hardship or revision clause (clauza de revizuire). This clause is not automatic; it acts at specific intervals, taking into consideration the changes in economic circumstances, requiring the parties to review the services.[41] If the parties are not able to agree upon renegotiation, the judicial authority can intervene and order the enactment of the clause.

The question arises: what is the relationship between the legal institution of unforeseeability and the aforementioned clauses?

Investigating case law and doctrine preceding the explicit regulation of the legal institution of unforeseeability, we could see that there was no consensus regarding the application of the principle. Since there have been various decisions in this topic, the rebalancing of synallagmatic relationships was not always secured. In order for the parties to eliminate this uncertainty, the conclusion of a clause was recommended ensuring the renegotiation of the contract in any case.

The new Civil Code regulates the legal institution of unforeseeability, and as such it orders the renegotiation of the contract in the absence of such a clause. According to the principle of contractual freedom,[42] the parties have the opportunity and are even recommended to include such a clause. The above statement can be explained by the fact that—due to several shortcomings—the present legal regulation is difficult to enforce: the criteria of excessive burden[43] are not defined, it is difficult to identify at the conclusion of the contract the events that cannot be reasonably foreseen. The law does not offer a solution to or even a definition of these problems, and that is why judicial bodies, in a sovereign way, evaluate in each case whether execution is more burdensome[44] or excessively burdensome for one of the parties.[45] However, if the parties conclude a contract with an unforeseeability clause, the law of unforeseeability will not be applied. If judicial intervention takes place, it will order the execution of the clause and not the adaptation (the equitable distribution of losses and profits between the parties) or the termination of the contract.

Answering the above question, we can state that in cases where the parties include an unforeseeability clause in the contract, as the result of which the agreement is—peacefully or judicially—renegotiated, we talk about the principle of the binding force of contracts and not about the principle of unforeseeability or its legal effect. Thus, the legal institution of unforeseeability can be applied only in the absence of explicit clauses.

---

[41]Turcu, I.: *Noul Cod civil, Legea nr. 287/2009, Cartea V. Despre obligații*, Articles 1164–1649, Editura C. H. Beck, Bucharest, 2011, p. 336.

[42]Lisievici, A., *op. cit.*, p. 105.

[43]New Civil Code, Article 1271, para (2).

[44]New Civil Code, Article 1271, para (1).

[45]Voirel, G.; Viorel L. A.: *Configurația impreviziunii în Codul civil. (Legea nr. 287/2009, Republicată).* Dreptul, 2/2012, p. 30.

11.8 Conclusions

During the performance of contracts, circumstances are subject to change compared to the time of conclusion of the contract, and can become excessively burdensome to one or both parties than at the time of conclusion. In today's economic climate, especially in the case of progressively executed contracts, financial obligations are subject to significant risk. Such unforeseeable economic risks include for example the collapse of the real estate market, the increase in the Lei/Euro exchange rate, more difficult access to credit, the radical restructuring of the conditions of supply and demand, the collapse of the commodity markets, economic agents becoming insolvent.[46] The occurrence of such factors can destabilize services. The legal regulation of contract renegotiations was preceded by contradictory case law and debates in the scholarly literature.

With the entry into force of the new Civil Code, the judicial authorities are no longer required to rely on the legal bases of doctrine and previous jurisprudence regarding the revision of contracts. Now Article 1271 ensures the application of the legal institution of unforeseeability, stipulating the conditions, as well as the limits and the level of intervention. Although the legal institution now is explicitly regulated, we however cannot expect a smooth and seamless application in case law, as the text of the law is not clear in every aspect. As the text gives way to interpretation, it will result in non-uniform judicial practice. In order to eliminate such problems, the law should give precise and detailed definitions of the basic concepts: these are criteria that differentiate "excessively burdensome" execution from simply "burdensome" execution; the replacement of the "reasonable deadline" phrase that is at the disposal of the debtor to invoke the adapting of the contract with a well-defined time interval.[47]

After having analysed the case law preceding the specific regulation of the principle, we can state that the conditions of the application of the principle were the same as those of the new CC. The new regulation gives two solutions to eliminate the effects caused by unforeseeable changes in circumstances: the adaptation of the contract as well as the termination of the contract.

Before the regulation of the legal institution of unforeseeability, imbalanced contracts could be renegotiated only in certain cases. Therefore, it was recommended that the parties conclude contracts with a clause referring to unforeseeable circumstances that provide shelter in the case of changes in economic circumstances. The renegotiation of the contract was secured if it was explicitly stipulated by the parties, determining the conditions and manner of renegotiation. The clause reinforced the binding nature of the contract, as the parties and the judicial authorities were bound by the clause.

According to the new regulation, the parties have the possibility—under freedom of contract—to conclude contracts with clauses that determine the renegotiation of

[46]Papp, T.: *Opuscula civilia. Magánjogi látlelet.* Lectum Kiadó, Szeged, 2013, p. 137.

[47]Voirel, G.; Viorel, L. A., *op. cit.*, p. 46.

the agreement if circumstances change. Moreover, in order to avoid inconveniences, the clause is recommended, as the new regulation has some shortcomings.

As a conclusion we can state that there are several solutions to restore balance in services that have been upset by changes in circumstances. One of them is stipulated by law based on the provisions of the principle of unforeseeability, the other is the clause of unforeseeability, agreed upon by the parties to prevent damages cause by changes in economic circumstances occurring after the conclusion of the contract.

References

Anton, G.: *Teoria impreviziunii în dreptul român şi dreptul comparat.* Dreptul, 7/2000.

Beleiu, Gh.: *Teoria impreviziunii – rebus sic stantibus – în dreptul civil român.* Dreptul, 10-11/1993.

Bobaşu, C. M.: *Consideraţii privind teoria impreviziunii.* Dreptul, 3/2006.

Chelaru, E.: *Forţa obligatorie a contractului, teoria impreviziunii şi competenţa în materie a instenţelor judecătoreşti.* Dreptul, 9/2003.

Costin M. N.; Deleanu S.: *Dreptul comerţului internaţional.* Vol. II. Special part, Ed. Lumina Lex, Bucharest, 1995.

Dobrev D.: Impreviziunea, o cutie a Pandorei în Noul Cod Civil? *Noul Cod Civil al României, Comentarii,* 2nd edition, Editura Universul Juridic, Bucharest, 2011.

Földi A, Hamza G.: *A római jog története és Institúciói.* Nemzeti Tankönyvkiadó, Budapest, 1996.

Lisievici, A.: *Clauza de impreviziune.* Dreptul, 6/2010.

Lukács N.: *A clausula rebus sic stantibus* elv az ókori és középkori jogtudomány tükrében - article. Iustum Aequum Salutare. XI.2015.1.

Munteanu C.; Ungureanu O.: *Reflecţii privind moneda în dreptul privat.* Revista de drept privat, 2/2010.

Papp, T.: *Opuscula civilia. Magánjogi látlelet.* Lectum Kiadó, Szeged, 2013.

Pătru, R. S.: *Teoria impreviziunii din perspectiva dimensiunii economice şi juridice a analizei contractului.* Juridical Tribune, Volume 1, Issue 1, June 2011.

Pop, L.: *Tratat de drept civil, Obligaţiile, vol. II, Contractul.* Editura Universul Juridic, Bucharest, 2009.

Pop, L.; Popa, I. F.; Vidu, S. T.: Tratat *elementar de drept civil. Obligaţiile conform noului Cod Civil.* Editura Universul Juridic, Bucharest, 2012.

Turcu, I.: *Noul Cod civil, Legea nr. 287/2009, Cartea V. Despre obligaţii,* art. 1164–1649, Editura C. H. Beck, Bucharest, 2011.

Veress E.: Drept civil. Teoria generală a obligaţiilor, ed. 2, Editura C.H. Beck, Bucharest, 2016.

Viorel, G.; Viorel L. A.: *Configuraţia impreviziunii în Codul civil. (Legea nr. 287/2009, Republicată).* Dreptul, 2/2012.

Zamşa, C. E.: *Teoria impreviziunii. Studiu de doctrină şi jurisprudenţă.* Editura Hamangiu, Bucharest, 2006.

Chapter 12
Perceptions of Simulated Contracts in the Hungarian and Romanian Legal Systems

Krisztina Constantinescu

Abstract Simulating is part of human nature, present in every walk of life, sometimes used willingly or unintentionally. Just like law, simulating is present since ancient times and has emerged in different social institutions. That is why it was needed to be regulated from the legal point of view. The question arises however, whether simulating is inherently evil and reprehensible, or the issue is much more nuanced. Actually, we can get different answers to this question throughout history, but there is no uniform regulation, so the question remains.

12.1 Introduction

Simulating is a complex legal process with three essential elements: a secret legal transaction, a public legal transaction and an agreement regarding simulating. The simulation of purchase price is such an example: in this case the parties include a price in the public contract that is different from the one decided upon in the secret contract, and agree to have the actually payable amount in the secret contract. Simulated contracts already existed in Roman times, and were regulated by the Codex Iustinianus.[1] Over the years it changed and was interpreted in various ways; it was the 19th century when the idea similar to present-day perception was beginning to take shape, meaning that simulated contracts are not always deemed invalid.[2] It is a universally discussed topic, as the different legal systems treat them differently, including them in different taxonomical categories. There are systems

[1]It was created during one of the most important codification processes in history, ordered by Emperor Justinian. Roman law forbade simulation and deemed simulated contracts to be invalid. See Zimmermann, Reinhard: The Law of Obligations. *The Roman Foundation of the Civilian Tradition*. Juta & Co Ltd., Cape Town, 1992, pp. 647–648.
[2]Pop, L.—Popa, I. F.—Vidu, S. I.: *Tratat elementar de drept civil. Obligaţiile*. Universul Juridic, Bucharest, 2012, p. 217.

K. Constantinescu (✉)
Attorney, Cluj-Napoca (Kolozsvár/Klausenburg), Romania
e-mail: krisztina@veress.ro

A. Menyhárd and E. Veress (eds.), *New Civil Codes in Hungary and Romania*, Ius Gentium: Comparative Perspectives on Law and Justice 63, DOI 10.1007/978-3-319-63327-5_12

where they are deemed to be invalid in every case, in others they can figure as valid legal transactions and have detailed regulations.

The present article aims to analyse the reasons for this two-way development of the present regulations, mainly focusing on contracts. Narrowing the topic is important as simulating is present on too many areas, as it is regulated by various laws and presents specific cases. By avoiding these we have the opportunity to continue the analysis in a much cleaner form. The study covers the Romanian and Hungarian legal systems: they were chosen because although they are neighbouring countries, they still regulate simulation differently. At the same time, as they used the French and German Civil Codes as models in their codification processes, the present study analyses the legal systems of these countries as well, and compares them from the point of view of simulation regulation.

12.2 Historical Overview

12.2.1 Simulation in Roman Law

One of the main characteristics of archaic law was fidelity to form, meaning that an essential condition of the validity of legal transactions was compliance with formalities. Thus, the expressed will was favoured to the internal will of the parties.[3] According to some authors,[4] in this period we cannot speak about simulation from the legal point of view, as only those legal transactions had legal effect, that were compliant with formalities. At the same time, however, the simulated transaction, which was actually the public legal transaction, was considered valid as it complied with formalities.[5] Since this pre-classical age, the exclusively formal legal transactions lost ground, and the element of will became more important through formless agreements. With the development of Roman society and the transformation of law, simulation appeared in various forms and in different legal transactions, such as[6]:

1. The simulation of a non-existent quality: the simulation of the quality of trustee or creditor in order to obtain a certain amount of money. Such cases were regarded as theft.
2. Simulated contracts: for example popular simulated sales contracts the goal of which is often to make possible for the debtor to salvage its property under the

[3]Nótári Tamás: *Római köz- és magánjog*. Scientia, Cluj-Napoca, 2011, p. 303.

[4]Baias, Flavius A.: *Simulaţia. Studiu de doctrină şi jurisprudenţă*. Ed. Rosetti, Bucharest, 2003, p. 22.

[5]Cf. Nótári Tamás: *Római köz- és magánjog*. Scientia Kiadó, Cluj-Napoca 2011, p. 174; Zimmermann, Reinhard: The Law of Obligations. *The Roman Foundation of the Civilian Tradition*. Juta & Co Ltd., Cape Town 1992, p. 647.

[6]The aforementioned cases can be found in: Baias, Flavius A.: *Simulaţia. Studiu de doctrină şi jurisprudenţă*. Ed. Rosetti, Bucharest, 2003, pp. 22–25.

creditor's claim, thus, although selling the property, preserving in fact, ownership. Justinian ensured avoidance actions, that is *actio Pauliana* against actors in bad faith, meaning that they had to give the property back, while the actors in good faith answered for property obtained freely in cases of enrichment. Another form of simulated contracts aim to circumvent the ban on gifts between spouses by simulating the subject or title of the contract.
3. Simulation in private law: it was present mainly through fictitious marriages. Simulating aimed to resolve the lack of inheritance capabilities: if the given person got married within 100 days from the opening of the inheritance, they could inherit. In addition there was fictitious divorce, in which the wife could claim her dowry before her husband's creditors, thus saving a part of thc property from under the creditors' claims.
4. Simulating in procedure: in case of property claims, one of the parties simulated ownership so that the original owner could acquire the property through adverse possession.

In the above described cases it can be observed that simulation appeared in a number of areas, and there was need for its regulation. Accordingly, the Justinian Codex states the basic principle of interpreting simulation, which reads as follows: „plus valet quod agitur quam quod simulate concipitur" or "the real deeds are more important, than the simulated ones".[7] This is the basis of the general assumption that in Roman law simulated legal transactions were declared void as a rule.[8] Nevertheless, there are legal academics who have opposite opinions, such as Partsch, who concluded that simulation was generally present in classical Roman law, or Giovanni Pugliese, according to whom simulation was not always valid or invalid, calling it case-specific.[9] In the light of the above we can state that there is no single theoretical framework on provision in Roman law regarding simulation; it is regulated in individual cases and that is why jurists do not share a common standpoint.

12.2.2 The Changes in the Interpretation of Simulation in History

Canon law moralized the issue of simulation and considered that it can be used for good as well, however there were no significant changes from the legal point of

[7]Zimmermann, Reinhard: *The Law of Obligations. The Roman Foundation of the Civilian Tradition*. Juta & Co Ltd., Cape Town, 1992, p. 648.

[8]Cf. Nótári Tamás: *Római köz- és magánjog*. Scientia, Cluj-Napoca 2011, p. 174; Zimmermann, Reinhard: The Law of Obligations. *The Roman Foundation of the Civilian Tradition*. Juta & Co Ltd., Cape Town, 2011, p. 174.

[9]Zimmermann, Reinhard: *The Law of Obligations. The Roman Foundation of the Civilian Tradition*. Juta & Co Ltd., Cape Town, 1992, p. 647, note 159.

view, thus simulated legal transactions remained mainly null and void. The issue of the protection of the third party was regulated only in the 19th century, and in this respect those *bona fide* third parties, who acted based on the simulated legal transaction, could not be punished because of the secret agreement between the two parties.[10] That is the reason why the legal transaction could not have an effect upon them. Not every legal system joined this standpoint, for example the German Civil Code rejected the possibility, and so did the Hungarian CC. As a contrast, the French, Italian, Austrian and Romanian CCs accepted the standpoint and offered protection for the third party.

12.3 Definition

The definition of simulation raises a number of questions; nevertheless it is a universally accepted fact that in simulation there is a public, simulated will and a secret, concealed will. As for its manifestations, the different legal systems operate with different concepts. The following names are used: in Romanian law public and secret contract, in Hungarian law simulated and concealed contract, in French law counter-statement, in German law apparent and hidden legal transaction.[11] Hungarian and Romanian jurists define simulation differently, as they apply different approaches. In the light of the above, let us examine the defining elements of simulating that are generally accepted in the Romanian legal system.

- Apparent contract: by its public nature it can be known by the third party, and it does not contain the real will of the parties.
- Concealed contract: it contains the secret agreement of the parties, which is the true expression of their will, however it is necessary to manifest it in writing, the existence of the agreement is enough for the existence of simulation.[12]
- Agreement regarding simulation: it expresses the will of the parties meaning that the concealed contract should have legal effect and not the apparent contract. This is what connects the sham contract with the concealed contract.[13]

Hungarian legal science sees the definition of sham transactions as a vitiated consent. According to this, the determining elements of simulating are the following[14]:

[10]Zimmermann, Reinhard: *The Law of Obligations. The Roman Foundation of the Civilian Tradition*. Juta & Co Ltd., Cape Town, 1992, p. 649.

[11]Baias, Flavius A.: *Simulaţia. Studiu de doctrină şi jurisprudenţă*. Ed. Rosetti, Bucharest, 2003, pp. 37–38.

[12]Ungureanu, C. T.—Răducan, G. et al.: *Noul Cod civil. Comentarii, doctrină şi jurisprudenţă. Vol. II*. Ed. Hamangiu, Bucharest, 2012, p. 621.

[13]Chivu, Gabriela: *Simulaţia în teoria şi practica dreptului civil*. Agronaut, Cluj-Napoca, 2001, p. 19.

[14]See Gellén Klára: *A színlelt szerződés*. Pólay Elemér Alapítvány, Szeged, 2008, pp. 30–40.

- The subjective note:
  - Lack of will: although the consciousness and intent to declare will as well as the knowledge of legal effect exists, there is no intent.
  - Awareness: both parties are aware that they are concluding a simulated contract, as Bálint Kolosváry[15] points out, contractual will is based on free will, and it remains valid here as well.
  - Bilateralism: both parties have to accept the existence of simulation, this element plays a role to differentiate simulation from mental reservation, when only one of the parties simulates the conclusion of the contract.
  - Community of purpose: the parties agree not only regarding simulation, but also regarding its content.
- The objective note:
  - Creation of appearance: the open and at the same time simulated declaration of will, which is knowable by third parties.

By examining how the definitive notes of simulation are deconstructed by the two legal systems in order to make simulating identifiable in case law, we can discover several differences, however the main points are overlapping. By combining the key elements of the two legal systems, it can be observed that in both cases there are subjective and objective notes. The subjective notes include the arrangement regarding simulating and the secret agreement included in the concealed contract, which is not necessarily materialized, but is imbued with a consistent content due to the community of purpose of the parties. At the same time, the lack of will, meaning that there is no valid will behind the public contract, does not have legal effect. In addition, the agreement contained by the arrangement of the parties, as its name also shows, is based on the free and conscious will of the parties, and this implicitly means bilateralism. The objective side of simulating is what is visible to a third party, the sham contract, the aim of which is the creation of appearance. This is what the parties make public and thus conceal their true intentions.

12.4 The Forms of Simulation

French legal science has addressed the theoretical aspects of simulation in detail: long before the entry into force of the Napoleonic Civil Code there were jurists who discussed several aspects of simulation as well as the issue of validity against a third party. Already in the 16th century, the French jurist Bertrand d'Argentré[16]

[15]Kolosváry Bálint: *A magyar magánjog tankönyve. Kötelmi jog. Családjog. Öröklési jog.* Budapest, Politzer Zsigmond és fia Könyvkiadó, 1904, p. 57 in: Gellén Klára: A színlelt szerződés. Pólay Elemér Alapítvány, Szeged, 2008, p. 32.

[16]Baias, Flavius A.: *Simulația. Studiu de doctrină și jurisprudență.* Ed. Rosetti, Bucharest, 2003, p. 27.

distinguished absolute and relative simulating, a classification which later became generally accepted. Accordingly, this typology can be found in legal systems, where simulation is considered a vitiated consent. For example, Elek Dósa in his 1861 study on private law uses the following categories: simulated conclusion of contract, which corresponds to absolute simulation, as well as concluding a contract with a different title, which is considered relative simulation.[17] Later, inspired by Italian legal literature, Hungarian legal science takes over the concept of absolute and relative simulation.

Jurists have developed several forms of classification based on various criteria, nevertheless, the categories created were similar to the above.[18] Based on the topic of the agreement between the parties they want to conceal by simulating, we differentiate absolute and relative simulation. We talk of absolute simulation when the aim of the parties is to declare the concluded contract to be non-existent and as such without any legal effect. In case of relative simulation, the agreement between the parties aims to modify some elements of the simulated contract. Among the latter we can distinguish two categories depending on the element of the contract simulation aims at. Thus, relative simulation can be objective if it affects the title or content of the contract; similarly we can differentiate fully or partially concealed contracts. In addition, relative simulation can be subjective, in this case the concealed contract masks the parties.[19]

12.4.1 Absolute Simulation

In this case the apparent contract receives a fictitious character, and the agreement of the parties refers to the lack of any legal effect of the concluded contract. The parties conclude the sham contract for the sake of appearance, their real purpose being the preservation of the status-quo from before the conclusion of the contract. This form of simulation is characterised by the lack of the secret document, as an agreement is sufficient for the parties to consider the concluded contract not valid.

Absolute simulation can take different forms in practice. One of the most common case is when the debtor sells an asset through a fictitious contract in order to rescue it from under the claims of the creditor, but still retains ownership over the asset by agreeing with the buyer that the sales contract does not have any legal

[17]Dósa Elek: *Erdélyhoni jogtudomány. Második könyv. Erdélyhoni magyar magánjogtan.* Rom. Kat. Líceumi Nyomda, Cluj-Napoca, 1861, p. 452. http://mek.oszk.hu/08100/08118/pdf/dosa2_02.pdf (19. 03. 2014.).

[18]Baias, Flavius A.: *Simulaţia. Studiu de doctrină şi jurisprudenţă.* Ed. Rosetti, Bucharest, 2003, p. 97.

[19]Baias, F.A.—Chelaru, E.—Constantinovici, R.—Macovei I. (ed.).: *Noul cod civil. Comentariu pe articole.* Ed. C.H. Beck, Bucharest, 2012, pp. 1359–1360.

effect. Another example is the fictitious division of property, which does not change the original situation of the parties and only aims to maintain appearance.[20] Scholarly literature also mentions the conclusion of overpriced fictitious sales contracts in order to gain a larger compensation in cases of expropriation on grounds of public interest.[21] On the same basis, there are fictitious companies, the concealed aim of which is to rescue property from creditors.[22] Through the establishment of the capital of the company, ownership is transferred to the legal entity whose assets the personal creditors of the investor can no longer follow. It can be observed in the previous examples that this form of simulation is mainly aimed to evade a third party or law itself, that is why it is declared null and void in Hungarian and German law. On the other hand, Romanian law does not declare it null and void as a general sanction; instead we speak of inopposability regarding a third party, however, in certain cases it is absolutely null and void.

12.4.2 *Relative Simulation*

When simulation concerns a particular element of a public contract, there is a consensus regarding simulation and a secret document, more exactly a secret agreement, which does not take a material form, and it contains the true will of the parties. Relative simulation is more complex than absolute simulation, as the parties do not agree upon the complete invalidity of an apparent contract, but only regarding one of its elements. Thus, apart from this one element, the public contract has in fact a legal effect by the will of the parties, but not exactly in the form it is presented to the public.

There are two main forms of relative simulation: on the one hand it can be objective, meaning that it concerns the title of the contract or its elements, or subjective, if it concerns the identity of the contracting parties. A detailed analysis of objective simulation reveals that the agreement between the parties regarding simulation can modify the public contract partially or as a whole, thus we can speak about completely simulated or partially simulated contracts. In order to thoroughly understand the nature and form of each of the above, we need to examine them separately.

12.4.2.1 Objective Simulation—Completely Simulated Contract, the Concealment of Title

As a form of simulation, it can be distinguished from the others by the fact that the parties conclude another type of contract than what is in the public contract.

---

[20]Chivu, Gabriela: *Simulaţia în teoria şi practica dreptului civil*. Agronaut, Cluj-Napoca, 2001, p. 22.

[21]Baias, Flavius A.: *Simulaţia. Studiu de doctrină şi jurisprudenţă*. Ed. Rosetti, Bucharest, 2003, p. 100.

[22]Chivu, Gabriela: *Simulaţia în teoria şi practica dreptului civil*. Agronaut, Cluj-Napoca, 2001, p. 22.

The statement of will of the parties is identical with the content of the contract, but in fact they conclude a bond of a different title.[23] In some cases such simulation is explicitly prohibited by law. For example, Article 992 of the Romanian CC penalizes with relative nullity the covering of the lack of power of action via free benefits with a contract for pecuniary interest. Such a case is when a person who has come of age secretly enters into a donation agreement in favour of the legal guardian, however publicly this appears as a contract for pecuniary interest. Under Hungarian law, if it is found that there is a case of simulation, the simulated contract is declared null and void, while the concealed contract can have legal effect only if it is not against the law.

One of the most widespread manifestations, also known in Roman law, is pretending that a donation agreement is in fact a sales agreement; in this case there is no payment obligation in the transfer of ownership. In case law, however, it has occurred that a maintenance contract was presented as a sales contact, or the sales contract in fact hid a usury.

12.4.2.2 Objective Simulation—Partially Simulated Contract, the Simulation of the Content of the Contract

In this form, simulation refers to only one element or clause of the contract. Accordingly, this part of the simulated contract does not have legal effect based on the real will of the parties, or it is not made public, thus found only in the concealed contract. Further, in cases where simulation concerns a given element of the contract, it can modify it. Such an example is the modification of the price in contracts for pecuniary interest by determining a bigger or smaller price in the concealed contract by the parties. The simulation of the purchase price is the oldest strategy to avoid paying taxes as it was present not only in Roman times, it existed in 14th century Italy as well. This form of simulation is mostly used for the evasion of taxes and contributions. It is not rare in real estate sales contracts to include a smaller price in the public contract, while the secret agreement contains a significantly larger amount, and as a result the payable tax is much lower. In addition, it is also a common procedure when the tenancy agreement contains a smaller price for the tenant to pay, and as a result the landlord will have to pay a much lower tax.

12.4.2.3 Subjective Simulation—Simulation of the Subject

This form of simulation occurs when the identity of the parties in the simulated contract is not identical with the ones against whom the contract has a real legal

[23] Dósa Elek: *Erdélyhoni jogtudomány. Második könyv. Erdélyhosni magyar magánjogtan.* Rom. Kat. Líceumi Nyomda, Cluj-Napoca, 1861, p. 452. http://mek.oszk.hu/08100/08118/pdf/dosa2_02.pdf (19. 03. 2014.).

effect. The public contract is concluded between two parties, however there is a secret contract concluded between one of the contracting parties and a third party, and based on this the contract has in fact legal effect against the third party. The role of the intervening person is only formal, the aim of its presence is to conceal the third party from public view. As for the agreement regarding simulation, opinions differ. According to some, simulation needs to exist between all three parties in order to stand, thus the party concluding the public contract is aware of the simulation. This criterion is the result of simulation of the subject, and it is necessary to be met, as simulation is based on the declaration of will of the contracting parties, so if it is not valid on each party, we speak of a different legal operation.[24] Other authors argue that this is not a necessary element of simulation, as simulation is present even if the party concluding the public contract does not know about the agreement.[25] From the point of view of Hungarian law this latter statement is not acceptable, as simulation of the subject means that there is need for the conscious consent of all three parties in order to declare the simulated contract null and void. If the contracting party is not aware of the agreement, he or she concludes it in the hope it will have legal effect; the agreement of the other party needs to be treated as a mental reservation, in the light of which the concluded contract remains valid. Hungarian scholarly literature calls it a "stróman" ('straw man') transaction, and differentiates it from the concept of simulation. In this case, as the name suggests, the intervening party is in fact only a "straw man" and acts as the effect of a hidden will, the BGB discussing it separately among fiduciary transactions.[26]

In practice, the simulation of the subject is used to circumvent law, that is why the legislator explicitly prohibits the practice of simulation in certain cases. For example, based on Articles 1653 and 1564 of the Romanian CC, in the case of the lack of ability to buy under litigation law, simulating the person automatically results in absolute nullity. Hungarian CC does not mention it separately, as according to the general rule of simulation, every simulated contract is considered null and void, and as such there is no need to emphasize cases when simulation is aimed to circumvent the law.

---

[24]Cf. Baias, Flavius A.: *Simulaţia. Studiu de doctrină şi jurisprudenţă*. Ed. Rosetti, Bucharest, 2003, p. 114 and Baias, F.A.—Chelaru, E.—Constantinovici, R.—Macovei I. (ed.): *Noul cod civil. Comentariu pe articole*. C. H.Beck, Bucharest, 2012, p. 1360, as well as Gellén Klára: *A színlelt szerződés*. Pólay Elemér Alapítvány, Szeged, 2008, p. 54.

[25]Cf. Pop, L.—Popa, I. F.—Vidu, S. I.: *Tratat elementar de drept civil. Obligaţiile*. Universul Juridic, Bucharest, 2012, pp. 226–227.

[26]Gellén Klára: *A színlelt szerződés*. Pólay Elemér Alapítvány, Szeged, 2008, pp. 56–57.

12.5 Legal Effect of Simulated Contracts and Validity Issues

As regards the legal effect of simulated contracts, the Romanian and Hungarian legal systems differ the most significantly. If we take into consideration the taxonomic classification, it becomes obvious that while Hungarian law considers simulating a vitiated consent and sanctions it with nullity, Romanian law does not consider it *a priori* null and void, instead the sanction is inopposability.

12.5.1 The Legal Effect of Simulated Contracts According to the Romanian CC

As opposed to the old Romanian CC, the new one regulates in detail the legal effect of simulation between the parties, as well as towards successors, third parties and creditors. According to the CC, only the secret contract can have legal effect between the parties, and this corresponds to the principle of will, thus the real will of the parties prevails. As a result, the sham contract does not have legal effect, as its aim is only to create appearance, and its content is not supported by the real will of the parties. At the same time, the elements of the sham contract which are not affected by simulation remain valid, thus, in the case of relative simulation, when the parties simulate the title or a particular content element of the contract, every other provision of the contract remains valid, as it complies with the provisions of the secret contract. For example, in the case of the simulation of price, we speak about a valid contract except for the element of the price. During the simulation of the subject, the contract does not have effect against the intervening party, but according to the real will of the parties, it has a legal effect against a third party. In contrast, in the case of absolute simulation, the public contract is absolutely invalid and does not have any legal effects between the parties, as the parties did not in fact want to conclude a contract.[27]

The code separately regulates simulation against a third party mainly to protect the *bona fide* third party from the prejudice caused by the secret contract. Accordingly, the sanction of the legislature is that the secret contract is inopposable to the third party, thus, if the third party gained ownership of an asset in good faith and based on a public contract, from his or her point of view the simulated contract prevails. The same is valid for the universal or universal title heirs, if the secret agreement harms their interests. The legislator provides more rights to the third party, thus balancing the negative effects of simulation. As a result, the third party —in accordance with its interests—can request inopposability to the secret contract,

---

[27]Baias, Flavius A.: *Simulaţia. Studiu de doctrină şi jurisprudenţă*. Ed. Rosetti, Bucharest, 2003, p. 170.

which does not have any legal effects on the third party, but if the simulated contract violates some of his or her rights, he or she can request the implementation of the concealed contract. For example, when the testator conceals a donation contract with a sales contract, the given part of the property cannot be calculated into the inheritance. Since this clearly violates the right to the inheritance of the heirs, by establishing simulation they can request to have the secret legal transaction implemented against them as well, and as a result, the secret donation is calculated into the property.

12.5.2 The Legal Effect of Simulated Contracts According to the Hungarian CC

Both the new and the old Hungarian CC sanctions simulation—as the result of deliberate lack of will—with the most serious consequence of invalidity: nullity. Accordingly, simulated contracts do not need to be contested, they are *ipso iure* invalid from the date of their conclusion. Since we are talking about a void contract, the restoration of the state that existed at the time of conclusion is necessary. If we analyse absolute and relative simulation separately, it can be observed that in the case of absolute simulation, this obligation is cancelled as the parties conclude the simulated contract not to have any legal effect. In contrast, in the case of relative simulation there is a concealed contract the law considers valid, as it contains the real will of the parties. Thus, the simulated contract is replaced by the concealed contract, and this needs to be examined in order to determine the rights and obligations of the parties. As the concealed contract is examined separately, it needs to meet the general criteria of validity as any other contract, meaning that it has to comply with specifications regarding content and form.[28]

Legal effects against third parties are not regulated separately by Hungarian law, however, as it sanctions simulation with nullity against the parties, the contract concluded in order to deceive the public cannot prevail against the third party either. On the other hand, the *bona fide* third party who confides in the public contract known by him or her, can only rely on the general rule of compensation (CC 6:115), which reads as follows:

> A person who has, in good faith, believed in the existence of an invalid contract, may demand compensation for damages resulting from the contract from the party responsible for the invalidity of the contract. The parties shall be equally liable to provide compensation if they are equally responsible for the invalidity of the contract

Based on the above, both parties are equally liable to provide compensation to the third party in case of simulation.

---

[28]Cf. Gellén Klára: *A színlelt szerződés*. Pólay Elemér Alapítvány, Szeged, 2008, pp. 113–115.; Wellmann György: *Polgári jog. Kötelmi jog. Az új Ptk. magyarázata V/VI.* HVG-ORAC, Budapest, 2013, p. 131.

Comparing the regulations of the two legal systems, it can be observed that similarly to the German BGB, Hungarian law is much more restrictive based on the fact that simulation is mostly created to deceive and circumvent third parties. In contrast, Romanian law is more permissive as it does not attach any positive or negative meanings to simulation: it considers neutral, making it possible for it to take both legal and illegal forms. According to Romanian jurists, the sole aim of simulation cannot be considered to be the circumvention of a third party or of the law itself, as this means a unilateral approach to simulation; it can be aimed at legal activities as well.[29] The neutral nature of simulation[30] means that simulation in itself does not cause nullity, however if the contract does not comply with the criteria of validity stipulated by law, it is considered void.[31] Similar to Hungarian regulation, simulation can be void, however this is an exception and not a general sanction of simulation. Both legal systems consider concealed contracts containing the will of the parties to be valid, and this—based on the principle of will—has in fact legal effect. The most important difference is that under Romanian law this secret contract may be enforced only between the parties, while Hungarian law does not have such a restriction, and as such, the contract applies to everyone. This is closely connected to the issue of protection of the *bona fide* third party: under Romanian law it is the person who was reliant on the public contract in good will; in this case the concealed contract cannot be enforced against him or her. This form of protection of legitimate expectations is applied by the Romanian, French, Italian and Austrian Civil Codes; it is however not used in Hungarian law, thus the *bona fide* third party can only be compensated for damage. Since in many cases this is not satisfactory for the third party, some Hungarian jurists[32] have admitted that the application of the concept of trust makes the simulated contract relatively enforceable towards a third party, and it could provide appropriate sanctions against the simulating parties.

12.6 Conclusions

Although the two legal systems have developed different sanctions, it can be observed that if the aim of the conclusion of a simulated contract is the circumvention of a certain legal requirement, it results in similar decisions. While Hungarian law sanctions simulated contracts with *a priori* nullity, Romanian law is much more flexible, as it focuses on the interests of the third party; if the rights of

[29]Ungureanu O.—Munteanu C.: *Drept civil partea generală.* Universul Juridic, Bucharest, 2013, p. 296. Such a case is when the donating party wishes to keep its identity secret.

[30]Baias, Flavius A.: *Simulaţia. Studiu de doctrină şi jurisprudenţă.* Ed. Rosetti, Bucharest, 2003, p. 165.

[31]Ungureanu, C. T.—Răducan, G. et al.: *Noul Cod civil. Comentarii, doctrină şi jurisprudenţă. Vol. II.* Ed. Hamangiu, Bucharest, 2012, p. 621.

[32]Gellén Klára: *A színlelt szerződés.* Pólay Elemér Alapítvány, Szeged, 2008, p. 122.

the third party are violated by the sham contract, it makes possible to invoke the secret contract or vice versa. On the other hand, both legal systems recognize the contract containing the real will of the parties to be valid, moreover, as every other contract, it needs to meet the criteria of validity. The only insurmountable difference occurs if the *bona fide* third party receives certain rights based on the public contract: the Hungarian CC states that the simulated contract is null and void, and cannot be validated by the faith of the third party, and the only solution is compensating for damage. In contrast, the Romanian CC makes it possible for the simulated contract to be valid regarding a *bona fide* third party, and as such its faith in the agreement receives protection. We can thus conclude that even if Romanian law is more permissive than Hungarian law, the penalization of the secretive parties is better ensured by always keeping the interests of the *bona fide* third party ahead of the interests of the simulating parties.

References

Baias, Flavius A.: *Simulaţia. Studiu de doctrină şi jurisprudenţă*. Ed. Rosetti, Bucharest, 2003.

Baias, Flavius A.—Chelaru, E.—Constantinovici, R.—Macovei I. coord.: *Noul cod civil. Comentariu pe articole*. C. H. Beck, Bucharest, 2012.

Chivu, Gabriela: *Simulaţia în teoria şi practica dreptului civil*. Agronaut, Cluj-Napoca, 2001.

Dósa Elek: *Erdélyhoni jogtudomány. Második könyv. Erdélyhoni magyar magánjogtan*. Rom. Kat. Líceumi Nyomda, Cluj-Napoca, 1861.

Gellén Klára: *A színlelt szerződés*. Pólay Elemér Alapítvány, Szeged, 2008.

Nótári Tamás: *Római köz- és magánjog*. Scientia, Cluj-Napoca, 2011.

Pop, L.—Popa, I. F.—Vidu, S. I.: *Tratat elementar de drept civil. Obligaţiile*. Universul Juridic, Bucharest, 2012.

Ungureanu, C. T.—Răducan, G. et al.: *Noul Cod civil. Comentarii, doctrină şi jurisprudenţă. Vol. II*. Ed. Hamangiu, Bucharest, 2012.

Ungureanu O.—Munteanu C.: *Drept civil partea generală*. Universul Juridic, Bucharest, 2013.

Wellmann György: *Polgári jog. Kötelmi jog. Az új Ptk. magyarázata V/VI*. HVG–ORAC, Budapest, 2013.

Zimmermann, Reinhard: *The Law of Obligations. The Roman Foundation of the Civilian Tradition*. Juta&Co Ltd., Cape Town, 1992.

Chapter 13
Marriage and Cohabitation in the New Hungarian Civil Code—Answering the New Challenges

Orsolya Szeibert

Abstract The new Hungarian Civil Code's Fourth Book contains family law regulations. It has resulted in the HCC replacing the Hungarian Family Act. The debate on whether family law is an independent branch of the law or part of the civil law is analysed in the thesis, which brings marriage and cohabitation into focus. There are three kinds of partnerships in the Hungarian law, namely marriage, registered partnership and cohabitation; among them, marriage is by far the most prestigious institution. Family law is based traditionally on marriage and it is reflected in the new rules, as well as the detailed and deeply regulated rights and obligations of spouses, which are in the foreground. Solidarity is required from the spouses towards each other henceforward but also their autonomy is supported via marital property agreements. Just to the contrary, cohabitation has remained a contract, even after long debates. Cohabitation as a contract is not contained in the Fourth Book. Nevertheless, if cohabitants have a common child and they live together at least one year, so-called family law consequences may emerge, and these are regulated within family law. This solution endeavours to fulfil the requirement to protect of the child's best interest. This chapter gives an introduction to the regulation of marriage and cohabitation (registered partnership is mentioned in a nutshell) and sketches the main trends in family law while analysing the shaping of the regulations in the course of the codification process. Finally, some aspects of the new rules are dealt with also in the context of the Principles of European Family Law of the CEFL (Commission on European Family Law).

This chapter was presented at the conference "New Civil Codes in Hungary and Romania I" held on 24th May 2013 at the Sapientia University. The written paper has been partly updated in 2015.

O. Szeibert (✉)
Civil Law Department, ELTE Eötvös Loránd University, Budapest, Hungary
e-mail: szeibert@ajk.elte.hu

A. Menyhárd and E. Veress (eds.), *New Civil Codes in Hungary and Romania*,
Ius Gentium: Comparative Perspectives on Law and Justice 63,
DOI 10.1007/978-3-319-63327-5_13

The Fourth Book of the new Hungarian Civil Code (HCC) is the Family Law Book, which entered into force on 15 March 2014. Before the HCC, Family Law was regulated in the framework of an independent Act, the Family Act, namely Act No. IV 1952 on marriage, the family and guardianship. Following the decision on the recodification of the Civil Code, the question of whether the regulations on family law should be incorporated into the Code of civil law emerged.

13.1 Different Viewpoints on Where Family Law Belongs

Although family law is *traditionally part of private law* and regulated in the codes on private law, marital and familial relationships in Hungary had been incorporated in an independent Family Act. It was the result of the comprehensive codification of family law for the first time in Hungary. At the time of the codification of the Hungarian Civil Code of 1959 (HCC of 1959) it seemed to be unquestioned that family law was a legal branch on its own within the (socialist) legal regime.[1] The family, from an ideological perspective, was maintained as a field of law free from the property relations that characterise civil law. Although family law has always shown a special character—even while being an unquestioned part of civil law—the separate character of family law became evident in the Hungarian judiciary until the nineties.[2] Later on, in that decade, the viewpoint, according to which family law as an autonomous legal branch was denied, accepted the peculiar features of the regulation of family and marriage.

The self-reliance of the family and the requirement to maintain that status quo were supported by several factors, such as the continuous strengthening of its peculiarities, the diverse interpretation of coordinating involved persons, the diverse forms of state intervention and the special principles which govern the judicature such as the priority of the child's interests.[3] Another, rather cautious attitude did not demand the unconditional reservation of an independent family act but drew attention to the fact that preserving the unity of the family law rules was necessary, just like the ensuring harmony between the civil law rules and those concerning familial relationships.[4]

[1]Kőrös András, A PTK. és a családjog kapcsolata – a gyakorló jogász szemével. [The Connection between the Civil Code and Family Law from a practitioner's view], Polgári Jogi Kodifikáció 1999, 1. 4.

[2]Weiss Emilia, Az új Polgári Törvénykönyv és a családjogi viszonyok szabályozása, [The new Civil Code and Regulation of Family Law Relationships], Polgári Jogi Kodifikáció 2000, 2. 5.

[3]Weiss 7-8.

[4]Kőrös 8.

13.2 The Legal Background: Marriage, Cohabitation and Registered Partnership in Hungary

Although only marriage and cohabitation existed as partnerships between a man and a woman at the end of the nineties, three forms of partnerships have been regulated since 2009. This thesis deal exclusively with marriage and cohabitation and not with registered partnership; however, for the sake of relative completeness, this institution is briefly mentioned here.

In the era preceding the HCC, *marriage* was regulated in the Family Act while rules on *cohabitation* were contained in the HCC of 1959. An independent Act, namely Act No. XXIX of 2009 on registered partnership and the facilitation of the proof of cohabitation was approved in April 2009 and this Act has not been affected by the HCC. A *registered partnership* can only be established by same-sex partners. It is to be mentioned that, according to the literal translation, the institution is called 'registered cohabitation' but in terms of its content it corresponds to the institution of registered partnership, as this terminology is generally used in this context in Europe. Registered partnership creates a status just like marriage and the process of establishing a registered partnership is the same as with marriage. A main rule is that in issues not regulated by the Act on registered partnership, the rules of the Family Act concerning marriage were to be applied analogously but there remained some important exceptions concerning the possibility of legally having a common child.[5]

Registered partnership is hardly referred to at all in the HCC, but Act No. XXIX of 2009 on registered partnership is also to be applied under the regime of the HCC.

13.3 Regulation of Marriage and Cohabitation in the Family Act and the HCC of 1959

As it mentioned earlier, before the HCC marriage was regulated in the 1952 Family Act while rules for cohabitation were contained in the HCC of 1959. Both rules concerning marriage and those regarding cohabitation were modified several times after their entry into force. Although the HCC entered into force in March 2014, the regulations of the FamilyAct and especially the HCC of 1959 are to be applied in the long run in judicial practice according to the rules of Act No. CLXXVII of 2013

[5]Registered partners cannot use their partner's surname, at least according to their status. They cannot adopt a child together. Joint adoption means that registered partners are not permitted to adopt a child as adoptive parents together. Step-parent adoption is also excluded so a registered partner cannot adopt the child of his or her registered partner and it is irrelevant whether the child is related by blood or was adopted. Besides, registered partners cannot take part in medically assisted reproduction processes.

concerning the provisional measures of the HCC and with regard to the fact that family law relationships are generally durable ones.

13.4 Marriage Was Not Discussed While Cohabitation Was One of the Most Debated Issues, Even in 2003

The Concept and Regulatory Syllabus of the HCC in 2003 anticipated the legislators' attitudes to marriage and unmarried partnership.[6] In the following, the rules in the Family Act concerning marriage and those in HCC of 1959 concerning cohabitation are dealt with in the context of the Concept and Regulatory Syllabus and also with regard to the new rules in effect.

13.4.1 Marriage

The legal consequences of marriage seemed to be mainly untouched.[7] The *Family Act* provided *comprehensive rules for marriage* which were also protected at the level of *principles of family law contained in the Family Act.* The formation of marriage, its substantive and formal requirements and its invalidity and termination, including divorce, were traditionally regulated in detailed way. Besides, several legal consequences were attached to marriage and marital life in the Family Act. There was no discussion concerning the preservation of these kinds of regulations.

The Family Act also protected the institution of marriage and the family, in accordance with the *Fundamental Law*, and guaranteed the spouses' equality, both in the marriage and in the family life. Although these are not designated as principles they were taken into consideration as main principles of family law. (While it was not planned to be strengthened, the unequivocal protection of marriage nevertheless became stronger later on.)

Issues of marital status and personal consequences have been preserved as well. According to the earlier regulations and those of today, a new status emerges when entering into a marriage and the consequences of this married status permanently fixed. Regarding the *personal consequences,* the spouses have to reach common decisions on issues belonging to their matrimonial life and they should support each other. Besides, fidelity is required of them. As the issue of name-bearing is strictly regulated in Hungary, there are detailed rules of how the spouses can bear their family names, including the possibility of a common family name or linked names. Nevertheless, a whole list of variations is provided, including the traditional

[6]The Concept and Regulatory Syllabus were published in the Hungarian Official Gazette (Magyar Közlöny). Special Edition, 2003.

[7]Concept 13-14. Regulatory Syllabus 37-53.

Hungarian form according to which the husband's family name or his whole name is lengthened by a short, two-letter-long extension which means that the woman belongs to that man, analogous to a 'traditional American wife' being called "Mrs. John Smith".

With regard to the *property consequences* of marriage, the default matrimonial property regime has been the community of property regime since 1952. Spouses have been able to enter into a matrimonial property agreement, in which they may deviate from the rules of the default regime, since 1986. The property consequences of marital life were regulated very laconically in the Family Act, in keeping with the socialist attitude to family law. It was the point where the need for modernisation was emphasised. The Concept, among the main topics to be discussed at principle level, highlighted the urgent need for reshaping the matrimonial property rules. Even so, it did not refer to any other issue concerning marriage and the matrimonial relationship.

In accordance with the requirement of solidarity, the spouses are obliged to cover the costs of the common household together. These costs are to be paid from their common property and, if those are not enough, each spouse is obliged to contribute to the maintenance of the common household from his or her separate property. The strict and wide notion of solidarity requires either spouse to cover all costs alone if the other spouse has no separate property. There was no plan to modify this legal attitude.

A marriage may be terminated by either spouse's death or by divorce. The Family Act codified the no-fault divorce and there it was also held to be a proper solution in the early 2000s. Marriage can be dissolved only through a judicial process if it is completely and irretrievably broken down. Although the irretrievable breakdown is the sole ground for divorce, the spouses' consent has a partly independent legal meaning and legal requirements. The spouses had to reach agreement on each ancillary issue namely the "placement of the child"; contact with the child, child support, the maintenance of the divorced spouse, the usage of the common dwelling and the arrangement of the property relations. Although the requirement of the consent on ancillary issues was held as good evidence for the complete and irretrievable breakdown of the marriage, the scope of these issues has somewhat changed.

The Concept emphasised completing the provisions of community property law. It was not planned or suggested to change the rules but rather to lift the crystallised judicial practice into the HCC. The community property regime terminates when the matrimonial community of life ends. Either of the spouses may claim for the distribution of the joint property; it usually happens when they divorce. As solidarity does not terminate automatically with divorce, one of the spouses sometimes may be obliged to maintain his or her former spouse. Although a main point is that both former spouses are responsible for themselves, the moral weight of marriage may result in prolonged responsibility. The requirements, both on the claimant's and the debtor's side, are strictly regulated, leaving some discretionary power to the court at the same time. The matrimonial community of life results in a right to use the common dwelling, which does not terminate automatically either. The Family

Act regulates the possibilities of maintaining the right to remain in the former family home, especially if the parental responsibility concerning common child makes it necessary.

The Regulatory Syllabus dealt with the need for the special family law principles which reflect and represent the independence and separateness of family law and with the matrimonial law in detail. Although several provisions were listed with the aim of modification, these seemed to be recommendations to alter the marital regulations to only a limited extent. No modification was submitted which would have fundamentally altered the rules on marriage and/or its consequences.

13.4.2 Cohabitation

Cohabitation had been regulated in the HCC of 1959 since 1977. The regulations were amended in 1996 and 2009. The HCC of 1959 provided a definition for cohabitants, according to which unmarried partners, if there is no rule of law regulating the situation differently, are two persons—either of different sexes or same-sex persons—who live together, without entering into a marriage or registered partnership, in a common household, in an emotional fellowship and in an economic partnership (community of life). They cannot be related to each other in direct line, cannot be siblings or half-siblings and neither of them can live at the same time in a matrimonial community of life, a community of life within a registered partnership or in another cohabitation with a third person. This definition was not discussed in the Concept; nevertheless, the maintenance of its *de facto* character and the avoidance of compulsory registration were already mentioned and emphasised.[8]

While marriage was held to be maintained, the issue of cohabitation was underlined as one of the most debated points. The Concept indicated the need for a careful balance between giving more rights and obligations to cohabitants and keeping the legal distance between marriage and cohabitation. The need to guarantee further rights for them was not questioned but it was planned to be achieved in a way which would not weaken the institution of marriage. Some rights, such as the usage of the common family home and the maintenance of the former cohabitant, were to be granted only to a cohabitant following a long-lasting relationship.

The Regulatory Syllabus admitted that cohabitation was very similar to marriage and arrived at a compromise, according to which a *de facto* unmarried partnership has to be regulated according to the norms of family law but it cannot result in the same regulation for cohabitants and for spouses. The Regulatory Syllabus was unambiguous about retaining the difference between the property relations of spouses and those of cohabitants, at least with regard to the default property regime. It was planned from the very beginning that a cohabitant should acquire ownership or have a claim for compensation only pro rata to his or her contribution in

[8]Concept 14. Regulatory Syllabus 42, 50-51.

acquiring the assets. The maintenance of a former cohabitant and usage of the common dwelling in the child's interest were also mentioned.

Concerning the "formation" and "termination" of cohabitation, it did not seem to be proper to create an obligatory registration system, so the *de facto* character of this partnership was not to be modified.

While marriage has always had far-reaching legal consequences, the same was not true of cohabitants, as only the property relations of *de facto* unmarried partners were regulated in the HCC of 1959. The cohabitants acquired common property during the community of life in proportion to the contribution they made in acquiring the property. If this proportion could not be calculated, the property was considered to have been equally acquired. Any work done in the household was considered to be a contribution to acquiring this property.

Although these rules seem to be beneficial for cohabitants, the judiciary developed a strict and restrictive interpretation on both the requirements of cohabitation itself and the requirements of acquiring common property. Besides, the cohabitants did not have a right to use a common or linked family name or even to change their family name on the basis of being cohabitants. A cohabitant could not claim maintenance if the cohabitation terminated, nor did they have any right to use the common dwelling after end of cohabitation. However, according to the judiciary, solidarity was required from both of them while they were living together in unmarried.

Cohabitation always followed the factual model, as cohabitation comes into existence through the cohabitants' real community of life and terminates by finishing the community of life. Although there is no obligatory registration system, a Registration of Cohabitants' Statements was introduced by the Act of 2009.[9] The registration system is maintained and managed by the public notaries. The essential feature of the factual model is not affected by this registration, as it only has a declaratory character and the registration of the cohabitants' common statement of the existence of their cohabitation does not create any status. Registration establishes a presumption on the existence or non-existence of the cohabitation. It has importance in cases in which whether the partners lived in cohabitation is disputed between them, mostly in connection with one cohabitant's property claim. The registration's non-obligatory character is reflected in the fact that while a common statement of the cohabitants is needed for the statement's registration, only one cohabitant's negative statement is enough for the declaration's cancellation from the register. In the latter case, the public notary informs the other party of the cancellation.

Although this declarative character was not to alter the legal features of cohabitation, not even originally, one important legal consequence was attached to the registration provisionally, only in 2010. During 2010, registration was a basis of paternal presumption for different-sex cohabitants. If the mother did not become married in the period between conception and the birth of the child, even for a short time, the man with whom the mother lived between conception and birth of the

[9]Registered Partnership Act, namely Act No. XXIX 2009 on registered partnership and the facilitation of the proof of cohabitation.

child, even for a short time, in cohabitation as proved by the Registration of Cohabitant's Statements, had to be regarded as the legal father of the child.[10]

13.4.3 Child-Parent Relationship

Although the legal relationship between spouses and cohabitants are sharply differentiated, there is a family law issue where cohabitants have the same rights as spouses, and this is the relationship between the parent living in a de facto unmarried partnership and the child which was born from this relationship. The parent-child relationship and the partnership were not linked to each other in the Family Act and it was of course not suggested that this position should be changed.

The parental responsibilities of cohabitants are the same as those of spouses concerning their common child. The Family Act does not provide any special rules for cohabitant parents because the parent-child relationship does not depend upon the parents' marital status. If the mother and father are the legal parents of the child, the rights and obligations of the parents living in cohabitation are the same as those of married parents. The same is true, as a general rule, if the parents' partnership, either marriage or cohabitation, breaks up. The difference flows from the fact that with marriage there is a legal bond while cohabitation exists *de facto*. The court has the power to decide, even *ex officio*, on parental responsibilities if a marriage is dissolved; however, if cohabitation ends then one or both of the partners has to request a decision on this issue.

Regarding parental status, the woman who gives birth to a child is the legal mother of that child, while the paternal status is created upon presumptions. The father who is the mother's husband will be automatically the legal father, by the operation of law. If the parents are not married, the father can gain paternal status through the child's recognition. A man who maintains he is the father may recognise the child if no other man has to be considered as the legal father by the operation of law and he is at least sixteen years older than the child. Recognition has to be made in person and the consent of the mother is also needed.

The Public Health Act makes it possible for both spouses and heterosexual cohabitants to take part in medically assisted reproduction procedures. Either artificial insemination or in vitro fertilisation without egg or sperm donation, or assisted reproduction techniques, which involve sperm or egg donation, are available for them. For *de facto* unmarried partners, neither of them may live in marriage to another person and the cohabitants must give a declaration of cohabitation in deed. However, while spouses may adopt a child jointly, as they may adopt a child who is not a family member, or one of them can adopt their spouse's child, even if that child is that spouse's adopted child, joint adoption is not provided for cohabitants at all.

---

[10]Orsolya Szeibert, How cohabitants and registered partners can or cannot be a child's legal parents in Hungary with a special view to the 'pater est' principle for cohabitants, in: Bill Atkin (ed.), The International Survey of Family Law, 2011, Jordan Publishing, 211-220.

13.5 The 2006–2012 Period in the Codification Process

13.5.1 Marriage and Cohabitation

The paragraphs on marriage and cohabitation that were formulated during 2005 and 2006 according to both the Concept and Regulatory Syllabus and expansive consultation reflected the main points anticipated in 2003. The submitted and published paragraphs on marriage[11] remained almost untouched until the acceptance of the HCC and even in the period between 2006 and 2012. Although small changes and modifications were proposed and discussed, the structure and the main content of the regulations on marriage remained intact. It seems to be self-explanatory, as marriage is a universal and generally revered legal institution, the characteristics of which have almost never been questioned. Besides, it was continuously emphasised that marriage should be maintained as the main and primarily protected form of partnership between a man and a woman. In the meanwhile, the context at the level of the legal acts, as we outline below, changed and those new developments even reinforced the legal status of marriage and that of spouses.

Just the opposite happened to cohabitation. Following the decision according to which cohabitation should have been included in the Civil Code, two crucial questions emerged, namely in which Book cohabitation should be regulated and what kind of legal rules should be created.

The new structure for cohabitation was created in late 2005.[12] According to the submitted paragraphs, all the regulations on cohabitation would have been included in the Family Law Book and the legal consequences of cohabitation would have been widened by the original aim, i.e. to give more protection for cohabitants but not endanger the primacy of marriage. As there is no bond in the case of cohabitation and no formal, procedural termination is needed, several legal consequences were planned to be preserved for spouses (such as bearing a common or linked family name). The regulations would have contained the definition of cohabitation, the cohabitants' property relations, the maintenance of the former cohabitant and the usage of their common dwelling after cohabitation. Significance would have been attributed to stable and long-term partnerships and those cohabitations within which the cohabitants have not lived so long together but do have a common child.

---

[11]Kőrös András, „Fontolva haladás" – az új Ptk. Családjogi Könyve. 3. Rész: A házastársi vagyonközösség. [Cautious progress. The Family Law Book of the New Civil Code, Chapter 3. Community of Property of Spouses.] Családi Jog, 2005, 4, 1-15.; Kőrös András, „Fontolva haladás" – az új Ptk. Családjogi Könyve. 4. Rész: A házassági vagyonjogi szerződés. [Cautious progress. The Family Law Book of the New Civil Code, Chapter 3. Marital Property Agreement.] Családi Jog, 2006, 1, 11-17.

[12]Kőrös András, „Fontolva haladás" – az új Ptk. Családjogi Könyve. 1. Rész: Az élettársi jogviszony szabályozásának szakértői javaslata [Cautious progress. The Family Law Book of the New Civil Code, Chapter 1. Experts' Proposal on the Regulation of Cohabitation] Családi Jog, 2005, 2, 1-10.

This well-founded structure was discussed and the discussions revealed between 2006 and 2012. While the developments and legal changes mentioned below strengthened the regulation and institution of marriage, otherwise protected, they had precisely the opposite effect on cohabitation and its regulation.

13.5.2 The Hungarian Fundamental Law and the Family Protection Act

The Fundamental Law, which entered into force in April 2012, fixed that *Hungary shall protect the institution of marriage, the conjugal union of a man and a woman based on voluntary and mutual consent. Hungary shall also protect the institution of the family, which it recognises as the basis for the survival of the nation*. The Fundamental Law referred to a new cardinal Act, which was finally passed in late 2011. This Act on the protection of families stated that the basis of the family is the marriage between a man and a woman or lineal affinity or guardianship.[13] This strict concept of the family in the Family Protection Act was deemed to be unconstitutional and annulled in December 2012 by the Constitutional Court.[14] In March 2013 the Fundamental Law was amended a fourth time so that, according to the actual wording of Article (L) of the Fundamental Law, "Hungary shall protect the institution of marriage, the conjugal union of a man and a woman based on voluntary and mutual consent and the family as the basis for the survival of the nation. The basis of the family is marriage and the parent-child relationship".

Even the procedure of creating a notion of the family heavily influenced the legal attitude to marriage and cohabitation, not only in the context of the HCC but also in the normative texts.

13.6 Detailed Rules on Marriage and Cohabitation in the HCC

13.6.1 Principles of the Family Law Book

Four principles introduce the Family Law Book with the aim of emphasising that family law is a special branch of civil law. The principles are the following: the protection of marriage and the family, the protection of the child's interests, equality of spouses, fairness and the protection of the weaker party. All principles

[13]See on the Fundamental Law and Family Protection Act in family law context: Orsolya Szeibert: Partnerships in Hungary in the Light of the New Legal Developments: Status or Contract? in: Bill Atkin (ed.), The International Survey of Family Law, 2012, Jordan Publishing, 115-122.

[14]Decision of the Constitutional Court No. 43/2012 (XII. 20.).

affect both the children's rights and interests and those of the partners. The principle on the protection of the child's interests deals explicitly with an issue related to public law and not civil law as, according to this principle, the child has the right to be brought up in his or her own family. If this is not possible, it has to be guaranteed that the child should be brought up in a familial environment as far as possible and that his or her family relationships are maintained. According to the last paragraph, the rights of child to be brought up in his or her family or familial environment and maintain the family relationship can only be restricted in legally determined cases, exceptionally and exclusively in the child's interest.

13.6.1.1 Protection of Marriage and Family

Although the Expert's Proposal[15] promoted the protection of family relationships in the first-mentioned principle instead of the protection of marriage and the family, the HCC's wording coincides with that of the Fundamental Law. Section 4:1 states that the Act protects marriage and the family and the harmony between family interests and personal interests are to be guaranteed when applying the Act. The phrase "family relationships" would have included not only the relationships coming into being by law as marriage but also *de facto* familial relationships, such as cohabitation.

The principle explicitly protects only marriage, with the tacit exclusion of any other forms of unmarried partnership, and this protection is reflected in the method of regulation, because the rights and obligations of spouses are regulated more thoroughly than those of cohabitants. Regarding the family, according to the academic and judicial commentary to the principles it has to be understood in a wide sense as the real contain of a familial relationship deserves protection.[16]

13.6.1.2 Equality of Spouses

A classic and traditional family law principle is the equality of spouses [Section 4:3]. The equality and equal rights and obligations of spouses guarantee their equal status, both in their matrimonial life and family life, obviously towards their common child. This provision is parallel with the protection of spouses. Although the cohabitants' equal position is not guaranteed at principle level, partners' rights and obligations are of course equal in the context of an unmarried partnership. That equality is obvious, both in the partners' relationship and in their relationship towards their common child.

---

[15]Vékás Lajos (ed.), Szakértői Javaslat az új Polgári Törvénykönyv tervezetéhez, [Experts' Proposal for the Draft of the new Civil Code], Budapest, Complex, 2008.

[16]Kőrös András, Alapelvek. In Kőrös András (ed), Családjog [Family Law], Budapest, Complex, 2008, 24-26.

13.6.1.3 Fairness and Protection of Weaker Party

Fairness and the protection of the weaker party [§ 4:4] is a new family law principle although both had already been cautiously applied in some family law issues in judicial practice. In the Family Act, fairness was required of the court when it rendered the spouses' property relations and it is interpreted in the judiciary in a rather restricted way.

13.6.2 Marriage

The complexity of the regulation on marriage has been preserved in the HCC.[17] The Second Part deals with the legal position of spouses in the context of detailed rules. The formation of marriage, invalid marriage and the legal consequences and procedural background of invalidity have remained untouched in their essentials. Regarding divorce, irretrievable breakdown as a governing rule has also been preserved. If there is no mutual consent on divorce, the breakdown has to be assumed by the court; however, the new rules add some objectivity to the determination of whether the marriage was broken down. Whether the matrimonial community of life has finished and there is no prospect of its restoration are to be taken into consideration by the court. For divorce by mutual consent, the scope of ancillary issues upon which the partners have to reach agreement has been reduced in the new HCC. The spouses do not have to arrange the distribution of their common property. The modifications of the ancillary issues show the adaptation to the new family law trends and provide easier access to divorce at the same time.

Marriage has the widest spectrum of personal legal consequences in comparison with other partnerships. Fidelity is required of spouses and they should cooperate with each other to reach common aims and support each other. According to the Family Law Book, spouses should reach common decisions on the issues of their marital and family life while they should decide on their own for their own personal issues but with regard to the common child's and the other spouse's interests. An emphasised right of the spouses remains, according to which they may choose their family name after marriage.

The property relations of spouses are regulated much more expansively than in the Family Act [18]. The Family Law Book contains regulations concerning the property relations of spouses, the default matrimonial property regime, alternative matrimonial property regimes, usage of the common dwelling and the maintenance

---

[17]Marriage is regulated in the Second Part of the Fourth Book under the title "Marriage" [§ 4:5-85].

[18]See the Hungarian answers (Orsolya Szeibert and Emilia Weiss) on the detailed rules of Hungarian matrimonial property regime as regulated in the Family Act in: Katharina Boele-Woelki, Bente Braat and Ian Sumner (eds.), European Family Law in Action Vol. IV: Property Relations Between Spouses, 2009, Intersentia.

of the former spouse. The community of property regime is maintained as the default matrimonial property regime, as it creates a balance between the spouses' properties, their work and contribution to the common life. As the spouses are free to deviate from the rules on the community of property regime, two kinds of so-called model rules of the regime of participation in acquisitions and those of separation of property also appear in the HCC, besides the default regime.

The rules of maintenance of the former spouse[19] are kept in the Family Law Book and the conditions for maintenance have not been changed. These requirements are the lack of means and the absence of unworthiness on the claimant's side and the ability of the debtor to pay. Unworthiness depends on the behaviour of the claimant during the marital life. Although the regulations concerning spousal maintenance preserve the rules of the Family Act, some brave new rules appear.

13.6.3 Cohabitation

The idea which had been upheld, even if debated, during almost the whole period of codification concerning the regulatory method of cohabitation, was left aside in late 2012. According to that idea, cohabitation was held to be a family and not a special type of contract. Contrarily, the HCC commits itself to the contractual perception of cohabitation. Cohabitation itself is regulated in the Sixth Book while the so-called family law consequences of cohabitation are in the Fourth Book.

The Sixth Book of the Civil Code provides rules for the definition of cohabitation, the property issues and the possibility of arranging the use of their common house after the termination of the cohabitation by contract.[20]

The notion of cohabitation does not change, since cohabitants are two persons, whether different sex or same sex, who live together, without entering into a marriage or a registered partnership, in a common household, in an emotional fellowship and in an economic partnership (community of life) and they are not related to each other in direct line; they cannot be siblings or half-siblings and neither of them can live at the same time in a marital community of life, a community of life in a registered partnership or in cohabitation with a third person.

With regard to their property relations, the default property regime resembles the regime of acquisitions of property and is an alternative property regime for spouses. Just as with marriage, cohabitants are encouraged to enter into a property contract and the cohabitants may create the contractual terms as freely as spouses, even if there are cogent rules in both cases.

[19]See the Hungarian answers (Orsolya Szeibert and Emilia Weiss) on the detailed rules of Hungarian spousal maintenance as regulated in the Family Act in: Katharina Boele-Woelki, Bente Braat and Ian Sumner (eds.), European Family Law in Action Vol. II: Maintenance Between Former Spouses, 2003, Intersentia.

[20]Cohabitation is regulated as a special contract in the Third Part of the Sixth Book [§ 6:514-517]. Family law consequences are contained in Third Part of the Fourth Book [§ 4:86-95].

The family law impacts of cohabitation may be claimed if the partners have lived together for at least one year and they have a common child. These consequences concern the maintenance of a former cohabitant and the possibility of claiming for a court decision on the use of the common flat by the former cohabitant. Both the rules of maintenance and those of the usage of the common flat derive from the marital regulations. Nevertheless, there are clear distinctions in both cases, with the objective of not providing as strict ruling as for spouses.

It is not regulated definitely but it goes without saying that, in the field of parental responsibilities, cohabitants have the same rights and obligations as spouses. The establishment of parental status does not happen in the same way as for spouses. Paternal status does not emerge automatically and cohabitants cannot adopt a child together. However, they can take part in medically assisted reproduction procedures, provided they are different-sex persons.

13.7 The Demographic Context

The number of marriages has been continuously falling for years. In the last decade not only the number of first marriages but also those of second or third marriages have decreased. Contrarily, the number of cohabitations has been slowly but also continuously increasing. (It is worth mentioning that we are almost sure that the notion of cohabitation used in the demographic literature does not cover the civil law phenomena of cohabitation perfectly, as it not as measureable as marriage and people often think they live in a state of cohabitation but their method of living together does not implement the cohabitation in its civil law sense.) Hungarian society seems tolerant towards non-marital partnerships, even if the partners have a common child. Although cohabitation does not function as something for life and these partnerships generally break up faster than marriages, its significance should not go unnoticed.[21]

The latest published demographic analyses definitely confirm these tendencies. The number of cohabitations is continuously growing and while in 1990 the proportion of women cohabitants was below 5% in all researched age-groups, in 2011 this rate is above 10% in all age-groups except for the women above 60. Earlier it was mostly divorced and widowed persons who lived in cohabitation in Hungary, today cohabitation not only precedes marriage but it seems to be an alternative to marriage. The demographers remark that this phenomenon will not disappear.[22]

---

[21]Pongrácz Tiborné, A párkapcsolatok jellegzetességei. [The Characteristics of Partnerships.] In: Monostori Judit et al. (ed.), Demográfiai Portré 2009, KSH Népességtudományi Kutató Intézet 9-17; Pongrácz Tiborné: A párkapcsolatok jellegzetességei. [The Characteristics of Partnerships.] In: Őri Péter – Spéder Zsolt (ed.), Demográfiai Portré 2012, KSH Népességtudományi Kutató Intézet 11-20.

[22]Murinkó Lívia – Spéder Zsolt, Párkapcsolatok. [Partnerships.] In: Monostori Judit – Őri Péter – Spéder Zsolt (ed.), Demográfiai Portré 2015, KSH Népességtudományi Kutató Intézet 9-26.

13.8 Answering the New Challenges—Balancing Solidarity and Autonomy in the Case of Spouses

Three issues are to be dealt with in detail to provide examples of how the Family Law Book balances the requirement of solidarity of the spouses towards each other and another requirement, namely autonomy in the matrimonial life. The rules of all the three fields mentioned below, namely divorce, maintenance and property rules, have generally maintained the regulations of the Family Act, although there are brand new rules on every subject-matter which deviate, even if very gently, from the traditional path.

13.8.1 Divorce—Simplification for Divorce by Mutual Consent

Divorce is based upon the irretrievable breakdown of marital life and this principle has been preserved in the HCC, just like the possibility of divorce by mutual consent between the spouses. With regard to mutual consent, there are outcomes, so-called ancillary issues, upon which the spouses have to reach an agreement as this shows the final character of their decision. The circle of the issues the spouses have to agree upon is very wide and contains the main issues affecting their common child and the main issues affecting the spouses' property relations [§ 4:21].

The HCC enforces the availability of divorce by mutual consent, as the spouses will not have to reach an agreement on the distribution of common property. In judiciary practice, this issue is a crucial one. The Family Law Book does not intend to make divorce more complicated if the matrimonial life really has broken down and the spouses' real intention is to follow their lives on separate paths. The omission of property issues from the ancillary ones was not debated, even when the protection of marriage was strengthened independently of the civil law codification.

The Concept and the Regulatory Syllabus stated that the distribution of common property was sometimes so difficult that it laid an extra burden on the spouses when divorcing by mutual consent.[23] The simplification has not yet been debated. Nevertheless, I remark that another change in the ancillary issues affects parental responsibility, and joint parental responsibility is underlined. As the divorcing parents often quarrel on their parental responsibility and the possibility of alternative residence is also debated, it distracts the attention.

It was also held in the Regulatory Syllabus that the Hungarian divorce law was in harmony with international trends, especially with regard to the principle of irretrievable breakdown as grounds for divorce. When comparing the Hungarian

[23]Regulatory Syllabus 40.

rules to the Principles of CEFL on European Family Law Regarding Divorce,[24] it can be seen that although Hungarian substantive family law does not know a reflection period,[25] it allows divorce upon the spouses' mutual consent. Regarding the content and form of the spouses' agreement, the principles suggest consent in the division of property.[26]

13.8.2 Maintenance—Clean Break in the Foreground

The new Family Law Book emphasises the fidelity of the spouses and their obligation to support each other. They have to cooperate and maintain each other. Maintenance may be claimed even after the end of the community of life or even after the divorce. The maintenance of ex-spouses perfectly shows the idea of solidarity.

On the other hand, the new rules manage short marriages differently. According to that provision, when the matrimonial community of life lasted only one year and there was no common child, the duration of maintenance after divorce may not last longer than the community of life [§ 4:29]. Although marriage is marriage and gives status, this example represents a new style of thinking. Autonomy of the spouses seems to win in the provision regarding clean break. According to that rule, the parties may agree on performing the maintenance in a lump sum. Although spousal maintenance normally has the character of providing the ex-spouse with a subsistence allowance, this new expressed possibility shows another trend.

This regulation was unknown before in Hungary and it is partly in harmony with the Principles of CEFL on European Family Law Regarding Maintenance Between Former Spouses.[27] These Principles allow the competent authority to order a lump sum payment.[28] Although the court does not have such competence in Hungary, the spouses may agree on this issue. According to the national reports in the context of CEFL research, a lump-sum payment was possible in most of the national systems which took part in the project in the early 2000s.[29]

[24]Katharina Boele-Woelki et al., Principles of European Family Law Regarding Divorce and Maintenance Between Former Spouses. 2004, Intersentia.

[25]Principle 1:5 Katharina Boele-Woelki et al. 33.

[26]Principle 1:7 Katharina Boele-Woelki et al. 43.

[27]Katharina Boele-Woelki et al. Principles of European Family Law Regarding Divorce and Maintenance Between Former Spouses. 2004, Intersentia.

[28]Principle 2:5 Katharina Boele-Woelki et al. 96.

[29]Katharina Boele-Woelki et al. 97.

13.8.3 Promotion of Matrimonial Property Agreements

The default matrimonial property regime is the community of property. Community of property is the regime of today as well, and it was decided to retain it. An important motive for not modifying the default regime was the conviction that this regime was to serve solidarity in the best way. Community of property protects the weaker party immanently, as they acquire common property as a general rule. The essence of the system has not changed at all in the new Civil Code. [30]

On the other hand, the Family Law Book very strongly promotes matrimonial property agreements. The Family Act also knows the matrimonial property agreement but it is not used so widely in practice. With the goal of supporting these agreements, the Civil Code gives special provisions for two alternative property regimes. One is the so-called community of accrued gains; another is the separation of property. The separation of property regime prohibits any agreement that would exempt one party from bearing the costs of the common household and child-raising [§ 4:73]. Nevertheless, separation of property is far from solidarity if the separation relates to all assets.

The possibility of entering into a matrimonial property agreement was only reintroduced in 1986, as it was not permitted earlier in the socialist era. The emphasis on this option in the HCC is in harmony with the Principles of CEFL of European Family Law Regarding Property Relations between Spouses[31] as they regulate the marital property agreement in an independent chapter. (Nevertheless, there are several differences in the detailed rules which are worth mentioning, e.g. there is a possibility for the spouses to create their own regime in a matrimonial property agreement within the wide frames of the family law regulations.)

13.9 Answering the New Challenges—Cohabitation Is a Contract Which May Have Family Law Consequences

While the balance between solidarity and autonomy may be surveyed in the case of marriage, other points are in focus with regard to cohabitation. Although the weaker party is protected in the HCC, the greater autonomy of cohabitants is self-evident in comparison with the position of spouses. This is reflected generally and in the default property regime in particular. The balance is between the non-protection of cohabitation and cohabitants as partners and the protection of cohabitants as parents. This balance is reflected in the fact that cohabitants as partners are regulated as

[30] See also Kőrös András, New Features of Hungarian Matrimonial Property Law in the Draft of a New Civil Code, in Bea Verschraegen (ed), Family Finances, 2009, Jan Sramek Verlag, 677-678.

[31] Katharina Boele-Woelki et al., Principles of European Family Law Regarding Property Relations Between Spouses. 2013, Intersentia.

contractual partners, while cohabitants as parents may claim for maintenance after the end of cohabitation and for the arrangement of their common dwelling's usage.

If the cohabitants do not have a common child, no family law outcome may be claimed for. It is disadvantageous for cohabitants who do not want a common child or are elder persons. Sometimes marriage has a high prestige for people and after the death of their spouses they are reluctant to enter into another marriage. If a widow(er) does not marry but lives in cohabitation, this partnership remains a contract. The same is true if someone does not want to enter into a marriage for the sake of not hurting his or her children's feelings. In these cases a prestigious marriage and the avoidance of so-called serial polygamy (which is tolerated in Europe nowadays) results in disadvantage according to civil law. It may be presumed that the lawmaker, when they regulated cohabitation as a pure contract, was thinking about young persons who are reluctant to commit themselves.

The existence of the cohabitants' common child results in family law impacts. Although this is one of the two conjunctive requirements, the other requirement does not require too much, as one year of common life is sufficient. The judicial practice interpreted the definition of cohabitation strictly. It will be seen whether the application of the definition will change under the regime of the HCC. Nevertheless, one year is not too much to perform. That demonstrates the HCC's commitment to protect the child's interests. This is in harmony with the principle of the primacy of child's best interests as they are protected in the New York Convention on the Rights of the Child.

References

Boele-Woelki, Katharina et al., Principles of European Family Law Regarding Divorce and Maintenance Between Former Spouses. 2004 Intersentia.

Boele-Woelki, Katharina et al., Principles of European Family Law Regarding Property Relations Between Spouses. 2013 Intersentia.

Kőrös András: A PTK. és a családjog kapcsolata – a gyakorló jogász szemével. [The Connection between the Civil Code and Family Law from a practitioner's view] Polgári Jogi Kodifikáció 1999. 1.

Kőrös András, „Fontolva haladás" – az új Ptk. Családjogi Könyve. 1. Rész: Az élettársi jogviszony szabályozásának szakértői javaslata [Cautious progress. The Family Law Book of the New Civil Code, Chapter 1. Experts' Proposal on the Regulation of Cohabitation] Családi Jog, 2005, 2, 1–10.

Kőrös András, „Fontolva haladás" – az új Ptk. Családjogi Könyve. 3. Rész: A házastársi vagyonközösség. [Cautious progress. The Family Law Book of the New Civil Code, Chapter 3. Community of Property of Spouses.] Családi Jog, 2005, 4, 1–15.

Kőrös András, „Fontolva haladás" – az új Ptk. Családjogi Könyve. 4. Rész: A házassági vagyonjogi szerződés. [Cautious progress. The Family Law Book of the New Civil Code, Chapter 4. Marital Property Agreement.] Családi Jog, 2006, 1, 11–17

Kőrös András, New Features of Hungarian Matrimonial Property Law in the Draft of a New Civil Code, in Bea Verschraegen (ed), Family Finances, Jan SramekVerlag, 2009.

Kőrös András, Alapelvek. In, Kőrös András (szerk), Családjog [Family Law], Budapest, Complex, 2008,

Murinkó Lívia – Spéder Zsolt, Párkapcsolatok. [Partnerships.] In: Monostori Judit – Őri Péter – Spéder Zsolt (szerk.), Demográfiai Portré 2015 KSH Népességtudományi Kutató Intézet

Pongrácz Tiborné: A párkapcsolatok jellegzetességei. [The characteristics of partnerships.] In: Monostori Judit – Őri Péter – S. Molnár Edit – Spéder Zsolt (szerk.): Demográfiai Portré 2009. KSH Népességtudományi Kutató Intézet 9–17;

Pongrácz Tiborné: A párkapcsolatok jellegzetességei. [The characteristics of partnerships.] In: Őri Péter – Spéder Zsolt (szerk.): Demográfiai Portré 2012. KSH Népességtudományi Kutató Intézet

Szeibert Orsolya, How cohabitants and registered partners can or cannot be a child's legal parents in Hungary with a special view to the 'pater est' principle for cohabitants, in: Bill Atkin (ed.), The International Survey of Family Law, 2011 Jordan Publishing,

Szeibert Orsolya, Partnerships in Hungary in the Light of the New Legal Developments: Status or Contract?, in: Bill Atkin (ed.), The International Survey of Family Law, 2012 Jordan Publishing, 115–122.

Szeibert Orsolya and Weiss Emilia, Hungarian Answers on the detailed rules of Hungarian spousal maintenance as regulated in the Family Act in: Katharina Boele-Woelki, Bente Braat and Ian Sumner (eds.), European Family Law in Action Vol. II: Maintenance Between Former Spouses, Intersentia, 2003.

Szeibert Orsolya and Weiss Emilia, Hungarian Answers on the detailed rules of Hungarian matrimonial property regime as regulated in the Family Act in: Katharina Boele-Woelki, Bente Braat and Ian Curry-Sumner (eds.), European Family Law in Action Vol. IV: Property Relations Between Spouses, Intersentia, 2009.

Vékás Lajos (szerk.), Szakértői Javaslat az új Polgári Törvénykönyv tervezetéhez, [Experts' Proposal for the Draft of the new Civil Code], Budapest, Complex, 2008.

Weiss Emilia: Az új Polgári Törvénykönyv és a családjogi viszonyok szabályozása. [The new Civil Code and Regulation of Family Law Relationships] Polgári Jogi Kodifikáció 2000. 2.

Chapter 14
The Law of Succession in the New Hungarian Civil Code

Hella Molnár

Abstract It is said the law of succession is one of the most durable parts of civil law. If this statement were true, there would not be anything new to report and I should write about the unchanged succession rules. However, in the new Hungarian Civil Code, there are many important changes in this area. On March 15th 2014, the new Book Seven of the Hungarian Civil Code, containing the new law of succession, entered into force. Succession can occur under the law or by testamentary disposition. If the deceased has left a last will and testament then it determines the order of succession. If there is no testamentary disposition, the law provides for the order of succession (Article 7:3—Titles of Succession). In the NHCC, the structure of the succession law will follow the logic of the legal titles of succession but this article will not. Above all, the intestate succession needs to be examined because the testator can make his or her last will and testament only if the rules of intestate succession do not live up to their expectations. At the end of this article I will spend a little time on the changes in the rules on compulsory shares as well.

14.1 Introduction

After a person's death, the property and debts of this person will pass to those who survive. Such passing (or transfer) of property and debts belongs to the area of property law. Traditionally, however, in succession matters the general rules of property law are supplemented by special rules concerning to whom and how a person's property passes upon his or her death: the law of succession.[1]

These rules are influenced by socio-cultural, socio-economic and sometimes also religious factors. Generally, succession law does not develop by rapid and radical

[1]Sjef van Erp, *New Developments in Succession Law*, Electronic Journal of Comparative Law, vol. 11.3 December, http://www.ejcl.org/113/article113-5.pdf, 1.

H. Molnár (✉)
Civil Law Department, ELTE Eötvös Loránd University, Budapest, Hungary
e-mail: hella.molnar@ajk.elte.hu

A. Menyhárd and E. Veress (eds.), *New Civil Codes in Hungary and Romania*,
Ius Gentium: Comparative Perspectives on Law and Justice 63,
DOI 10.1007/978-3-319-63327-5_14

changes, as for example, does contract law. This may be due to the fact that succession law does not have to respond to the more usual and more rapid changes of business and economic practices and necessities. Its roots reach deeper into the fundamental concepts of justice, morals and society.[2]

Act IV of 1959 on the Civil Code of the Republic of Hungary (hereinafter the HCC) was enacted in the socialist era. Prior to that time there had been no private law code in Hungary; there had been several acts in force, but fundamentally a case law system had applied. It was promulgated on 1st May in 1960 and provided detailed rules for the private law of succession. Hungarian civil law is quite similar to German and Austrian law, but in the law of succession there are several rules that differ from those in the two Germanic systems. After 1989–1990 the socialist type of social system collapsed and the restrictions on private property were removed. Due to the social and economic changes, the role of the law of succession became increasingly important. The range of assets that could be held by private individuals also expanded (shares in companies, intellectual property). Despite that, the civil law provisions on succession remained basically unchanged; neither the provisions on intestacy nor the assets that can be inherited were amended. That part of the HCC went practically unchanged since its creation (i.e. since 1959). As a result, owing to the court practice of nearly fifty-five years, it had become a consistent and transparent area with a huge volume of case law.[3]

The first problem to be solved in succession matters is how the estate of the deceased is transferred to the heirs.[4] The new Hungarian Civil Code (Act V of 2013 on the Civil Code of Hungary, hereinafter referred to as NHCC) does not change the definition of succession: "The estate owned or controlled by a person at the time of decease shall pass in its entirety to the heir."[5] In Hungary there is no estate without a claimant, succession occurs automatically on the strength of law at the moment of the deceased's death.[6] The term "universal succession" is of modern derivation, and is descriptive of the succession which occurs upon an individual's death. Universal succession means succession by an individual to the entirety of the estate, which includes all the rights and duties of the deceased.[7] The NHCC

---

[2]Urve Liin, *Laws of Succession in Europe and Estonia: How We Got to Where We Are and Where We Should Be Heading*, Juridica International 2001. VI. 114.

[3]Zoltán, Csehi, *The Law of Succession in Hungary*, Miriam Anderson and Esther Arroyo i Amayuelas (ed.), The Law of Succession: Testamentary Freedom: European Perspectives, CSIC Press 170.

[4]A brief discussion relating to terminology is inserted here to acquaint the reader with some of the vocabulary used throughout this article. The word "heir" is generally used as descriptive of all persons who share in the estate, either by testacy or intestacy.

[5]NHCC, Article 7:1 – HCC, Article 598.

[6]The fact that the succession is considered as having been passed over to the heir in its entirety on the death of the deceased person does not prevent the heir from disclaiming it.

[7]George A. Pelletier Jr. and Michael Roy Sonnenreich, *A Comparative Analysis of Civil Law Succession*, Villanova Law Review, 1966, Vol. 11, Issue 2, Article 3. 324–325.

expressly states that the claim to inheritance is exempt from the statue of limitations; it is a perpetual claim to ownership (Article 7:2—Succession Claims).

14.2 Intestate Succession

In the absence of a testament, the intestate succession will be transferred to the heirs, designated according to the legal principles on the devolution of succession. Basically, these principles are founded on consanguinity, with preference to descendants, excluding more distant relatives.[8] Rules of intestacy are regarded as subsidiary: they are applied only if the testator has made no will or if the will does not include provisions for the disposal of the whole estate.

14.2.1 The General Order of Intestate Succession

In the rules of intestate succession the most radical change is the succession of the spouse. The need to protect the surviving spouse is a generally accepted rule. Although not a blood-related person, the spouse is recognized to have a legitimate claim towards the succession of his or her partner. In considering the position of the surviving spouse, one should also take into account what the surviving spouse receives through the liquidation of the marital property system.[9]

It must generally be considered that the spouse, as a rule, is the person closest to the deceased and therefore, the protection and enhancement of the interests of the surviving spouse is fully understandable and entirely appropriate. In doing so, it is also necessary, however, to consider the perspective of surviving children and other close relatives, who likewise have an interest in having the inheritance estate remain in the family. Accordingly, several conflicting interests and perspectives converge in this question, and reaching a resolution fair to all parties is not an easy task.[10]

The general order of intestate succession under the HCC stated that the child of the deceased is the priority heir under intestate succession. If there is more than one child, each of them inherits in equal shares. The children of any disqualified child or of any further descendant replace the latter and each of them inherits in equal shares.[11] The spouse inherits only beneficiary ownership (the usufruct or enjoyment) of the estate (inheritance, bequest) which is called the right of survivorship

[8]Alain-Laurent Verbeke and Yves-Henri Leleu, *Harmonization of the Law of Succession in Europe*. In: Arthur S. Hartkamp — Martijn W. Hesselink — Ewoud H. Hondius — Chantal Mak — C. Edgar du Perron, *Towards a European Civil Code, Fourth Revised and Expanded Edition*, 2011, Kluwer Law International BV, The Netherlands, 459.

[9]Verbeke – Leleu 2011, 466.

[10]Liin 2001, 119.

[11]HCC, Article 607, paras (1)–(3).

(also called "widow's right").[12] Only the descendants may request restricting (limiting) the usufruct at any time; however it can only be limited to the extent of still ensuring the needs of the spouse, with a view to the items of property inherited by him or her, as well as his or her own property and the gains of his or her occupation. Both the spouse and the heirs may request the redemption of the usufruct. No redemption may be requested with regard to the usufruct of the place of residence shared with the deceased, along with its furniture and equipment. The spouse is entitled to a share of the redeemed property equalling—in kind or money —the share he or she would inherit intestate as the deceased's child, together with the other descendants. Redemption may be requested during the probate procedure or, in the absence of it, no later than in one year from opening succession at the notary public otherwise having jurisdiction to conduct the probate procedure.[13] In the absence of any descendant, the spouse or the registered partner inherits the estate.[14] From that point, the HCC utilises the system called Parentelen (statutory heirs), under which blood relatives are grouped into classes corresponding to their relationship to common ancestors.[15] The first Parentelen consist of the parents of the deceased and their descendants; the second the grandparents of the deceased and their descendants, and the third is an incomplete Parentelen. In the absence of any descendant, spouse or registered partner, both parents of the deceased inherit the estate in equal shares. The descendants of a disqualified parent replace the parent in the order of succession in the same manner as the descendants of a disqualified child replace that child. If the disqualified parent has no children, the other parent or his or her descendants are the sole heir(s).[16] If there are no descendants, spouse or registered partner, parents, or descendants of parents then the grandparents of the deceased and their descendants become the legal heirs.[17] If neither the grandparents of the deceased nor their descendants are eligible for inheritance, more distant ancestors of the deceased become legal heirs in equal shares.[18] In the absence of any other heir, the estate will be obtained by the state.[19]

As one can see contrary to many other European legal systems, a Hungarian spouse does not inherit property from the deceased if the descendants are still alive. The spouse only inherits property as a legal heir in the absence of descendants. The existence of only one child of the deceased, regardless of whether from the present or a previous marriage, or a born out of wedlock, leaves the spouse with "empty hands". The HCC solves this problem by declaring that the spouse inherits usufruct in all property not otherwise inherited by the spouse. This legal right is created

[12]HCC, Article 615, para (1).

[13]HCC, Article 616.

[14]HCC, Article 607, para (4).

[15]Pelletier Jr.—Sonnenreich, 1966, 336.

[16]HCC, Article 608.

[17]HCC, Article 609.

[18]HCC, Article 610.

[19]HCC, Article 599, para (3).

automatically for the benefit of the deceased's spouse, and provides an unlimited right to use the property. This may create difficult legal situations, e.g. the children of the deceased inherit property which is of no value to them because of restrictions arising from the beneficial interest of the spouse.

According to the NHCC the child of the deceased is the priority heir under intestate succession only if the deceased has no surviving spouse or registered partner.[20] Article 3, para (1) Point (c) of the Act XXIX of 2009 on Registered Partnership and the Modification of Rules in connection with Registered Partnership and the Facilitation of Cohabitation unaltered states that the rules for the widow of the deceased shall apply to the registered partners. If the deceased has a surviving spouse we have to divide the estate (inheritance, bequest) into two parts. The heirs of the flat shared with the deceased and of the furniture and equipment used in common are the children of the deceased, and the spouse inherits only the usufruct of it. From the rest of the estate (inheritance, bequest) the spouse is entitled to a share he or she would inherit intestate as the deceased's child, together with the other descendants.[21] So if the deceased has two children, the spouse is entitled to usufruct on the flat shared with the deceased (on its furniture and equipments) and the ownership on one third of the rest of the estate (inheritance, bequest). The matrimonial home and its contents are used by the entire family, though they undoubtedly have particular importance to the surviving spouse as a major asset that may largely determine his or her standard of living in widowhood. Thus, to the extent that the application of succession law and the preferences it provides to the surviving spouse help ensure the perpetuation of the same living conditions as those that existed prior to the death of the intestate spouse, they provide stability and security not only in the financial sense, but also spiritually and emotionally. Average life expectancy has increased substantially, which has also meant that in most instances, the death of the intestate occurs when his or her children are largely middle-aged and financially secure with their own homes and families. Thus, surviving children are not likely to depend on the matrimonial home and contents for their own habitation, which will, however, continue to be of vital importance to the surviving spouse.[22] If a spouse or registered partner remarries or enters into another registered partnership, his or her usufruct will not cease to exist. The usufruct cannot be limited and only the spouse has the right to request the redemption of usufruct at any time.[23] It is unchanged that the spouse is entitled to a share of the redeemed property equalling the share he or she would inherit intestate as the deceased's child, together with the other descendants.[24] The testator's spouse is debarred from succession if they were separated at the time of the opening of the succession and it is manifestly evident from the circumstances that there was no

[20]NHCC, Article 7:55, para (1).

[21]NHCC, Article 7:58, para (1).

[22]Liin 2001, 121.

[23]NHCC, Article 7:58, para (2).

[24]NHCC, Article 7:59, para (2).

reasonable expectation of reconciliation. Debarment of the testator's spouse can only be alleged by a person who, as the result of debarment, would himself inherit or would be exempted from an obligation or other burden to which he is bound by virtue of the testamentary disposition.[25]

In the absence of any descendant, the spouse or the registered partner inherits the estate only if the deceased has no parents.[26] If the deceased has parents we have to divide the estate (inheritance, bequest) into two parts. The heir of the flat shared with the deceased and of the furniture and equipment used in common is the spouse with no beneficiary ownership of the parents. The spouse inherits the half of rest and the other half goes to the parents. If one of the parents is disqualified, the other parent and the spouse take the disqualified parent's place.[27] So for example if the father of the deceased is deprived of inheritance, the spouse inherits the flat shared by the deceased (with its furniture and equipments) and five eighth part of the rest (half plus one eighth) and the mother of the deceased inherits three eighth part of it (one fourth plus one eighth).

In the absence of any descendant, a spouse or a registered partner, the heirs are the parents of the deceased and its descendants.[28] If there are no descendants, spouse or registered partner, parents, or descendants of parents; the grandparents of the deceased and their descendants become the legal heirs.[29] But the NHCC introduces one more Parental with the great-grandparents of the deceased and their descendants. According to the new rules if neither the grandparents of the deceased nor their descendants are eligible for inheritance, not the more distant ancestors of the deceased become legal heirs in equal shares but before them the great-grandparents of the deceased and their descendants.[30] It was a great need in practice to expand the inheritance by collateral heirs.

14.2.2 Lineal Succession

The NHCC does not abolish lineal succession, which substantially means that certain properties are returned to the deceased's family if the deceased leaves no children or descendants, instead of going to the spouse. This is a special form of succession, originally made to replace feudal restrictions to the principle of the freedom of inheritance. Linear succession ensures that any assets belonging to the family of the deceased are returned to their family and not to another person,

[25]NHCC, Article 7:62 – HCC, Article 601, paras (1)–(3).

[26]NHCC, Article 7:61.

[27]NHCC, Article 7:60.

[28]NHCC, Article 7:63.

[29]NHCC, Article 7:64.

[30]NHCC, Article 7:65.

particularly the spouse of the deceased. Assets falling under the rules of linear inheritance are an independent sub-category of the estate.

If the legal heir is not a descendant of the deceased,[31] a property that has come down to the deceased from an ancestor by inheritance or by donation is subject to lineal inheritance. Property inherited or donated from a brother or sister or his or her descendant is also subject to lineal inheritance if the property had been inherited or donated by the brother or sister or their descendant from their and the deceased's common ancestor. Whosoever would inherit under the title of lineal succession shall prove the lineal nature of the property.[32]

A parent shall succeed to property that has come down to the deceased from them or one of their ancestors. Descendants of a disinherited parent shall succeed in his or her place according to the general provisions on intestate succession. If there is neither a parent who is entitled to succeed to a lineal property nor a parental descendant, the grandparent, and if there is no grandparent, a more distant ancestor of the deceased shall inherit the property that has come down to the deceased from them or one of their ancestors.[33] The spouse inherits the usufruct of the linear property and, after redemption, the spouse receives one third of it. The usufruct cannot be limited and both the spouse and the lineal heir have the right to request the redemption of usufruct at any time for future considerations with one exception: redemption from the spouse relating to usufruct on the apartment used together with the deceased, including its furniture and equipment, may not be requested.[34] Redemption of the usufruct shall be carried out in due consideration of the reasonable interests of the holder of usufruct and the heir to the property.[35] If there is no lineal heir, lineal property shall be treated the same as the deceased's other property.[36] Lineal property shall be inherited in kind. If succession in kind appears to be impossible or impractical, the court may—at the request of either of the parties affected — order payment of the monetary value of the lineal property.[37]

Under the HCC, provisions relating to lineal succession cannot be applied to lineal property that no longer exists at the time of the decedent's death, or to property that replaced lineal property, or to property purchased for the value of

[31]The total absence or disinheritance of descendants who could be regarded as legal heirs (particularly children, grandchildren, and great-grandchildren) is the first criteria necessary to qualify for linear succession.

[32]NHCC, Section 7:67 [Lineal property] – HCC, Section 611.

[33]NHCC, Section 7:68 [Lineal heirs], paras 1–2. — HCC, Section 612, paras 1–2.

[34]Under the HCC no inheritance, under the title of lineal succession, may be claimed with regard to furniture and equipment of the apartment used in common from the surviving spouse after fifteen years of marriage. Section 613, para 3.

[35]NHCC, Secion 7:69 [Spouse's usufruct on lineal property] — HCC, Section 615, para 1 and Section 616, para 4.

[36]NHCC, Section 7:68 [Lineal heirs], para 3. — HCC, Section 612, para 3.

[37]NHCC, Section 7:71 [Lineal estate] — HCC, Section 614.

lineal property.[38] The judicial practice exceeded this rule and allowed lineal inheritance when the donation was money in order to buy something, for example a house. The practice said that the real donation was the house; the donor just simplified the transaction.[39] However, it should be remembered that the donor could not have bought the house because of the restrictions on obtaining property in the era of socialism. After lifting the controls the reason for this practice ended but it still exists. The NHCC incorporates into law that a property that has replaced lineal property or was purchased for the value of the lineal property can be the subject of the lineal inheritance.[40] I think this rule will result in many evidence problems.

14.3 Testate Succession

In Hungarian law, the types of testament are the last will, contract of inheritance (contract of succession) and testamentary gift[41] (donatio mortis causa). The minimal requirements for a testament are proof that: the declaration was made by the testator and contains their testament (i.e. a testament cannot be made by an agent) and it contains a declaration that makes it obvious the testament has the character of a "real" testament. A declaration lacking one of these two characteristics is not regarded as a testament and is treated by law as a "non-existing testament". The notary public who is in charge of the procedure is obliged to verify ex officio the existence of the minimal requirements.[42]

---

[38]HCC, Section 613, para 1. Gifts of common value are also exempt from these provisions. Substitution or compensation for the value of lineal property that does not exist at the time of the deceased's death (e.g. property that was transferred, consumed, or has perished) is not affected according to para 2.

[39]PK No. 81, Point a).

[40]NHCC, Section 7:70 [Property excluded from lineal succession]. The provisions on lineal succession shall not apply to gifts of ordinary value. The provisions on lineal succession shall not apply to any property that no longer exists at the time of the testator's death, however, they shall apply to any substitute property or a property purchased from the proceeds received for such property. No claim can be filed, on the grounds of lineal succession, for furnishings and/or household accessories of common value against the deceased's spouse.

[41]Testamentary gift is a special testament. If a gift has been given under the condition that the donee outlives the donor, the regulations governing gifts shall apply to the contract, with the exception that the formal requirements to be applied shall be the same as those for contract of inheritance. A testamentary gift shall be deemed valid only for a bequest that would qualify as a specific legacy in a will. NHCC, Section 7:53 [Testamentary gift].

[42]Lajos Vékás, *Öröklési jog (Law of Succession)* 2013, Eötvös József Könyvkiadó, Budapest, 39.

14.3.1 Formal Requirements

The basic form of will in Hungarian law is the written will. Oral wills are only regarded as valid if they were made under life-threatening conditions and the lack of an ability to write.[43] According to the HCC, written wills can be divided into public wills (made with the aid of a notary public or before a court),[44] private wills (are made in three different forms: holographic wills, allographic wills and wills deposited at a notary public). A private will can only be written in a language that the testator can understand, read and write, not exclusively in Hungarian.[45] Non-standard forms of writing (e.g. shorthand, cryptography, Cyrillic or Arabic characters) are not valid, even if the person using them is capable of writing and reading such characters.[46] The document must be identified as a last will, specify the date of creation and the place where it was made, and include the signature of the testator. If composed of more than one sheet, every sheet (not page) has to be numbered and signed by the testator and witnesses. A holographic will is hand-written and signed by the testator. An allographic will is valid if signed by the testator in the presence of two witnesses or, if previously signed, the signature is declared to be his or her own before two witnesses. The witnesses′ knowledge of the contents of the will and their awareness that the testator has drafted a will are not conditions for the validity of the will. A will is regarded as invalid if a witness cannot verify the testator's identity, or if the testator is a minor or legally incompetent or illiterate. Private wills do not have to be written by the hand of the testator; however, the testator must sign the will and may deposit it personally with a notary public, either as an open document or a sealed document, specifically marked as a will.[47]

According to the new rules, a public will must be drafted with the cooperation of a notary public and cannot be taken before a court.[48] The formal requirements for a valid last will are simplified in the NHCC, in order to give more weight to substance (the deceased's intent) than to form (validity rules). The NHCC does not require the testator to indicate on the last will the place where it has been made.

14.3.2 Joint Wills

A last will made in any form by two or more persons within the same deed is invalid in order to prevent abuses.[49] However, under the NHCC, spouses can make

[43]HCC, Section 634 — NHCC, Section 7:20 [Exceptional nature of oral wills].

[44]HCC, Section 625, para 1.

[45]HCC, Section 627.

[46]HCC, Section 628, para 3.

[47]HCC, Sections 629–630.

[48]NHCC, Section 7:14 [Notarial will], para 1.

[49]NHCC, Section 7:23 [Joint will], para 1. — HCC, Section 644.

joint wills at the time of their coexistence if they meet several formal requirements. A written joint testament is valid if one testator writes it with their own hand from the beginning to the end, and signs it; and the other testator declares with their hand in the same deed that the document includes also their testament. If the testament consists of several separate sheets, it is valid only if all of its sheets are numbered in a continuous order and all sheets are signed by the other testator as well. A joint testament written by another person is valid if both testators sign it in the joint presence of two witnesses, or—if it had been signed by them before—acknowledge in the presence of two witnesses the signatures as their own signature. A testament written by another person consisting of several separate sheets is only valid if all of its sheets are numbered in a continuous order, and all sheets are signed by the testators and by both witnesses. The joint will is also valid if it is a public will drafted before a notary public.[50]

The joint will is inoperative if they live in legal separation after the time of making the will and they do not reconcile the marriage before opening succession. The joint will become inoperative if, after making the will, both or one of them has a baby (including adoption), except if there is other provision in the contract.[51] In some countries (for example, in France) joint wills are not permitted due to the belief that there is a difficulty in revoking such wills.[52] In Germany spouses are permitted to execute joint wills, and frequently do so. Any revocation during the lifetime of both spouses requires a publicly certified declaration addressed to the other spouse. After the death of one spouse, the surviving spouse can only affect a revocation by first renouncing all rights under the will of the deceased spouse. About this problem, our new codex says that the unilateral revocation (withdrawal) is invalid if the testament excludes it or it happens without the other testator's notification. The valid unilateral revocation (withdrawal) makes the other testator testament inoperative only if neither of them would have made the testament without the other.[53] It is remarkable that our legislator treats spouses as they were one soul in two bodies, but needless to say that unfortunately most of the time it is not true to life, so I am afraid that joint wills will be breeding grounds for abuses.

14.3.3 Reversionary Succession

Another important change is connected with reversionary (substitute) succession. Any testamentary disposition according to which the original heir is replaced by another heir with regard to the estate or a part of that from a given date or in the case a certain event would happen is invalid. However, in the event of the death of

[50]NHCC, Section 7:23 [Joint will], para 2–3.

[51]NHCC, Section 7:43 [Annulment and revocation of joint wills], paras 1–2.

[52]Pelletier Jr. — Sonnenreich, 1966, p. 348.

[53]NHCC, Section 7:43 [Annulment and revocation of joint wills], paras 3–4.

the heir named as the primary heir, an heir enters as an alternate heir if the conditions thereof have been satisfied.[54] In the HCC, the rules are completed here but the NHCC rules are continued. The appointment of a reversionary heir, naming an heir for the case of the decease of the spouse, is valid and does not affect the spouse's contingent right of disposition and their right of donation no more than the gift of common value. The appointment of a reversionary heir is also lawful in cases of *substitutio pupillaris* (for a child who has no testamentary capacity at the time of the descent and distribution and dies without getting it).[55]

14.3.4 Contract of Inheritance

According to the HCC, in a contract of inheritance the deceased undertakes to make the other contracting party their heir against receiving maintenance or life annuity.[56] The obligation to provide maintenance includes general care, medical treatment, nursing, and burial.[57] Life annuity is a specific sum of money or a specific quantity of agricultural produce periodically.[58] In an inheritance contract, the testator may also make other testamentary disposition; the other party has no such right.[59] That's why its formal requirements follow those of a last will with two exceptions. The provisions on private wills shall be applied regarding the validity of contracts of inheritance, with the exception that the consent of the legal representative and the approval of the guardian shall be required for the validity of a contract of inheritance made by a person of limited capacity and, furthermore, that the formal requirements of wills written by other persons shall apply to contracts of inheritance, even if they are drafted in the handwriting of one of the parties.[60] This contract has a fiduciary nature and continuous service must be provided; it must be concluded for a long term. If the provider pays a life annuity then the fiduciary, personal relationship is not that important.[61] The contract of inheritance concluded by spouses as deceased with a third person is considered valid, even if it is drafted in the same deed.[62] The deceased may not dispose *inter vivos* or *mortis causa* over their property that has been made the subject of a contract of inheritance. With regard to real estate subject to a contract of inheritance, restraint on alienation and

[54]HCC, Section 645, para 1. — NHCC, Section 7:28 [Reversionary heir], para 1–2.

[55]NHCC, Section 7:28 [Reversionary heir], para 3–4.

[56]HCC, Section 655, para 1.

[57]HCC, Section 586, para 3.

[58]HCC, Section 591, para 1.

[59]HCC, Section 655, para 2.

[60]HCC, Section 656. — NHCC, Section 7:49 [Validity of a contract of inheritance].

[61]BH 1996. 534. — Legf. Bír. Pfv. V. 22.148/1995. sz., BH 2000. 105. - Legf. Bír. Pfv. III. 20.539/1995. sz.

[62]Section 73 of the Decree-Act No. 11 of 1960.

encumbrance must be recorded in the land registry for the benefit of the party who has concluded the contract with the deceased.[63] The prohibition on alienation and encumbrance is based on the law (on the HCC provisions). Once it has been recorded in the land registry, the acquisition of the contractual heir is guaranteed with the effect of property rights. In exceptional cases, the courts acknowledge that the testator may make another last will, if they have already started the procedure or lawsuit with the purpose of ceasing or terminating the contract of inheritance.[64]

The definition of a contact of inheritance is much wider in NHCC. The contract can be concluded for a third person's (for example for spouse's) maintenance, life annuity or just for care. If the contracting party's obligation is a third person's maintenance, life annuity or care, after the deceased's death, the real estate subject to a contract or right of support must be recorded in the land registry for the benefit of the third person.[65] The contract of inheritance concluded by spouses as deceased with a third person is considered valid, even if it is drafted in the same deed. If there is no other contractual provision, the surviving spouse inherits usufruct on the flat shared with their wife or her husband with its furniture and equipment.[66] The contracting parties can exclude a restraint on alienation and encumbrance.[67]

14.4 Compulsory Share

Compulsory share has existed in Hungarian law since 1852. The Hungarian rules upheld this institution, which was adopted from the Austrian ABGB. The compulsory share has become an integral part of the Hungarian private law culture; this cultural tradition practically survived the modifications of the Civil Code and it remains unaffected by re-codification.[68] The reason is that the basis of society is the family and not the single individual. The basis of social coexistence is not the unrestricted and unconditional free will of the individual but rather the written and unwritten rules of social life. This situation of social coexistence is manifested in the compulsory share.[69] One should distinguish between the Anglo-American legal systems, where the freedom of will has traditionally been unlimited, and to a large

[63]HCC, Section 657, para 1.

[64]BH 1994. 80. — Legf Bír. Pfv. II. 20 791/1993. sz.

[65]NHCC, Section 7:48 [Contract of inheritance], paras 1–2.

[66]NHCC, Section 7:51 [Contract of inheritance concluded by spouses].

[67]NHCC, Section 7:50 [Transfer of estate], para 1.

[68]The elimination of compulsory share has been raised in the Hungarian legal literature, see Lajos Besenyei, *De lege ferenda gondolatok az öröklési jog köréből. [De lege ferenda Reflections on the Law of Succession]* In: Acta Universitatis Szegediensis de Attila József Nominatae, 2008, LIII, 33–43.

[69]Csehi 2011, p. 177.

extent still is.[70] As opposed to that, the civil law countries defend the notion of forced share, thereby stating that the estate does not exclusively belong to the deceased but at least partially also to their family, who may not be deprived of the entire estate.[71]

The institution of compulsory share reflects the attachment of the estate to the family; certain persons who were the closest to the testator are entitled to the minimum share to be taken primarily from the estate. The deceased's descendants, spouse, registered partner and the deceased's parents are entitled to a compulsory share if, at the time of the opening of succession, they are an intestate heir of the deceased or they would be an heir in the absence of testamentary disposition.[72] Under the HCC, the descendants and the parents are entitled to a compulsory share equalling half of the share they would receive as an intestate heir – calculated according to the basis of the compulsory share.[73] The basis for the calculation of a compulsory share is the net value of the estate plus any donations granted by the testator during their lifetime at the time of their donation. However, if the net value of a donation at the time it is made is unjust to any person concerned, the court is entitled to determine the value of the donation in the light of the circumstances.[74] If the spouse would be entitled to usufruct as intestate heir, their compulsory share is the limited extent of the usufruct covering their needs, with account to the items of property inherited by them as well as their own property and the results of their work. The spouse would otherwise be entitled to a compulsory share equalling half of their share as an intestate heir.[75]

The extent of the compulsory share is changing in the NHCC. Those entitled to a compulsory share receive a compulsory share equalling one third of the share they would receive as intestate heir — calculated according to the basis of the compulsory share. If the spouse would be entitled to usufruct as intestate heir, their compulsory share is the limited extent of the usufruct covering their needs, with regard to the items of property inherited by them. The spouse who is entitled to usufruct as a legal heir is entitled to lay claim to his or her compulsory share as if his or her usufruct had been redeemed.[76] It would only be proper to ask what the

[70]In the Anglo-American jurisdictions, freedom of a will is not restricted, but those persons whom the deceased was bound legally or morally to support during their lifetime may claim a right of maintenance from the estate. The courts are given a discretionary power to award a so-called family provision.

[71]Verbeke — Leleu 2011, p. 468.

[72]HCC, Section 661. — NHCC, Section 7:75 [Compulsory heirs]. In Europe there is a tendency towards reducing the class of heirs entitled to a forced share. Descendants are invariably recognised as being entitled to a forced share. Often also the surviving spouse is protected through a reserved right. Forced share rights for ascendants have been limited or abandoned. Reserved rights for brothers and sisters are very rare and seem to have been increasingly excluded. Verbeke — Leleu 2011, p. 468.

[73]HCC, Section 665, para 1.

[74]HCC, Section 666, paras 1–2.

[75]HCC, Section 665, para 2.

[76]NHCC, Section 7:82 [Extent of compulsory share of inheritance].

reason for this reduction is. I do not know what to say to you, because it was not a prepared and conscious modification, just a political one and every competent person was very surprised.[77]

Compulsory share is not a claim to inheritance: its term of limitation is five years.[78] The right to a compulsory share does not amount to succession, even if it is linked to the testator's death. It is, in fact, a claim under the law of obligations, which those entitled to the compulsory share must enforce. It must be filed at the probate proceedings and enforced against the obligors. Belgian law still applies, with few exceptions, the traditional Napoleonic forced share property right upon the assets of the succession. The German *'Pflichtteil'* represents only a claim in money for the protected heir; he or she has no property rights upon the assets of the succession. Under the new Dutch legislation, since 2003, the protected heir is reduced to a creditor of the succession. In France, the entitlement of a protected heir to the assets of the succession was limited to the relationship towards third parties. In the internal relationship between heirs, the forced share right has been reduced since 1971 to a right in value. Under the new French legislation in force since 2007[79] the forced share right has been reduced to a right in value in all cases.[80]

Although the law of succession is generally considered rather fixed and static, especially as compared to contract law or even family law, the last fifty years have seen many important changes in this body of law.[81] The social problem to be solved by the law of succession is the issue of transferring property after death, and how and to whom. Even considering all of Europe as part of the modern Western capitalist world, the social problem involved is of a morally and culturally more delicate nature than contract law. Perhaps the law of succession (even more than family law) is a field reserved to local rules and customs, a field in which the desire or need for unification seems to be moderate.[82] In many European jurisdictions, the law of succession is currently undergoing reforms or has been reformed. From the perspective of contemporary comparative law, the law of succession constitutes part of a country's cultural heritage. It differs from all of the other branches of private law in that it most closely reflects a given society's traditions, achievements, beliefs, practices, views and legal customs. The law of succession is to a large extent influenced by local rules, moral values and cultural conventions. For these reasons, a harmonised and unified law of succession is neither feasible nor

[77]See further Lajos Vékás, *Bírálat és jobbító észrevételek az új Ptk. Törvényjavaslatához (a zárószavazás előtt). [Comments, criticisms and improvements on the new Civil Code (before the final vote)]* In: Magyar Jog [Hungarian Law], 2013, Nr. 1, 1–7.

[78]NHCC, Section 7:76 [Lapse of right to compulsory share].

[79]See Act of 23 June 2006.

[80]Verbeke – Leleu 2011, p. 468.

[81]Liin 2001, p. 124.

[82]Verbeke – Leleu 2011, p. 462.

desirable. However, were one to evaluate the current state of the law from the perspective of whether the Hungarian law of succession has considered the thrust of current developments throughout the world, one would have to answer affirmatively.

References

Besenyei, Lajos (1998) De lege ferenda gondolatok az öröklési jog köréből. [De lege ferenda Reflections on the Law of Succession] In: Acta Universitatis Szegediensis de Attila József Nominatae, LIII, p 33–43

Csehi, Zoltan (2011) The Law of Succession in Hungary. In: Miriam Anderson and Esther Arroyo i Amayuelas (ed.) The Law of Succession: Testamentary Freedom: European Perspectives, CSIC Press, p 167–190

Gárdos, Péter (2013) Öröklési jog [Law of Succession]. In: Vékás, Lajos (ed.) *A Polgári Törvénykönyv magyarázatokkal* [The Civil Code with Commentaries], Complex, Budapest, p 985–1031

Liin, Urve (2001) Laws of Succession in Europe and Estonia: How We Got to Where We Are and Where We Should Be Heading. In: Juridica International VI. p 114–124

Pelletier Jr., George A. and Sonnenreich, Michael Roy (1966) A Comparative Analysis of Civil Law Succession. In: Villanova Law Review, Vol. 11, Issue 2, Article 3. p 323–356, http://digitalcommons.law.villanova.edu/vlr/vol11/iss2/3

van Erp, Sjef (2007) New Developments in Succession Law. In: Electronic Journal of Comparative Law, vol. 11.3 December, http://www.ejcl.org/113/article113-5.pdf

Verbeke, Alain-Laurent and Leleu, Yves-Henri: Harmonization of the Law of Succession in Europe. In: Hartkamp, Arthur S. – Hesselink, Martijn W. – Hondius, Ewoud H. – Mak, Chantal – du Perron, C. Edgar (2011) Towards a European Civil Code, Fourth Revised and Expanded Edition, Kluwer Law International BV, The Netherlands, p 459–479

Vékás, Lajos (2013) Bírálat és jobbító észrevételek az új Ptk. Törvényjavaslatához (a zárószavazás előtt). [Comments, criticisms and improvements on the new Civil Code (before the final vote)] In: Magyar Jog [Hungarian Law], Nr. 1, p 1–7

Vékás, Lajos (2013) Öröklési jog [Law of Succession]. Eötvös Kiadó, Budapest

Chapter 15
Law of Succession in the New Romanian Civil Code

János Székely

Abstract This study outlines several novel elements of the law of succession, which were introduced by the new Civil Code of Romania, and compares them to earlier rules set forth by the Romanian Civil Code of 1864. A brief historical overview of Romanian civil law in general, and the law of succession in particular, is provided. Subsequently some of the issues raised by the legal literature relating to this field are examined. Among them are the opening of the estate, the prerequisites for succession, and disqualifying factors, such as unworthiness. Representation *per stirpes*, the rights of the surviving spouse over the estate, and the partially repealed prohibition of fideicommissary substitution are examined in more detail. For the sake of comparison, reference is made to the rules of succession contained in the new Hungarian Civil Code (as the Hungarian recodification of civil law largely coincided with that of Romanian civil law), in order to elicit the common concerns of the two legislators.

15.1 A Brief History of the Romanian Civil Code and Law of Succession

The Romanian Civil Code was adopted in 1864 and entered into force in 1865. Even though later subjected to numerous amendments (and some major 'amputations', when parts of its text were repealed or moved to other codes or statutes), it constituted the first modern codification of Romanian civil law, and remained in force until the 1st of October, 2011. A major achievement of Romanian legal science at the time, the Civil Code of 1864 was characterized by the scholar Constantin Nacu in his work "*Comparaţiune între codul civil român şi codul Napoleon*" cited by Ticu (2006) as "*[…] a mostly less than ornate translation of the*

J. Székely (✉)
Sapientia University, Cluj-Napoca (Kolozsvár/Klausenburg), Romania
e-mail: szekely.janos@kv.sapientia.ro

A. Menyhárd and E. Veress (eds.), *New Civil Codes in Hungary and Romania*,
Ius Gentium: Comparative Perspectives on Law and Justice 63,
DOI 10.1007/978-3-319-63327-5_15

Napoleonic code […]" (due to its obvious pedigree). Hamza (2002) stated, based on contemporary accounts, that it was compiled in a period of just seven weeks. The Civil Code was therefore adopted with some haste, and was primarily (if not exclusively)[1] of French inspiration (Hamza 2009).

Its structure closely mimicked that of the Napoleonic Code of 1804, by use of the so-called "*institutio system*" (Stanković 2005) based on the "*Omne ius quod utimur vel ad personas pertinet, vel ad res, vel ad actiones*" organizing principle. Under this system it was divided into *three major structural units* (books) and an introductory title which set forth some general principles (by reproducing the contents of Articles 2–6 of the Napoleonic Code). "Book I" contained the provisions pertaining to persons and those governing family law, "Book II" held general provisions regarding property law while "Book III" (entitled "*The Various Means by Which Property is Acquired*") held all provisions of contractual and tort law, as well as those pertaining to the law of succession (the latter at Articles 650–799). This made it by far the bulkiest of the three books, upsetting the structural equilibrium of the Code (Ticu 2006).

15.1.1 The Law of Succession in the Civil Code of 1864

The law of succession in the Civil Code of 1864 closely resembled the French model under most aspects. As an example of this fact, the surviving spouse could only inherit the estate of the deceased (according to the rules of intestate succession) in case *de cuius* had no other inheritors—either legitimate or illegitimate[2] [Article 652, para (2), Article 679 and Articles 681–683]—up to and including the 12th degree (Alexandresco 1926),[3] just as the Napoleonic Code of 1804 provided, based on the Roman praetorian model (Bardoczi 2013). This provision would be the cause for many inconsistencies, finally resolved only by the new Civil Code of 2011.

---

[1]Other codes of civil law were taken into consideration during its codification, primarily the codes of Belgium and the Swiss Canton of Geneva, but some influences from the—then ongoing—Italian codification can also be discovered.

[2]The Romanian legislator strayed from the French model under two other aspects. The "poor widow" was instituted as a usufructuary for a share of the estate equal to that of the descendants. If there was only one descendant, the widow's share would be 1/3 parts. If only collateral relatives inherited the deceased, the widow would in turn inherit 1/4 of the estate as property. A right to alimony, for the duration of one year, to the benefit of the widow was also instituted. Both provisions had their roots in the code of Calimach, adopted in the mid-19th century.

[3]This provision was repealed by Act 3581/1921 which instituted the progressive inheritance tax. According to the new rules only inheritors of the fourth degree at most, or the surviving spouse could inherit, the latter considered by judicial practice as an inheritor of the fifth degree.

15.1.2 Attempts at Recodification

The first proposal for the recodification of the Romanian Civil Code came in 1940 with the reforms of King Carol II, but the chaos of World War II put an end to his grand initiative. Just a few years later, prompted by the realities of war, Act no. 319/1944 elevated the surviving spouse alongside the other classes of successors of the deceased, as a protected heir. The widower or—as was more often the case in war—the *widow* gained the right to a legal reserve, and a varying share of the estate, the extent of which depended on the class of successors he or she came into contest with. These classes of heirs in intestacy remained established according to the principles laid down by the Napoleonic Code and included (Deak 2001) the *descendants* of the deceased (the *first class*), the *privileged ascendants and privileged collateral relatives* (parents and siblings of the deceased and the respective siblings' descendants—the *second class*), the *ordinary ascendants* (lineal ascendants of the deceased, other than the parents—the *third class*), and *ordinary collateral relatives* (the siblings of ordinary ascendants and their respective descendants—the *fourth class*). Initially only the descendants and privileged ascendants of the deceased enjoyed a right to a legal reserve.

By Act 319/1944 the surviving spouse (regardless of gender) was also granted—alongside the rights already enjoyed by the poor widow according to Article 684 of the Civil Code of 1864—a *right to inhabit* the residence used jointly with *de cuius* prior to the opening of the estate, for a period of no less than one year, even if such a residence constituted the exclusive property of *de cuius*. The surviving spouse would also benefit from a *special right of inheritance* over the items of the household, to ensure that he/she would not be rendered destitute upon the opening of the estate. The law of succession in the Civil Code of 1864 not having been properly correlated to the changes, especially regarding the newly established legal reserve of the surviving spouse (Chirică 2003), the reform resulted in a lasting debate in legal literature on several issues, even such fundamental problems as the proper way to determine the reserved share to which the surviving spouse and each of the other reserved heirs were entitled to when they came into contest with each-other.

After King Carol II's attempt at comprehensive reform, and throughout the following decades, parts of the Civil Code of 1864 were repealed, and major sections, such as family law, the law of persons, or the statute of limitations were amended, and/or moved into newly created acts, and the Code of Family Law. In 1960 and again in 1971 there were fleeting attempts at comprehensive legal reform with two drafts for a new Civil Code proposed. They were not completely lost to history, as they would be mentioned as a source of inspiration by the framers of the new Civil Code (Guvernul României 2009).

15.1.3 The New Civil Code

The final, successful push for recodification came in 2004 when the need to unify and clarify Romanian private law arose as a result of the pending accession to the European Union. After several years of legislative effort, the new Civil Code was adopted under the title "Act no. 287/2009 regarding the Civil Code" and published in the 24th of July, 2009 issue (no. 511) of the official gazette of Romania. It would enter into force on the 1st of October, 2011, but only after undergoing large-scale amendments by means of Act no. 71/2011.

15.1.4 Sources of Inspiration and Structure

It is considered established wisdom, that the new Civil Code is based primarily on the Civil Code of Québec, Canada adopted in 1994, while the Civil Code of France (including its recent amendments in 2006), the codes of Italy and Switzerland, and some European Union norms also played their part in influencing its composition (Lupan 2011).

The recodification resulted in the breakup of the former code's cumbersome structure, and the adaptation of the structure of the Civil Code of Québec to suit the Romanian tradition. As a result of this reconfiguration, the law of succession came to be regulated in the new "*Book IV*" of the Romanian Civil Code[4] under the title "*Regarding succession and liberalities*". The Romanian legislator opted to treat *liberalities* (i.e. charitable devises) in the same structural unit as the law of succession due to the close link between the two topics, especially in the field of *legates* granted to particular successors in testacy, and *donations* by which the estate of the deceased may unduly diminish to the detriment of reserved heirs.

"Book IV" of the Romanian Civil Code is divided into four titles, as follows:

- Title I: Provisions Concerning Succession in General;
- Title II: Intestate Succession;
- Title III: Liberalities;
- Title IV: The Transmission and Partition of the Estate.

The drafters of the new Civil Code changed much more than merely the structure of the text, having introduced important novel elements into the substance of the law of succession. The remainder of our study is largely devoted to eliciting some of these elements by presenting some newly introduced institutions and the reconfigurations of some old ones.

[4]This order of topics differs from that the Civil Code of Québec, because—perhaps out of fidelity to the former *institutio* system—the Romanian legislator opted to place provisions of property law into "Book III" (as opposed to Book IV) of the Code, thereby inverting the order used in the Québec model, and more closely following the previous order of topics.

15.2 Novel Elements of the Romanian Law of Succession

15.2.1 A Definition of Inheritance

The first Romanian Civil Code lacked a definition of *inheritance*.[5] In a way similar to the solution found in § 7:1 (Vékás and Gárdos 2013) of the new Hungarian Civil Code (Act no. V from the year 2013, in force as of the 15th of March, 2013), such a definition is now provided at Article 953, albeit without reference to the *universal* character of the transmission of the estate from the deceased to the successors (i.e. the transmission of the entire estate or a share of that estate as a rule), an omission not found in the analogous Hungarian text. Inheritance is now defined, as "*[…] the transmission of the estate of a deceased natural person to one or several existing persons*". It is implied that the existing persons may be either natural or moral persons.

This improvement by the Romanian legislator is aimed at correcting a lacuna of the old text, but also at correlating the language of the Code to other modern norms, including Article 46 of the Romanian Constitution which refers to "*inheritance*" ("*moştenire*" in Romanian)—as opposed to "*succession*" ("*succesiune*" in Romanian)—as a way by which property is acquired (Bob 2010). Though it was, and still is customary to use the two expressions as synonyms, their meanings differ (Popa 2015) as the concept of successor ("*successor*" in Romanian) is also understood to refer to persons who acquire rights by way of *inter vivos* devices in certain contexts[6] (Veress 2012). Thus, more than just an aesthetic issue was corrected.

15.2.2 The Opening of the Estate

The time and place for the *opening of the estate* has been defined in a single rule (Article 954) by the new Civil Code. Previously several rules had to be correlated to determine this critical moment and location. Substantially, the text maintained the previous provisions, the time being the time of death and the place the last domicile of *de cuius* (Bob 2010).

---

[5] The term "inheritance" is used deliberately in this context instead of "succession" due to the language employed by the new Civil Code.

[6] Such a context exists when referring to successive owners of an item which was resold several times, the current owner being defined in Romanian legal jargon as the "*successor*" of the previous one.

15.2.3 Qualifications Required to Inherit

According to Romanian law, in order to qualify to inherit the deceased, an heir *must exist* at the time of the opening of the estate and *must be worthy* to receive the inheritance. Some important changes have occurred in the rules governing the heir's capacity to inherit, in reaction to problems which arose in practice and legal theory while the Civil Code of 1864 was being applied. In the following paragraphs, we shall attempt to analyse the way in which the new Romanian Civil Code regulates *situations when death occurs simultaneously* or *when the times of death are impossible to determine*, and the *unworthiness of a prospective heir.*

15.2.3.1 Simultaneous Death

Simultaneous death is the legal notion used to denote situations when several prospective heirs to one-another (the *commorientes*), perish in a way which renders the determination of the order of deaths impossible (such as during accidents, or acts of war). This problem has been known to civil law since Roman times (Eliescu 1966), and was mentioned explicitly in the Digest of Justinian, where some exceptional solutions were proposed to resolve such situations in the form of *presumptions of survivorship.* However, the Digest did not institute any general presumptions (Hunter 1903) of precedence in death, or of simultaneity of death for that matter. This last remark is important to note when we take into account the solutions adopted by the Romanian legislator over time.

The Civil Code of 1864 did not mention in any way the situation of simultaneous death, unlike the Napoleonic Code of 1804 which, at Articles 720–722 provided a complicated set of presumptions of precedence in death (Pelletier and Sonnenreich 1966) which were later repealed. Article 725-1, para (2) of the French Civil Code now provides a solution (Rouhette and Rouhette-Berton 2006) virtually identical to that of the new Romanian Civil Code.

The initial silence—*based on the Italian model* (Alexandresco 1926)—of the Romanian Civil Code of 1864 on the matter of simultaneous death was attributed by Alexandresco (1926), to the reasoning that instituting a legal presumption of simultaneity of death was by no means a more just solution to the problem, than any of the other more or less arbitrary presumptions proposed in other systems of law.

Due perhaps to the relative proximity of World War II at the time it was adopted, at Article 21 of Decree number 31/1954 pertaining to the law of persons, the Romanian legislator provided as follows: "*In case several persons die in the same circumstances without the possibility for establishing if one has survived the other, they are to be considered to have died at the same time.*" Undoubtedly this text instituted a presumption of simultaneous death for those deceased in the same circumstances. The solution however presented two major flaws: the first was that it still resolved the problem by means of instituting a presumption of an event which may or may not have occurred in the presumed way [an imperfect solution, as noted by Alexandresco (1926)] being no different in essence to other presumptions; the second that it left untreated the issue of persons who died at the same time—or at different times impossible to determine—but under different circumstances. It is worthwhile to mention for the sake of comparison, that the former Civil Code of Hungary (Act number IV from the year 1959) provided no text to resolve the situation of the commorientes, yet Hungarian legal science adopted without reservations (Deak 2001) the presumption of simultaneity of death, even when the deaths occurred in different circumstances.

Romanian legal literature favoured an improvement to the solution provided by Decree no. 31/1954, as a possibility *de lege lata*, or at the very least an option to be considered at the nearest recodification, *de lege ferenda*. With a view to this preference, the new Romanian Civil Code now provides at Article 957, para (2) an unambiguous rule which reads as follows: "*If in case of several persons' deaths, it cannot be determined that one has survived the other, they shall not have the capacity to inherit after one another.*" Apart from a slight inconsistency (the legislator uses the word "several" at the beginning of the sentence but then limited the rule to two persons, even though more than two *commorientes* may be prospective heirs to one another) the new text has largely resolved the old contentions. On the one hand, as a significant difference from the language (Vékás and Gárdos 2013) adopted by the new Hungarian Civil Code at § 7:4 para (1), which also aims to settle the same issue, while unwittingly restricting the scope of the rule to persons who die in the same dangerous circumstances, and from a possible solution proposed by Deak (Bob 2010), the final language of the Romanian Civil Code has the effect of depriving the *commorientes* of the *capacity* to inherit, doing away with the presumption of simultaneity of deaths. The Romanian solution is not based on a presumption that any person preceded another in death (or that their deaths had occurred at the same time), but instead on depriving a person of the right to inherit from another by the power of law, *for lack of capacity*. On the other hand, it is not limited to persons who die simultaneously under the same circumstances (as states the Hungarian rule), and can be readily applied to persons whose deaths occur simultaneously, but under different circumstances, or when the times of these deaths are materially impossible to determine.

15.2.3.2 Unworthiness to Inherit

In the field of unworthiness to inherit from the deceased, the provisions of Article 655 of the Civil Code of 1864 reproduced the wording of Article 727 of the Napoleonic Code of 1804, and disqualified the prospective heir from inheriting the estate of the deceased if said heir had been found guilty: 1. of either perpetrating murder or attempted murder against the deceased; 2. of having intentionally brought against the deceased an accusation for a capital crime which was later determined to be false; or 3. of having neglected to notify the authorities of the murder of the deceased, in this last case only if the prospective heir was an adult at the time he/she gained knowledge of the murder.

The new text (Articles 958–961) of the Romanian Civil Code draws inspiration from the Civil Code of Québec—even though its French roots were also emphasized (Boţi and Boţi 2011) by the legislator—when establishing a dual regime of unworthiness (Bob 2010) constituted by two reasons for *absolute* (*ex lege*), and three reasons for *judicial unworthiness*, and by instituting a possibility by which the unworthy heir may be forgiven. Both types of unworthiness produce the same effects: the unworthy prospective heir is excluded from inheriting the victim's estate, regardless of the succession being testate or intestate (Bob 2010) unless expressly forgiven (contrary to the solution adopted under the Civil Code of 1864 which disqualified the unworthy prospective heirs only from the intestate succession of the deceased).

Absolute Unworthiness

Absolute unworthiness to inherit is now restricted to just two grounds by Article 958, para (1) of the Civil Code: 1. the conviction of an heir for a crime perpetrated with the intention of killing *de cuius*, or 2. the conviction of an heir for a criminal act committed prior to the opening of the estate, with the intention of killing another person, who by his/her very existence would have diminished the perpetrator's claim to the estate of *de cuius*, if the opening of the estate had taken place at the time of the killing. Since the legislator, just as under the Civil Code of 1864 (Deak 2001) limits the scope of these grounds to *intentional* killings (Macovei and Dobrilă 2012), all actions of the prospective heir which result in the death of *de cuius* without this specific intent will be excluded from the scope of absolute unworthiness, including those committed *praeter intentionem* or out of negligence. Criminal acts directed against *de cuius*, other than those with an intention to kill, may be considered grounds for judicial unworthiness, as outlined below.

Another issue which must be addressed with regard to the grounds for absolute unworthiness is when a prospective heir finds him or herself in the position of *instigator* or *accomplice* (accessory) to the crime of which *de cuius* is the target or victim. Whereas authors of legal theory under the former Civil Code of 1864 based their opinions on judicial practice (Eliescu 1966), which quasi-unanimously accepted that being an accessory to the murder of *de cuius* in the form of instigator or accomplice results in the unworthiness of the prospective heir to inherit (Deak 2001), some commentators of the new Civil Code (Macovei and Dobrilă 2012)—in our opinion justly—consider that the formulation of the text (as opposed to that of the current Civil Code of France, which explicitly deals with such situations) when corroborated with the *exceptional nature of unworthiness as a civil penalty*, which thus cannot be construed in an extensive manner, *excludes instigators and accomplices from such a penalty*. The solution for the situation when the prospective heir *conceals* the killing of *de cuius* without being either a perpetrator of the deed, or an accessory to it, must be identical to the one outlined above. Given that the text of the Civil Code of 1864 did not provide for these situations of participation, yet jurisprudence (albeit contrary to the principle of restrictive interpretation of legal sanctions) extended the sanction to instigators and accomplices, we believe that future jurisprudence shall have an important role in settling this issue, hopefully in a way compatible with the general rules of interpreting the law, that is: by excluding the penalty of unworthiness in such cases.

Judicial Unworthiness

Alongside absolute unworthiness which excludes an heir from inheriting the estate by the effect of law, without a need for any judicial proceedings (Macovei and Dobrilă 2012), the legislator also provided rules for situations of judicial unworthiness. This may occur if certain circumstances are ascertained by a court at the request of an interested (prospective) heir.

Reasons for judicial unworthiness are defined by law as follows (Article 959 of the Romanian Civil Code): 1. the criminal—and if statutes of limitation bar such, then the civil—conviction of a person for intentional acts of *grave physical or moral violence* perpetrated against *de cuius* or other acts that resulted in his/her death; 2. the person who in bad faith *hid, altered, destroyed or falsified the will* of *de cuius*; 3. the person who by *fraud or violence prevented de cuius* from making, changing or revoking a will. The plaintiff must lodge an application for the establishment of judicial unworthiness, which produces the effect of tacit acceptance of the inheritance on his/her behalf (Macovei and Dobrilă 2012), within a compulsory time limit of *one year* after the opening of the estate [Article 959, para (3)] if the heir has knowledge of a reason for unworthiness, or within a period of one year after the guilt of a prospective heir has been established by a court decision, or has come to the knowledge of the petitioning heir after the opening of the estate by any other means [Article 959, paras (4) and (5)]. Even the Romanian State may invoke judicial unworthiness against an heir, by way of its local authorities, but only if it stands to profit from the heir's disqualification from inheriting the estate. After the time limit expires, the application becomes time-barred.

Possibility of Forgiveness

The new Civil Code (in view of the wider scope of unworthiness as compared to the Civil Code of 1864) now grants the possibility for *de cuius* to *expressly* forgive the unworthy successor during his/her lifetime, by either drafting a will or an authentic instrument (Veress 2012) whereby he/she absolves the unworthy prospective heir from under the effects of unworthiness (Article 961 of the Romanian Civil Code). Tacit forgiveness was not introduced, as opposed to the Canadian model (Boţi and Boţi 2011), for the situation when *de cuius* decides to gratify the prospective heir as a legatee, regardless of the acts this heir perpetrated against him/her, or having knowledge of the acts of the prospective heir, and a possibility to amend his/her will, *de cuius* still maintains the clauses by which the disqualified heir is gratified. As a result, unworthy heirs whom are not forgiven *expressis verbis* during the lifetime of *de cuius* remain disqualified from succeeding him/her.

Other Problems Regarding Unworthiness

The new Civil Code resolves an old debate in Romanian legal science by *omitting* a former reason for absolute unworthiness, that of the *slanderous capital accusation*. Some authors of Romanian legal literature (Deak 2001; Chirică 2003) debated the applicability of this text since the time capital punishment had been abolished in Romania, and reached the conclusion that it should either be considered inapplicable, or considered applicable to any slanderous accusation of a defamatory nature levied against *de cuius*, even though the latter remained a minority opinion (Bob 2010). Even if this problem has largely been considered as inconsequential (Bob 2010) in recent scientific debate, the hypothetical situation in which such an accusation is brought before a foreign jurisdiction which still applies the death penalty, should not be ignored. In such situations, to our opinion, the first cause of absolute unworthiness should operate, as the text proscribes any *crime* with the intention of killing *de cuius*. False criminal accusations constitute a crime under Romanian law (according to Article 268 of the Penal Code) while also likely to be criminalized under the law of most foreign jurisdictions, rendering it punishable also under Romanian law. If we contend that the intention to kill *de cuius* is the main reason for disqualification from the right to inherit under the first reason of absolute unworthiness, no other solution may be adopted.

Another important aspect to note is that the Romanian legislator, when regulating the effects of unworthiness, omitted to consider the situation in which the inheritance of the deceased is *collected by the minor descendant of a parent who has been disqualified from inheriting de cuius*. Thus, the inheritance is to be administered by the unworthy parent: a less than preferable outcome. This situation has been expressly regulated by the Hungarian Civil Code (Vékás and Gárdos 2013), and is also possible to resolve under Romanian law due to the provisions of Article 965 pertaining to representation *per stirpes*. This omission, however may only be corrected by means of an amendment to the law.

15.2.4 Representation Per Stirpes

In the field of representation *per stirpes* (whereby an heir from the class of descendants or that of privileged ascendants takes the place and assumes the rights of a—usually predeceased—ancestor in view of the settlement of the inheritance) which is partly linked to the problems of unworthiness, the new Romanian Civil Code did not fulfil all the expectations of domestic legal literature.

For much of the 20th century a debate existed between two major positions (Bob 2010): according to the first, an heir could *de lege lata* only represent a *predeceased* ancestor, while according to the second an heir could represent an ancestor who was either disqualified as *unworthy*, or even one who *rejected* the inheritance outright, or at the very least this should be the solution instituted *de lege ferenda* at the nearest recodification.

15.2.4.1 Representation of the Unworthy Heir

The new Romanian Civil Code vindicated those who maintained that a descendant of an unworthy heir should be entitled to inherit in his/her place. This is due mainly to the individual character of the effects of unworthiness as a civil penalty, but also to the revival of the Roman law concept of *inheriting in place of another* as opposed to the medieval concept of *representation*, the two being distinct. The former confers a right on the successor in virtue of maintaining equality between the branches of the same family, while the latter is based on a fiction of the law of a more recent origin, according to which the living descendant takes the place of the deceased ancestor when collecting his/her ancestor's share of the inheritance, a mechanism called *representatio in locum* (Bob 2011a).

At the same time the Romanian legislator dashed some hopes in another matter, because the final language of the legal text it settled for failed to reproduce the wording of the 2010 draft Civil Code, according to which an heir who renounced his/her heirship could also have been represented by his or her descendants (Bob 2010), not to mention the wording of the 2003 draft, which would have permitted representation *per stirpes* to operate even in the case of *commorientes* (Bob 2011a). The reason the legislator opted in this way was the sum of objections outlined by the National Union of Notaries Public of Romania, which raised concerns on grounds of uncertainty during the non-litigious devolution of the succession, and a potential increase in the duration of the procedure, had the new system been introduced (Bob 2011b). Another profound problem was that the Romanian legislator never reproduced the analogous provisions of the French Civil Code regarding trans-generational charitable devises, or those by which a prospective heir can renounce the succession prior to the opening of the estate (Bob 2011b). Thus, the initial drafts were rejected and the final version of Article 965 only provided for representation in case *de cuius* was *preceded in death* by a descendant or sibling (and—if applicable—descendants of the said sibling up to and including the fourth degree relative to *de cuius*) or in case such descendants or siblings came to be *disqualified from the inheritance as unworthy.*

15.2.4.2 Consequences of Representation per Stirpes on the Descendants of the Unworthy

A special situation arises out of this novel interpretation of the institution of representation: the possibility that the unworthy heir, subject to representation *per stirpes*, may later produce descendants not yet conceived at the time the estate had opened. These descendants, lacking capacity to inherit *de cuius* by means of representation *per stirpes* would be at a disadvantage in comparison to those descendants already conceived at the time the estate of *de cuius* opened. To remedy this perceived injustice, the legislator once again turned to the French model (Article 755 of the French Civil Code) and enshrined in Article 969, para (1) of the Romanian Civil Code a new obligation by virtue of which the descendants of an unworthy former heir, who were (at least) conceived at the time the estate of *de cuius* opened, are bound, once in turn the estate of the unworthy heir him or herself opens, to return to the estate of the latter the value of all that they have inherited from the original *de cuius*.[7] This text was much criticized, even by former proponents (Bob 2011a) on grounds that it extended representation to persons who were not in existence at the time the estate opened, and was therefore unjust, but made its way into the text of the Civil Code regardless.

15.2.5 Inclusion of Some Provisions of Act no. 319/1944 and Correlation with Those of the New Romanian Civil Code

A welcome aspect of the reformed text of the Romanian Civil Code is the *inclusion of some provisions of former Act no. 319/1944 pertaining to the rights of the surviving spouse* into the body of the law of succession (Articles 970–974) with some clarifications to resolve the most contentious issues, especially with a view to the calculation of the reserved share of the surviving spouse.

15.2.5.1 Calculation of the Reserved Share

The Romanian legislator finally resolved the old debate raging around *the proper way to calculate the share of the estate reserved for the surviving spouse.* Subsequently to Act no. 319/1944 authors of legal science began debating (Deak 2001) whether the reserved share of the surviving spouse should be deducted from the entire estate first, followed by the deduction of the shares owed to other reserved heirs from what is left of the estate (Eliescu 1966) or exactly the other way around, or should a proportional method of deduction be applied (Chirică 2003). The competition between the spouse and other categories of reserved heirs had inevitably resulted in some cases, in either the spouse or any of the other reserved heirs receiving a smaller reserved share than that provided by law. The debate arose from the fact that, while the original Code favoured the concept of a unified reserve for all reserved heirs, from which they all benefited according to their respective shares, provided for by law in case of intestate succession, Act no. 319/1944 in turn created a personal reserve for the surviving spouse (Bob 2011b) alongside the initial (global) reserve of the other reserved heirs.

The new Civil Code, for the first time, gave a definition for the *reserve* and the *disposable portion* of the estate (Article 1086 of the Romanian Civil Code), in

[7]The obligation to return what they inherited is however limited to the amount by which the assets exceeded the liabilities in the inheritance which they collected from the first *de cuius* by virtue of representation.

essence adopting the position of Deak (2001). It provides that the reserved share of the estate is in effect a *global* 1/2 part of the combined shares all reserved heirs would have inherited, had the succession been intestate, and had no charitable devises diminished the estate of *de cuius* (Bob 2011b). According to a position formulated by Popa (2015), this global character of the reserve is however only illusive, and is to be understood as the sum of the individual reserves of the reserved heirs, due to the fact that the renunciation of one reserved heir does not result in the increase of the reserved share owed to the others.

15.2.5.2 Right of Habitation

Act no. 319/1944 had granted the surviving spouse of *de cuius* a right to continue inhabiting the residence occupied prior to the opening of the estate, in case the spouse disposed of no residence befitting his or her needs, even if the residence inhabited was the exclusive property of *de cuius*. This provision begged the question whether the right of habitation was gratuitous or onerous? The law gave no answer, and despite the compelling logic of the argument in favour (Chirică 2003) of its onerous character,[8] the prevailing opinion remained that it constituted a gratuitous right (all the more so, because the intention of the legislator of 1944 was understood as being the protection of war-widows). Finally, the legislator settled this problem by declaring the right of habitation unalienable, not subject to seizure, and gratuitous, by Article 973 of the new Civil Code (Macovei and Dobrilă 2012).

15.2.6 Acceptance of the Estate

15.2.6.1 The Time-Limit for Acceptance

Under the Civil Code of 1864 (as another provision of French inspiration) an estate had to be either expressly or tacitly accepted by the heir. The lack of such an acceptance in the time provided made it impossible for the heir to later accept and ultimately to inherit the estate. The time limit provided for manifesting such an acceptance under the Civil Code of 1864 was set at a generous 30 years subsequent to the opening of the estate. This period was reduced in 1951 to just six months by Decree no. 88/21.06.1951, as calculated from the day of the opening of the estate on grounds of making property rights more secure. It was qualified as a period of *prescription* (i.e. with the effects of a statute of limitations) by Article 700, para (1) of the Civil Code as amended by the above Decree in 1954 (Bob 2011b).

---

[8]This right carried a minimal duration of one year unless the other heirs provided the spouse with an equivalent and suitable residence or the surviving spouse remarried. The residence could not be partitioned before the expiration of this period.

This time limit underwent further modification by the new Romanian Civil Code, and was set at *one year*, by Article 1103 which contains some welcome improvements regarding the calculation of the acceptance period—as opposed to the initial text—in cases when: 1. the opening of the estate occurred before the birth of an inheritor already conceived at the time of the death of *de cuius*; 2. when the estate is opened by a judicial declaration of death, or 3. in case an inheritor's filiation was only later established, or 4. a legatee gained knowledge of the legate in his/her favour only at a later time. In such cases the time limit is to be calculated from the date of these events, not the opening of the estate.

15.2.6.2 The Nature of the Acceptance Period

Although some authors (Genoiu 2012a) continue to qualify the time limit of the acceptance period as a *prescription* period, just as the text of the Civil Code of 1864 Article 700, para (1) as amended in 1954 once did, other commentators (Macovei and Dobrilă 2012) of the new Civil Code now offer substantiated arguments in favour of qualifying it as a time limit with the effect of forfeiture of rights. This second opinion is supported on the one hand by the fact that the text *no longer refers to prescription*, and on the other hand by the fact that certain rules pertaining to prescription periods—the application of which were extended to the case of the acceptance period [Article 1103, para (3) of the new Civil Code]—would not have been provided for expressly if the period was intended by the legislator to still be of prescription, and not of legal forfeiture (Macovei and Dobrilă 2012). Another authority and former member of the codification commission deduces this nature of the acceptance period from the *potestative* (*discretionary*) *character of the right to accept the estate* with which the drafting commission operated (Bob 2011b). The exercise of such a right being an act which the beneficiary does not have to justify, and which depends solely on his/her free will, this right cannot be construed to be subject to prescription, but may be subject to forfeiture.

15.2.6.3 Presumptions of Waiver and of the Acceptance of the Estate

Lastly, the new Civil Code regulates two situations when the waiver of inheritance is presumed (such presumptions were not widely accepted under the Civil Code of 1864). The first such presumption (Article 1112 of the new Civil Code) operates in case a person entitled to inherit had been aware that the estate opened, and that he or she was an heir to that estate, and said person still did not express an option in the sense of acceptance of the estate until the acceptance period had elapsed, while the second [Article 1113, para (2)] takes effect if the prospective heir has been summoned by a court to express an option to inherit the estate or to reject it, in a period shorter than the statutory one year (Genoiu 2012a).

If situations when the waiver of the inheritance is presumed are *exceptional*, then the *rule* must be that a waiver of inheritance cannot be presumed in other cases.

Such was and is the opinion of an overwhelming majority of authors (Genoiu 2012a). If we accept this reasoning, we must also be open to a proposal by Bob (2011b) whom, as a participant to the drafting commission of the new Civil Code was made privy to the initial intentions of the commission to institute a *presumption of acceptance of the inheritance* in case the heir did not express an option in the one year period provided. Although this proposal (too) was opposed by the National Union of Notaries Public on grounds of possible uncertainty over the number and quality of accepting heirs, and the final version of the Civil Code does not contain an explicit provision in this sense, it can be maintained (although this constitutes a minority opinion) that a general presumption of acceptance still operates in cases when no express waiver of the inheritance has been made but no situations of presumed waiver are present (Bob 2011b). This opinion strongly emphasizes the provisions of Article 13 of the new Civil Code which state that a waiver of any right may not be presumed, unless provided otherwise by law.

15.2.7 Fideicommissary Substitution

Fideicommissary substitution is an institution of civil law known since Roman times (Poenar 2013) which is defined by the new Civil Code (Article 993) as a compulsory disposition given by a *grantor* (who can be either a *donor* or a *testator*) to the *grantee* of a charitable devise (a donee, an heir or a legatee, called the *instituted*) by which the latter is ordered to conserve the object of the grant and to pass it on *mortis causa* to a third person (called the *substituted*) also designated by the initial grantor (Genoiu 2012b). It is regulated today by Articles 993–1000 of the new Civil Code.

As apparent from the definition, this mechanism of successive liberalities may span a single generation (*simple* or *unique* substitution) or several generations (*gradual* substitution), in case the grantor imposes the same obligations of conservation and retransmission upon the substituted as on the initial instituted, with a possibility for this chain of substitutions to stretch on to perpetuity (Macovei and Dobrilă 2012; Popescu 2015). Both versions of these liberalities were expressly prohibited by Article 803 of the Civil Code of 1864 (Popescu 2015), under the penalty of being considered null and void in their entirety, and constituted (along with the prohibition of pacts regarding unopened estates, and the rules concerning the legal reserve of heirs) one of the major limitations constraining the freedom of disposal over one's own estate (Genoiu 2012b). Such harsh treatment of fideicommissary substitutions was justified by legal science on three grounds: 1. it was thought to induce inequality between heirs as it could be used to maintain certain parts of the estate in the family of *de cuius* by means of repeated transmissions (to e.g. firstborn heirs); 2. it restricted the circulation of goods and credit by rendering certain items unalienable, and 3. it unduly reduced the freedom of disposal over the property of an heir, degrading him/her to the statute of quasi-usufructuary (Poenar 2013). To permit such provisions in reality would have also meant a concession to the aristocratic *ancien régime*, something the drafters of the original Napoleonic Code of 1804 were all too keen to avoid, a trait 'inherited' by the Romanian Civil code of 1864 as well.

This drastic treatment of fideicommissary substitutions was attenuated by legal science under several aspects which shall not constitute the object of our present analysis. We direct the reader to consult the works of Poenar (2013) and Popa (2015) for a well-documented review of these attenuations.

Through the adoption of the new Civil Code the prohibition of simple (unique) fideicommissary substitutions was effectively lifted (Article 994) while the legislator still maintains the prohibition of gradual substitutions [Article 996, para (3)] by use of a wording similar to that of the French Civil Code (Poenar 2013). The reasons for the—partial—lifting of the prohibition were summarized by Popescu (2015) as: 1. the necessity to ensure the trans-generational transmission of the estate by 'skipping' a generation, 2. the protection of the rights of children from a previous marriage of *de cuius*, and 3. the protection of the interests of descendants with disabilities.

The freedom of the grantor is by no means absolute even when the substitution is permitted. The conditions of capacity set forth by law for the charitable devise used must be met in the person of the grantor, in that of the instituted, and in that of the substituted as well (Poenar 2013), for the devise to produce its effects (Genoiu 2012b). However, an opinion has been expressed which maintains that a substituted may be a person not yet conceived at the time a *donation* is made by the grantor to the instituted (Genoiu 2012b), although this has been contested by other authors (Poenar 2013).

In the case of substitutions by means of a *legate* however the substituted legatee must undoubtedly be at least conceived to have capacity to inherit the grantor, since the substituted is considered to obtain the object of the grant directly from the grantor, even if the instituted is the one who effectively transmits that object. The instituted is required to conserve the object of the *fideicommissum* as a *trustee* prior to retransmission upon death, and may be required to present guarantees to the grantor or to insure the object (Macovei and Dobrilă 2012; Popescu 2015). In case the instituted is also a reserved heir of the grantor, in order to prevent the unjust reduction of his reserved share, the Civil Code provides at Article 998 (Macovei and Dobrilă 2012), that he/she shall only be bound to retransmit the share of the estate which exceeds his/her reserve (Genoiu 2012b).

15.3 Conclusions

The Romanian legislator, through the adoption of the new Civil Code attempted to update almost all institutions of the law off succession by the creative use of foreign models and domestic legal science. The result is a set of norms which now contain most institutions internationally known to the law of succession, making the Civil Code a modern piece of legislation under this regard. More importantly, by directing legislative efforts at such former problems as those surrounding the capacity to inherit, the extent of the rights of the surviving spouse or the waiver and acceptance of the inheritance, as well as fideicommissary substitutions, the new Civil Code now offers useful textual guidance to practitioners and theoreticians alike, as problems hitherto left to theoretical debate—and a not always unitary jurisprudence—have been resolved.

References

Alexandresco, Dimitrie. 1926. *Principiile dreptului civil român. Vol. II.* Bucharest: Atelierele Socec & Co. Societate Anonimă.

Bardoczi, Irina. 2013. Marchează Codul Civil din 1864 o evoluţie în materia drepturilor succesorale ab intestato ale soţului supravieţuitor? *SUBB Jurisprudentia* 1: 5–34.

Bob, Mircea Dan. 2010. Propter veteris iuris imitationem: Nou şi vechi în materie succesorală (I). *SUBB Jurisprudentia* 4: 53–73.

Bob, Mircea Dan. 2011a. Consideraţii asupra reglementării reprezentării succesorale în noul Cod civil. *Romanian Rev. Priv. L.* 1: 33–48.

Bob, Mircea Dan. 2011b. Propter veteris iuris imitationem: Nou şi vechi în materie succesorală (II). *SUBB Jurisprudentia* 4: 34–62.

Boţi, Iolanda, and Victor Boţi. 2011. Codul civil din Quebec: sursă de inspiraţie în procesul de recodificare a Dreptului Civil Român. *SUBB Jurisprudentia* 1: 5–19.

Chirică, Dan. 2003. *Drept civil. Succesiuni şi testamente.* Bucharest: Editura Rosetti.

Deak, Francisc. 2001. *Tratat de drept succesoral – Ediţia a II-a actualizată şi completată.* Bucharest: Universul Juridic.

Eliescu, Mihail. 1966. *Moştenirea şi devoluţiunea ei în dreptul Republicii Socialiste România.* Bucharest: Editura Academiei Republicii Socialiste România.

Genoiu, Ilioara. 2012a. Renunciation of Inheritance According to the Regulations of the New Romanian Civil Code and of French Law. *AGORA Int'l J. Jurid. Sci.* 1: 44–53.

Genoiu, Ilioara. 2012b. Substituţiile fideicomisare şi liberalităţile reziduale în reglementarea noului Cod Civil. *Romanian Rev. Priv. L.* 3: 147–163.

Guvernul României. 2009. Camera Deputaţilor. http://www.cdep.ro/proiecte/2009/300/00/5/em305.pdf. Accessed 05 September 2013.

Hamza, Gábor. 2002. *Az európai magánjog fejlődése – A modern magánjogi rendszerek kialakulása a római jogi hagyományok alapján.* Budapest: Nemzeti Tankönyvkiadó Rt.

Hamza, Gábor. 2009. *Entstehung und Entwicklung der modernen Privatrechtsordnungen und die römischrechtliche Tradition.* Budapest: Eötvös Univ. Verlag.

Hunter, William Alexander. 1903. *A Systematic and Historical Exposition of Roman Law in the Order of a Code.* (4th). London: Sweet & Maxwell Limited.

Lupan, Ernest. 2011. Căile grunzuroase ale Codului civil român. *Scientia Juris – Revistă româno-maghiară de ştiinţe juridice* 1: 5–10.

Macovei, Codrin, and Mirela Carmen Dobrilă. 2012. Cartea a IV-a – Despre moştenire şi liberalităţi. In *Noul Cod civil – Comentariu pe articole*, ed. Flavius-Antoniu Baias, Eugen Chelaru, Rodica Constantinovici and Ioan Macovei, 997–1214. Bucharest: Editura C. H. Beck.

Pelletier, George A. Jr., and Michael Roy Sonnenreich. 1966. A Comparative Analysis of Civil Law Succession. *Villanova Law Review* 11: 323–356.

Poenar, Florina. 2013. Eternizarea voinţei lui de cuius prin intermediul substituţiilor fideicomisare. *SUBB Jurisprudentia* 3: 5–66.

Popa, Ioan. 2015. Instituţii juridice controversate de drept succesoral menţinute sau existente în noul Cod civil român. *Dreptul* 7: 26–51.

Popescu, Radu-Romeo. 2015. Substituţiile fideicomisare în noul Cod Civil. *Analele Universităţii Bucureşti – Seria Drept*: 94–109.
Rouhette, Georges, and Anne Rouhette-Berton. 2006. Civil Code. http://www.legifrance.gouv.fr/content/download/1950/13681/version/3/file/Code_22.pdf. Accessed 15 September 2013.
Stanković, Emilija. 2005. The Influence of Roman Law on Napoleon's Code Civil. In *Ex Iusta Causa Traditum: Essays in Honour of Eric H. Pool*, ed. Rena Van den Bergh and Eric H. Pool, 310–315. Pretoria: University of South Africa.
Ticu, Mădălin Savu. 2006. Fundamentele filosofice ale Codului Civil român. *Revista de Ştiinţe Juridice* 2: 81–88.
Vékás, Lajos, and Péter Gárdos. 2013. *A Polgári Törvénykönyv magyarázatokkal*. Budapest: CompLex Kiadó Jogi és Üzleti Tartalomszolgáltató Kft.
Veress, Emőd. 2012. *Drept civil. Moştenirea. Liberalităţile conform Noului Cod civil*. Bucharest: Editura C. H. Beck.

CPSIA information can be obtained
at www.ICGtesting.com
Printed in the USA
BVOW06*0648250817
493085BV00011B/13/P

9 783319 633268